Evolving to Grace

By
Grace Lozada

A story of perseverance, strength, spiritual evolution, and the choices one must make to change one's path.

Published by Grace Lozada

Paperback ~ US - ISBN-10:1511858737
International ~ ISBN-13:978-1511858731

To my great loves

Duran Duran, thank you for being my comfort all those times when I wanted to throw in the towel. Because of your music, I dreamt my way through some of the darkest moments in my life and survived through one more day.

To my son, because of you, I truly learned what love is supposed to be. I learned to love and be loved in return. That is the greatest gift one could give another. Thank you. And, thank you for helping me find my happiness and humor again, teaching me all that you have and continue to teach.

Mister, thank you for the time we had. Because of this, I am completely evolving to this generous, giving heart that I knew was there but kept hidden inside me. You turned the lights back on, brought back that sparkle that was lost for too long. And, lastly, I picked up this work again I had set aside for twenty years. You truly inspired me to begin again and finish. There's something to be said when I say I'd redo my whole entire life again just so that I could meet you again. "Miss you more. See you on the flip side."

My biggest wish in life was for my son. I wished that he would grow up to be happy and successful. That wish has come true and I thank all the powers that be!

My second wish is that by sharing my story I can help at least one person to find the strength to not give up! Life is too sweet and sometimes you have to go through challenges to truly appreciate the beauty of life!

Find hope
Inspire others
and
Love

Some names have been changed in this book out of respect for the privacy of the individuals involved.

Table of Contents

1

Threats from a Pimp
"Excuse Me—Press Rewind"

"You talk too much."

It was late, and I was at Mike's condo in West Hollywood. I was twenty-three years old but sometimes had the maturity of a naive fifteen-year-old. I had met Mike over a year earlier when I was living in Orange County and running to the wild streets of Hollywood on the weekends. I moved to Hollywood months after meeting him when a close friend of mine had died. When I look back now, I realize that I was traumatized by my friend's death. I had never had anyone close to me die before. What made matters worse was that I had moved out of my apartment in Huntington Beach because I no longer could afford it. I was staying with my parents for a little while after my girlfriend's death because I was scared of being alone. While I was there, I pondered on where I was going to live. Moving back in with my parents was not the best option for me. The only other choice I thought I had was to move to Hollywood. Since I met Mike, he had been asking me to move there. I wasn't thinking straight when I decided to move. I packed up everything I could, I didn't give notice to my boss, and I moved to the City of Angels within a few days after my friend's funeral. But things rarely ever seem as they are. And here I found myself over a year later at one of Mike's places. I was in L.A., being threatened by a man who was now my ex-pimp/"manager." A man who just ten years earlier was a street pimp.

"You talk too much, and when you talk too much, you can get yourself hurt—this is not a threat; it is a fact," he said to me. It was just a week earlier that I was sitting in his car with him, and for the first time, I had seen in his eyes that he wanted to hit me. Thankfully, he didn't. My life had sunken so low, but how did I end up here? How did my life make me end up here of all places? I came from generations of successful, well-educated, affluent people who would have never thought I'd end up like this. Didn't I know better than this? Didn't I know better in all the other situations before this that I had been in or put myself in? When was I going to learn to change? When was I going to learn that I needed to change?

There are many journeys we all will take in our lifetimes—many roads leading us to whom we are destined to become or to the lives we desire to live. My journey has been a long one, sometimes extremely difficult to emotionally, mentally, or physically survive, but somehow I've made it so far—and standing on my own two feet. And throughout the last two decades, I have fought tirelessly to change my path. There are days, weeks, and months that are struggles, but I'd rather go through these challenging times than to live the life I more than likely would be living if I didn't have this deep desire to change; live in a positive light and with purpose and love, giving back as I believe we all should do; not being a victim, either by the hands from another or from self-victimization; and lastly, I didn't want to become like her, my mother.

When children are born, we can't see into their futures. We just hope that they will end up happy and healthy. We never envision that their lives will lead them down paths that could possibly harm them. I don't think my parents ever imagined that their youngest daughter would have ended up trying to kill herself a few times between the ages of twelve and fourteen, withdrawing almost completely from school at the age of fifteen—officially dropping out of high school at sixteen (never passing the tenth grade); would take drugs, drink until she'd blacked out constantly and/or threw up, and not stop drinking even though she would be raped at the age of sixteen because she was passed out; become a call girl at the age of twenty-one; and end up being a single mother on welfare at the age of twenty-four. I had a path of destruction—victimization and lack of success as I see it—that started shortly before I took my first breath in this lifetime. I continued these ways for my own life for many years even after I moved out on my own—though unknowingly for a long time, I had no idea that I could do something to change it. I would sometimes wonder, was it my destiny to have this life? I'd sometimes share with others how I just believed that there was a black cloud always following me or assumed that this was the way it was supposed to be. At other times, I pleaded, crying for forgiveness to whomever or whatever was out there. I wanted to know what I could have done so badly in my life or past lives to deserve this life that I had been given. For the first twenty years of my life, there was really never any insight that my life could be any different, free of so much pain and suffering. I had no faith that it could get better. My life always seemed hopeless. Would it always be like this? I often wondered.

I'm not sure when my story began. Does our life and journey really begin at birth, or does our lineage collide with us to lay the foundation to our journey once we are born? Is our spirit passed on from lifetimes before, making amends, learning, and trying to evolve? I've always felt that generations of my past did influence my upbringing. Some habits, traditions, stories, and experiences are passed on from generation to generation, good and bad, just as they are in any family. I'm a melting pot of different cultures—Peruvian, Spanish, German, Irish, and even immigrants that had been living in the U.S. for some time, but mainly my heritage for the last few generations is from a country that is somewhat foreign to me, Peru—a place unknown to me because we left there to move to the United States when I was just three years old.

I was born in Lima, the capital of Peru. It's referred to as the City of the Kings (Ciudad de los Reyes). Lima is on the coast facing the Pacific Ocean; I'd later hear that California reminded my parents of their home country.

My parents were also both born in Peru and so were their parents.

My paternal grandfather, unknown to me, was Santiago Polo Bahamonde. Born in 1906, he worked as a banker for thirty years in Peru. He came from a family "great in stature," says my father. My father's grandfather had a large law firm in Lima, his granduncle was the foreign minister, and his grandmother was one of the first women lawyers in Peru. This part of my family also held many official titles in government. What I have heard about my grandfather is that he was an extremely handsome man and that he was really not part of my father's life.

My paternal grandmother, Maria Esperanza Monroy Sotomayor, had my father when she was just seventeen years old. My father is the eldest of four kids but my grandmother did have another child that died at a young age, about the age of one. She had this boy either right before or after she had my father and sadly this child is rarely spoken of. This must have had an impact on my grandmother and therefore on my father, as well. At a very early age my grandparents had either divorced or separated.

My grandmother was a generous but domineering woman,

which I'd come to hear from my mother. Maybe my mom just took my grandmother's strength as a woman, which my mom doesn't have, as domineering. My mother, in my eyes, was very jealous of my paternal grandmother because of the loyalty my father had toward her. I don't ever recall hearing about her until right before she came to live with us for a while in Houston in the '80s. My grandmother had not finished her education because of her marriage to my grandfather. She was a runner, which I also would later be good at. My father recalls how she could have been a great athlete, and for many years, he had a large picture of her in her early teens on the first page of the sports section of the Lima newspaper, La Cronica, showing her crossing the finish line of the 100-meter dash and being the winner of the national tournament. My grandmother moved to the United States when she was fifty years old. She lived in Southern California, close to her two daughters and other son. She learned English within the first few years after she moved to the States. She died in December 1989.

My parents are both from affluent families, but especially my mother. Her father, my maternal grandfather, was a well-known surgeon in Lima. His name was Gerardo Miguel Lozada-Murillo. He owned a clinic in Lima, Clinica Lozada, for a period of time and was also recognized worldwide for delivering a baby to the youngest confirmed mother in medical history, Lina Medina. She had been brought down from her village by family members to have a doctor help her because it was thought that she had a tumor growing in her belly. After viewing the little girl, my grandfather knew she was pregnant. At the tender age of five, on May 14, Mother's Day, she gave birth to Gerardo, whom she named after my grandfather. It made medical history around the world and was written about in Life magazine, Time magazine, Los Angeles Times newspaper, and the New York Times and is even in the Guinness Book of World Records. She was sought after by Ripley's Believe It or Not, most notably, but my grandfather did not want Lina to become a circus show attraction, so he assisted her family with the ongoing requests for Lina and declined for her to appear anywhere. Gerardo, Lina's son, grew up healthy but died in 1979 at the age of forty of a bone marrow disease. In young adulthood, Lina worked as a secretary in my grandfather's clinic. He gave her an education and helped put her son through high school. Dr. Lozada was a grandfather that I'd never meet because of his death in 1960 and unfortunately all I ever heard about him was that he was a surgeon, helped Lina give birth to her son and helped Lina not become used by the curious media. Though I never met my grandfather, I know he is very much a part of me and was connected to my family for a long time, at least in spirit. I, as a child, had always felt his presence. He was born in Peru and was a teenager when he went to be educated to become a surgeon, my mother later told me. My mother, his daughter, will speak of him as a tender, considerate human being that came to understand the human weaknesses of people. Though very opinionated and a stern disciplinarian with his four daughters, he was a fragile man, she once said.

My maternal grandmother was Ethel Beatriz Montero-Messler. She was born in Peru on October 14, 1907. Her mom, Marie Dolores, came from a wealthy family from Philadelphia, Pennsylvania, in the United States. Her father, Emilio Manuel Montero Meyerhuber, had family in Peru, though his family had moved to England, and he was born in London. He was educated in New York at Peekskill Military Academy and the Rensselaer Polytechnic Institute, also in New York. After my great-grandparents married, they moved, possibly by railroad and sail, back to his homeland of his parents, Peru. My grandmother's parents had arrived in Peru from the United States only a few years prior to my grandmother being born. My grandmother's mother, Marie Dolores (Dolly), died when my grandmother was a very young girl. Over the years, I recalled hearing that my great-grandmother wanted to return with her young daughter back to Philadelphia where her uncles and mom lived but that she never made it due to her health. My great-grandmother's family in Philadelphia—two uncles, Joseph and Thomas, and Agnes, my great-grandmother's mother, the Clabbys— had built a row of stores, which later was known as the "Clabby Block" to us and was right on the Atlantic City boardwalk. They had begun their success by operating one of the first bathhouses on the Atlantic City boardwalk in Atlantic City, New Jersey, which eventually led into purchasing more property on the boardwalk and having a row of stores and a parking lot, which was leased out. The Clabbys became millionaires. I don't believe my grandmother's two uncles ever had children of their own, and I've been told that in 1933 when the Great Depression had been making thousands of people homeless and hungry, my grandmother's last inheritance was all the property in Atlantic City, New Jersey, and about $3 million. Not only was that a lot of money for that time but it also was a lot of money for someone who was living in Peru.

My great-grandfather on my maternal grandmother's side, Emilio, had also come from an affluent family, the Monteros, in Peru. Emilio was an engineer and had been the mayor of Pisco a few times. His brother, Juan Ramon, was one of the very first aviators in Peru. Their family managed multiple investments and businesses prior to their birth, but perhaps the most renowned of all these investments was when they were given the award to build, (using their own money) and operate the railroads in the highly profitable nitrate province of Tarapacá. After the death of Don Juan Bautista Montero Núñez, three of the five sons (including my great-great-grandfather's father, Ramon) partnered together all of their inheritances to establish The Montero and Brothers Company in 1868 and had its headquarters in both Peru and England. In 1872, to finance the project of the building of two railways—Pisagua and Iquique—the Montero brothers, contracted a loan in London for £1.2 million, setting aside a substantial equity, and then they asked for another additional loan of £45,000 in 1873. Prior to the war between Peru, Chile, and Bolivia, the Montero brothers transferred most of their rights to a company formed in London, which retained most of the shares of the company. After the war of control over the lands and with most of the railroads damaged and not in use because of war, the Montero brothers couldn't make some of their loan payments and had to sell their shares at £14 each when their price was £100, losing a considerable sum of money, thus ending the presence of Peruvian and Montero Tarapaquenos Railways. The Monteros still remained with much wealth, owning land and farms in Peru, even after this enormous loss.

The only memory I have of my maternal grandmother is as a kind and elder lady I had met in 1979 when we visited Peru before we moved to Texas. It was the last time I went to Peru and the only time my sisters and I had gone since moving to the United States. My grandmother was a woman with so much love toward her grandchildren even though she did not know who they had become in the prior six years. I've been told by my mother that she was a funny lady, a very happy and full-of-life person. But like her husband, she also had strong and very defined opinions. In later times, they had both become very separate thinkers. They had become their own persons, and once that had happened, they both became very difficult because their opinions were mostly wrong, my mother has said. My grandmother died of a heart deficiency on October 30, 1991, a little too soon before I could go back and see her before she passed away. I had wanted for years to go back and see the only one in our whole family that I thought truly cared for me and my sisters' well-being.

As mentioned earlier, my ancestors were a combination of Irish, German, Spanish, Peruvian, and possibly from what I've heard, also Scottish. While growing up there was an emphasis on the Irish side, even though I'd later find out that we had a huge history coming from the German side. Our mother may have emphasized the Irish side because her mother did also. While growing up in Ohio, we would later be introduced to other countries' traditions, like leaving our clogs or wooden shoes out for St. Nick.

I heard of the richness of only my mom's side of the family, not just the materialistic but also all the great things they achieved and where they came from and I couldn't stop to wonder of all the misfortunes we had while growing up and how maybe my mom's upbringing was somehow to blame. I think somehow my mom was crippled at an early age emotionally, and she was kept from doing the things she wanted to do for herself. Back in my grandfather's generation, men were the rulers of their castles, and that is how I believe my grandfather ran his house. I don't know all that went on or even what childhood was really like for my mother and her three younger sisters, but I believe it must have been tough. I've always thought that something must have gone wrong, despite being brought up in a grand home with the kind of money they had. They were taught in convents (which is like going to a Catholic private school), had maids, cooks, and nannies, and had an abundance of wealth that provided them with the luxuries of traveling in the United States, Europe, and Japan, going to college in New York, and having the finest of clothes and jewelry.

This is about the only truth I know of my mother's upbringing. I also do know that my mother went to college in New York and had wanted to stay longer and eventually go to France to further her education, but to my recollection of what I've overheard was that my grandfather would not allow her because her place in life was to become a wife and mother. My mother is not very judgmental when it comes to her father; in a way, she has always praised and adored him. But he must have done (or not done) something to have his children all end up as they did. Maybe they were just too confined and held back from pursuing their dreams. Maybe it is as simple as being too spoiled and not having to know or hear about real-life situations. Besides my mother being an alcoholic and having the emotional and mental inadequacy problems I believe she has, I've overheard that others in the family and past generations have also been or are possibly also addicts, along with possibly having emotional and psychological problems, as well. My mother and her sisters have fought constantly for decades, even without having any kind of contact for years at a time. I think the root of all the fighting had to do with greed and stealing from one another; it was fortunate that my mother moved so far away, because that kept her out of most of the fighting—but at a loss in the end. One of her sisters passed away in 2010, and we did not hear about it until a month later. I may never know the dynamics of my mom's family and what truly went on. I just believe there might have been enormous sadness, neglect, abuse, overindulgence, or all of the above in the house where they grew up. I may never know the truth of how my grandfather really was or what really went on in that house to make my mom so broken and fragile.

Growing up, I heard so many stories of my mom's side of the family, the history of the Clabbys, the Monteros and the Lozadas, like they were the only ones we came from. It would not be until later, recently, that we'd hear my dad speak (or be able to speak) about his family and his life prior to my mom. This probably happened because if you ever met my mother or really know her, she is a very selfish, self-centered person. Only her universe is important, and she dismisses everyone else's.

From what my parents both told me, all my grandparents were Catholic. On my mom's side, it was her dad who was the extremist, and on my father's side, it was his mother. Our parents raised us four girls as Catholic, but while growing up, we rarely went to church. As I saw it, we rarely went to church because my mother was either hungover or my parents didn't want to deal with their four complaining daughters who didn't want to go. All us girls were baptized and did have our first Communion. I remember the early years in Ohio, and we were taught to kneel next to our beds to say our prayers. From a very young age, I always thought that my parents weren't very religious when it came to acting like it. Maybe this was the beginning of my questioning organized religion and religious people. As far as my sisters and I go, we are all over the place when it comes to religion, our beliefs or spirituality.

My own view is that I don't know if there is a God. I say, "I'll see when I pass," and in the meantime, I just try to live a good life. I prefer not to be labeled or defined by a religion, but as I describe my beliefs to anyone, my son has pointed out to me and says that I'm Agnostic, which is okay, but I like to mix in a little bit of Buddhism in there. I have at times been in a Catholic church in Beverly Hills or in the missions throughout Southern California, which I find beautiful. If anything, I have felt connections to what lies out there beyond our sight, and before this life. I see the beauty in some of the art in religion, and I like some of the stories, but to me, they are just that—stories. Growing up I saw the judgmental, one-sidedness of organized religion, and because of this, I must say that I don't stand by most of what is preached in the Catholic Church or Christianity. I also feel that my childhood truly affected me when it comes to how organized religion is taught and perceived, that all you need is God in your life, and he will help you. No one helped me or my sisters while we were growing up. And, I saw and heard of so much suffering in the world and couldn't understand why God didn't stop it and doesn't stop it. Why would something make you choose it to believe in it—and then, only then, would it help you? It never made sense to me. My god, if there is one, loves, forgives, understands, and doesn't force you to do anything, like choose, especially choosing him over another. I believe that religion is a crutch that people use today, which is fine if that is what they need to get by, but I believe that it is used and has been used for so long to scare individuals into behaving. You don't need a religion to be a good person to yourself and to others or to live your life correctly and give back to humanity. And, I believe faith is very different from religion. I think many confuse the two and think they go hand in hand. My conflict with religion, because of my upbringing, led me to find a different crutch when I need something to believe in, something to help me go on, even if it was just for one more day. The conflict laid the foundation for me later in my twenties to learn to lean on myself and know that I'd get through just about anything. I would later learn to believe that I was strong and that I could—would—survive, even when at times I didn't want to. How greatly different this must be from my grandparents' lives and beliefs?

The house of my grandparents, the Lozadas, which still stands today in Lima, is one that I can only dream of ever having. I used to want to rebuild it here in the States if I were ever to become rich. It was sold in 2011 for about $1.3 million, and somehow, with all the fighting with my mom and her sisters, my mom's share was only 12.5 percent when she was supposed to have gotten 25 percent. After my grandfather's death in 1960, my grandmother, my mother, and her three sisters would never be the same again.

My father wed into a family that any man would envy from outside appearances. The Lozadas traveled worldwide, staying at the nicest hotels (the Waldorf Astoria and the Plaza in New York City), enjoyed shopping sprees at Bergdorf Goodman, Lord & Taylor, and Mikimoto, were well respected in their community, were well-educated, and had what seemed a vast fortune, but my father never saw that these women's lives were taking a new path—a path of destruction. They had for some reason fallen apart after my grandfather's death. Soon after his death, my mother and her sisters' problems truly evolved, and my grandmother had to deal with all her daughters falling apart.

I believe this was a true turning point—a crippling effect and a new path for possibly generations to come. But, I also believe their problems had already been planted little by little before this tragedy. My dad was probably too clouded to see any of the serious problems my mom had, but his foundation may have had just as strong of an impact as my mother's; his was just not so apparent. His family was also successful, but his dad had left while my father was still young and this seemed to have left a hole in his heart that was covered with anger.

Even though there was a legacy of success and wealth, there was a legacy of being broken. I wondered if my own misery already started by these wounded hearts? Could the achievements of past generations—being focused more on accomplishments and money—have left them not being connected to what was really important in life, have played a part too? Or was it just unluckiness that transpired and did life just happen to me the way it was supposed to happen?

I believe we all come with baggage; we all have issues, some more than others. We all have aspects of ourselves that have not been fully developed and nurtured. There are many things some of us were never taught and somehow have to learn for ourselves. Some of us go through life trying to fully develop ourselves and our life skills. We want to uplift our spirits so that we may leave a positive mark on people we touch, especially our children. Then there are some of us that don't see that anything is wrong, nothing needs to be fixed. The wounds hit so deeply that we cannot get back up and experience life to the fullest though. I didn't want that to be me. Traces of hurt are sprinkled behind to leave a trail and these family cycles continue. I wanted to try to find my own way to heal my wounds and this is my story on trying to find my way to evolve, find peace in my life and to break the cycle—changing the path that was laid down for me.

The evening I came home after being threatened, I cried and thought to myself—my life wasn't supposed to be like this. I wondered—what made my life veer so off course—when did it all go so wrong? Would I ever be able to learn to fully change my life, my path, my journey?

2

In the Beginning

My dad was born on December 9, 1933, in Peru. He grew up in Lima and lived with his paternal grandmother after his parents' divorce and his father couldn't take care of him, leaving my father to be raised without his father and rarely even seeing him; at least that is what I recall hearing. His mother had gotten custody of the other three children. My father's grandmother lived in a very distinguished area of Peru in a large colonial-style house. He told me he had no structure of a family; no one was really looking out for him as parents should. At the age of seven, my father got very sick because he was not well taken care of. Later, he had gotten into a fight with some kids, leaving him with a black eye. His mother found out about these things. She no longer cared of what the judge declared, and she retrieved her son from what she considered an undisciplined environment. And even though he would later move back with his mother and his siblings, the divorce and possible feelings of abandonment from both his parents may have had an effect on my father that could have resulted in his fierce anger later in life.

My father never graduated from high school, which may be the reason why it was so important that all his children get the best education they could and for it to be further than high school. He went to work in a bank, where his father had worked previously. Starting at entry level, he worked his way up. After four years, he went to work with a friend, a son from the well-known Prado family. The Prados had presidencies of Peru among their successes. The Prado family also had other businesses, like in the banking world with Banco Popular. My father and his friend were starting a company dealing with stocks and equity. After five years of doing business together, the company thrived and was becoming profitable. The brothers of my father's friend—who, prior to this time, wouldn't have invested five minutes of their time—wanted to be involved with the business because it was becoming very successful. My father says the brothers pushed my father out of the way, even though it was he and his friend who had built up the business. After leaving that position, he then returned to the bank at which he had formerly worked.

My mother was born on July 3, 1936, in Lima. She was raised in Pisco, Peru, a coastal town just south of Lima. She is the eldest of four girls. "Beautiful, beautiful childhood," my mother recalls. She had everything, she says, even though she had a very confined life. She wasn't allowed to go out to play with the children in the neighborhood until she began attending school at the age of eight. The only kids she could play with were her mother's friends' children, and that was only at birthday parties. She attended a private school that was run by nuns, Saint Ursula. She told me that for ten years she learned the necessities of an immaculate education but was never taught what went on in the real world or how to cope with the outside world, its circumstances, and most people.

Though it was a beautiful childhood, she says, it was a lonely one. She only played with one of her sisters while both of her parents worked. Their isolation from other children made her very shy, and when she went to school, it was hard for her to cope with situations, she says. When she started puberty, she began to realize the harsh regulations that her father was now imposing on her. On top of being overly sensitive about what other people would think of her, her father's fears of his first daughter growing up made it very difficult. It was eerie as she spoke of it, because it always seemed as though things were great in her childhood and that everything was always great between her and her father.

Around this time, it was taboo to speak about sex and just the natural developments everyone goes through in life, and it seems that my mother had a difficult time, because she was alone and couldn't go to anyone about life's transitions. Breaking through her dad's tight grip, though, she managed to get him to allow her to attend junior college for one year at Briarcliff College, an exclusive women's college located in the village of Briarcliff Manor in Westchester County, New York. The only young ladies that attended from out of the United States came from some of the wealthiest, most affluent families at that time. It was just another privilege from her upbringing and being from the family she came from.

It was the summer of 1959 when my father met my mother in Lima. And being one another's first love, my mom says, they knew within a month after meeting that they eventually would marry. My father says that before he met her, his perspective on marriage and love was minimal. My mother tells me that even after warning him that with her came the possibility of tremendous fighting among family members over the treasure my grandfather would leave behind after his death in 1960, he married her, anyway.

During my childhood, there were many accusations from my mother when she was drinking that he initially married her because she was so wealthy. She'd say things like that in front of us when she was drunk. Looking back, I don't believe those accusations, because he stuck by her, for better or for worse (in my eyes, it has been definitely worse) and for richer or for poorer (which, for the last twenty-seven years in comparison to my mom's lifestyle, has definitely been poorer). In February 1962, they married. Within a year, my mother gave birth to their first of four daughters. Her name was Candelaria. Within the next five years, they had two more daughters, Paoletta in 1964 and Guadalupe in 1968. During these years, they lived in a relatively small apartment in Lima. Though there was plenty of money on my mother's side of the family, my mother didn't participate in the constant asking for money or things as her sisters did up until it virtually all ran out.

On March 7, 1970, on a sunny Saturday afternoon, my mom gave birth to me. I've been told by my mother that I was a quiet baby. I guess I still remain quiet most of the time. After four girls, three miscarriages, and being still very religious and did not use birth control, my mother had her tubes tied, making me the baby of the family, though it's hard for me to recall being treated like that. When I look back at my childhood, Guadalupe was really treated as though she were the baby. It seemed like she always got her way and was the closest to my mother, and my mother just absolutely adored her.

The years we lived in Peru before we moved to the States must have been very tough for my parents, even though the four of us girls each had nannies, and my mother had her family close by. I believe that my mother at this time was already socially drinking, but she was drinking very often and more than likely a little bit too much. I believe that she drank while she was pregnant with all of us, but definitely with me, and she also smoked cigarettes. The reason I believe she did was because I've only known her to abuse alcohol and be a chain-smoker. I can't imagine a time when it wasn't this way. And even though I can hold conversations, write well, and do well in school and at jobs, there is the problem sometimes with my brain's response time. Let's just say it is slower than I'd like. I've walked away from situations, not being aware instantly that I was being insulted or being spoken to in a degrading way. And years ago, I read somewhere about a possible link with sugar addiction and drinking while being pregnant. I was teased all my life about my bad habit with sugar. It seems like the typical sweet tooth, but I can also eat powdered sugar for hours if it is in a bowl in front of me. In the '70s, it was still a time when it was unknown what effects smoking and drinking could do to an unborn baby and way before secondhand smoking was even thought of. Unfortunately at that time, the news wasn't there of these harms while being pregnant, and possibly her addiction already took hold. I don't want to blame her or her addiction, but sometimes I do wonder where the root lies with some of these things and if alcohol and smoking could have played a factor even before my birth.

Troubles through the family had been going on for close to ten years before my grandfather's death, my mother told me. I grew up hearing of how all this materialism and wealth that my mother's parents had received and established tore up the family. After my grandfather passed away, my grandmother couldn't or didn't know how to deal with her daughters and how to say no to them. She allowed them to take and take and take, my mother says. Some may say the Lozada daughters were spoiled. I think they all, including my grandparents, just knew how to spend and spend and keep spending. And once the only person who was actually physically working was gone and there were no more inheritances to supplement the actual working income, the money eventually did run out. I've heard of so many stories, like one of my mom's sisters flying on a whim to Spain to follow or see a matador; they were like rock stars back in those days, at least in Lima. Or there was another time when one daughter was able to get a brand-new Aston Martin. This was on top of the lavish trips to Europe, Japan, and New York and all the fancy stuff that was bought on a regular basis, even prior to my grandfather's death. And when they traveled, there were shopping sprees, they stayed at the top hotels, and they were chauffeured around in limousines. I don't believe that my mother and her sisters were educated on a basic fact about money—that you have to earn it or invest it, because if you don't, it definitely won't fall from the sky. They were kept down from the beginning of infancy to not learn this, as I see it. They were allowed to live as freely and lavishly as they chose for so long, just living as if money would always be there for them. So the appreciation surely wasn't there, either. They were also raised at a time when only men needed to know about money and weren't only the breadwinners but the sole providers. Most people thought like this at the time.

Before the time I was born, my parents had been talking about moving to the States. My parents wanted to move to the United States because of the problems that were happening politically. In the Peruvian government between 1968 and 1975, Juan Velasco Alvarado was a left-leaning Peruvian general who ruled Peru under the title of "President of the Revolutionary Government." He introduced radical reforms, which included agrarian reform, the expropriation of foreign companies, the introduction of an economic planning system, and the creation of a large state-owned sector. These measures failed to achieve their objectives of income redistribution and the end of economic dependence on developed nations.

One story I heard from my parents was about the expropriation of foreign companies. In the '60s, Peru was telling anyone who owned property or assets outside of the country that they'd have to sell them and hand over some or all the profits to the government, and if this wasn't done, the individuals would be put in jail. This was a difficult issue for our family, because my grandmother owned a whole block of the Atlantic City boardwalk at that time. Because of this reform, my grandmother had to sell the property in New Jersey, which New Jersey had also been pressuring her to sell because of "community remodification"—eminent domain. My parents and my grandmother were told by the State of New Jersey and its attorneys that if they didn't sell, it would be taken from her. My father and mother went with my grandmother Beatrice to help her negotiate a better deal in New Jersey. The Clabby Block was sold for about twice more than what they wanted to originally give my grandmother. I believe the sale price was a little over $500,000. To this day, my dad believes that it wasn't used for the intended purpose—remodification of the community—but for building casinos, which had been on New Jersey's radar for some time. With the money of the Clabby Block, my grandmother purchased some property in Philadelphia, which my mother then sold from her inherited property portion in 1991. The other reason for us having left our homeland was that my parents wanted a better life—really, a better education for their four girls, which we heard often while growing up. A good, well-rounded education was their primary reason. I'd heard that possibly Peru was being influenced by Fidel Castro's teachings and that it was education in the schools that was changing. The rumors and possibility of Fidel's literature in the schools was my father's final straw, he told me.

My father told my mother that he would go to the United States and find a job and then later send for us, but my mother's insecurities outweighed what he had in mind. She told me that she insisted that she and their daughters were going with him. She told me that she was in fact scared that he'd go and that he wouldn't send for us; she was scared that we'd never hear from him again. She wasn't going to have her children grow up without a father. This is one of only a few smart things that my mother did in her lifetime.

In April 1973, we went to New York, where my father had a friend who was a lawyer that handled immigration, among other things. Before we left Lima, he told my father that there would be no problem getting us residency and that we'd have it within a few weeks. It took almost three years, and even though we traveled legally, we ended staying up illegally after our visas ran out because the lawyer from New York couldn't help us.

My first vivid memory of my childhood is of us being in New York City. I remember loving the circular, revolving doors at the hotel and the unique, now old-school buttons in the elevators—Guadalupe and I fought over who was going to be able to push them—and when I see kids doing this nowadays, I just smile with fondness. We possibly stayed at the Plaza, which was one of the hotels where the Lozadas typically stayed, the other being the Waldorf Astoria. Another thing while we were in New York that I do recall was meeting this tall, blonde white lady and jumping on beds with two boys who were about my age and had fairer skin than I and blond hair like the woman's. It was my godmother and her sons. Another very smart thing my mother did do in her lifetime was to choose this lady to be my godmother.

My godmother was from a very wealthy family in Mexico City and was now living on Park Avenue in New York. She and my mother had gone to school together at Briarcliff. When I was born, my mother wanted her to be my godmother, but Tia, as I call her now, was moving to Paris, France. She explained to my mother that she couldn't be in my life in that fashion because her life was going across the Atlantic, and she didn't know when or if she was coming back to the States. My mother insisted and somehow convinced Tia to take on the role of being my godmother.

She has been truly a blessing in my life. Though she always remembered me at birthdays and Christmas, we truly didn't connect until I was sixteen, after my mom had called her drunk, begging her to take me in, and told her how I was dropping out of high school. My godmother called me right after she got off the phone with my mother, and I shared with her how my life had been growing up—the abuse, the neglect, and the alcoholism. She never took me in but has since encouraged me, supported me, guided me, and tried to be my strength and positivity when I couldn't do so for myself. It has been more than a gift to still have her in my life and share her with my son.

After knowing we couldn't get residency right away, we went to Cincinnati, Ohio, where my mother had other friends from college. They had told my mother that if she had ever intended to move to the United States, they would give her guidance and advice when the time came. After speaking and being connected with who could help, we were told that we had to obtain our green cards by going to Canada, filing the appropriate paperwork, getting another visa for the time being, and reentering the United States legally again. It was through the help of the senator of Ohio, not through the lawyer in New York we trusted, that we later obtained our green cards. At the time, the senator of Ohio was somehow related to former president Taft; my mother had gone to school with the senator's daughter. It really does help to make connections, especially in the right places.

For the first few years that we were here, only my father worked. He worked in the back of a restaurant owned by his friends the Comisars, helping as kitchen staff. We were almost like any other immigrants who move to the United States and had to start all over again. But I do acknowledge that we were a little bit different somewhat—privileged. We had flown over here. We had money to stay at hotels, eventually rented a condo, and had the means to travel from New York to Ohio and then from Ohio to Canada, even stopping to view Niagara Falls like we were tourists on vacation. Though I come from such a family, I do have a soft spot for illegal immigrants who have to travel by any means necessary just to have better lives, even at the cost of their own. I've been told that what money we came over with and what money my mom received from her family helped us to survive those first few years in our new homeland. Eventually, my parents bought a house within the Indian Hill School District, which is in the suburbs of Cincinnati and one of the best school districts in Ohio. The house, on a cul-de-sac in Heightmeyer Farms, was a four-bedroom, two-story house that had a sprawling backyard.

In 1976, my father, now legal to work in the United States, got a job at Conval International, an oil valve distribution company with headquarters in Chicago, Illinois. He told me he started in the shipping department, and within two months, he became the sales manager of Central America. After six months, he then became the sales manager for all of Latin America and the Caribbean. He was a man with no limitations on what he could do and accomplish. It seemed like things were great for our family and that we were back to climbing up the ladder of success. But our lives were not turning out as my parents had hoped, especially how my mom thought it would be.

My mom had grown up thinking she could have the large house and beautiful family, obedient and religious children, and a life with all or some of the wealth she had growing up, but that was never in the cards for us. She had never been without maids, cooks, and nannies. She probably didn't know how much work it took to maintain a home and kids. And here she was now living in this foreign country without her family, without any help, and with very tight financial resources that now needed to be earned by not only my father but by her, as well.

She has spoken over the years of how hard it was in the beginning because of the different cultural and social ways from what she had known. It was the '70s, and people were looser about their views on politics, sex, drugs, and their behavior. She wasn't accustomed to this. It was decades before she came to terms with how people thought and behaved here. I'm sure in Peru there were also freethinkers and people with loose attitudes, but never in her social and economic circles.

These early years of what I can remember weren't that bad for us as children. Not to mislead you, my mother was drinking a lot. Well, when she drank, I'm sure she got drunk. She'd often pass out after starting a fight with my father. I only have glimpses of the incidents that happened on occasion. I do remember seeing large cases of Budweiser or jugs of wine around the kitchen or in the garage, but I didn't know at this time it was a problem; I just assumed it was normal. At seven years old, do we question what is normal and what is not?

When I look back on these early years, I see two sides to my life. Because we were at times latchkey kids and it was the '70s—carefree and without many boundaries, just left to play outside to our hearts' content—my sisters and I were happy. When I look back at those times and picture my parents, though, for the most part, there was tension, fighting, and unhappiness. And unfortunately, for many years, I held on to this side of my life probably because I only knew how to hold on to the negative.

My dad seemed to be traveling often for business, and unfortunately, this is my memory of us in Ohio too. My dad's traveling left me to become very distant from him because I was so young. He was gone for what seemed extensive periods of time, but they were probably only for about a week or so. When he was home, he felt like a stranger to me to the point that my mom would have to ask me to give him a kiss good night before going to bed. That always felt awkward to me. I'd never give him a kiss; instead, I'd turn my face to have him kiss me on the cheek. I'd always dread when nighttime came and she'd ask me to do this. Most of the time, I felt as if he was just a distant friend of the family, but he was my father.

I remember Guadalupe being like Daddy's little girl. I may not have felt like Daddy's little girl, but I felt close to him when it came to driving and cars. We had those two things in common: we liked cars and loved driving dangerously. I loved having the chance to sit on his lap and handle the steering wheel while he was driving. Gotta love the '70s. I got a thrill when he'd drive fast down the circular ramps between the levels, exiting the parking lot that went down many levels. And he may have liked how I loved Hot Wheels cars instead of Barbie or other dolls. I used to love getting my Hot Wheels cars for Christmas, and I was especially happy the Christmas I got the Hot Wheels suitcase to store all my cars in. My love of cars and driving fast still remains today.

What I also recall mostly of our early childhood days in Cincinnati was of it being a time of innocence, the childhood that most of us had or wish we'd had. Long summers spent playing outdoors, catching fireflies at night, and picking strawberries out of our garden. Not coming in until it was after dark, knowing that our curfew was set only by when it got dark and the streetlights came on or when we'd hear our parents' whistle. We'd cherish those hot summer days when one of our parents would set the rotating sprinkler outside to cool us off. We'd lie out, blasting music from inside the house while our parents were off at work. My sisters and I spent a lot of time being outside playing in our enormous backyard, climbing trees, riding our bikes, and sledding in the winters. We all did activities like play soccer. My dad even coached my two older sisters' team. Guadalupe and I hated soccer, because we were so fearful of the physical contact, me especially. I hated how it seemed like the girls were coming after me, chasing me down to kick the ball, my legs sometimes being in the way; therefore, I'd be kicked in the shins repeatedly. To me, it was another form of being hit. I hated it. I was happy when we were no longer forced to play. Guadalupe and I also did gymnastics, in which she thrived. I became pretty good at my tumbling, backbends, and somersault skills. We also did ballet and took tap lessons, and I was in the choir at school.

I had a very two-sided childhood. On one hand, it was bliss and the wonderfulness of exploring and learning life. On the other hand, it was seeing the unpleasantries of what life could also offer if you have people around you who are unhappy. The joyful moments of an innocent, carefree childhood were intertwined with little jabs of meanness by a sister or clouded by parents arguing over things that made no sense at the time. It was bad enough that Guadalupe would jump at the chance to harm me, either with words or physically, but here were the people who brought me into this world who destroyed special moments, like birthdays and Christmases that we all hold so dear, with the exception of one of my birthdays, which had been the teacher's fault. I was in the first grade, and my mother later found out that the teacher had forgotten to pass out the birthday invitations. I had been all dressed up, waiting for everyone to attend my party at my house, but no one did. I was too young to understand. It just felt like no one liked me and didn't want to come to my birthday. With the exception of times like this and the in-between fighting, I think I mostly felt that life wasn't that bad because I was so young and didn't know anything different.

When my mom was sober or not working, she'd teach us how to bake. She'd also try to have sit-down meals at the kitchen table, but somehow that eventually was pushed by the wayside to converge around the television for dinner, like most families in the '70s did. What I remember about having dinner in the living room was the punishment Guadalupe and I'd get for not eating these adult-size portions my parents would serve us. Guadalupe and I were little, not as tall and lacking the bone size of our two older sisters, but we were expected to eat everything on our plates, even if that included the liver my mother enjoyed so much. And when we didn't continue eating, my mother would have us stand in a corner with our faces toward the wall until we said we were ready to finish eating. But when it came to the liver, that was sometimes a two-day process where she, my mother, would reheat it for us to eat, and it still wouldn't be finished the second time around, at least not completely. Liver is the worst thing to eat if you don't eat it right away. It gets very dry and tough and hard to chew, even with adding mustard to it (anything to make it taste good). It's the most difficult thing you can feed a child. We later made jokes in Houston, calling our mother "Mommy Dearest," because in the movie of the same title, this is done—the reheating and reattempting to eat the same plate of food the following day. I know she probably thought she was feeding us something healthy, but that was gross!

Another thing I remember from those times circled around the TV. My mom used to smoke like a chimney and I had such a dislike of cigarette smoke that one Christmas I bought her an ashtray that sucked in the smoke. I probably didn't like the smoke because I was allergic, and my nose would just close up. And there was one time that I reached for her glass of what I thought was water, and instead, it was the remains of her beer and a cigarette. I can still smell that smell that penetrated my nose prior to touching my lips and going down my throat. I gag just at the mention or thought of it. Smokers and smoking would eventually end up being my number-one pet peeve even though I'd smoke for a few years as a teenager.

Throughout my life, there were moments that were fond memories or that refined and educated us to some extent, but then there are memories that are complete nightmares. It is the life of an alcoholic home, a dysfunctional love and what we used to call discipline, which in our household was really mental, physical, and emotional abuse. As I see it and saw it, it was not always bad. We were not being tortured. We were being fed, clothed, and shown some social graces of being classy, well-mannered females. But that doesn't take away from the fact that we were significantly, spiritually, being changed and hurt. My mom did what she was raised to do—marry and have children. But I question if that is what she truly wanted. I don't think to this day if she knows what she wanted. I know if anyone were to ask her, she'd say that she loved having us and that she wouldn't have changed that. But no one knew how much of a broken, fragile soul she was when she set forth with these things called adulthood and parenthood. She wanted to pass on her customs and traditions that she was more than likely raised with. That sounds so easy and idealistic, but it is not, and when you come to a different country that has just come out of a time like the '60s, it is pretty impossible. She did try for a while to re-create the upbringing she had and the family she wanted for herself, but she found herself defeated time and time again by us, by her husband, and by her community.

In Cincinnati, I shared a bedroom with Guadalupe. We grew up hearing how we looked like twins, even though we are two years apart. Sometimes because of hearing this so often, I almost felt as we were meant to be as close as twins. My relationship with her is an interesting one. We've been at times as tight as they come, but I believe she had a love-hate relationship with me growing up and probably still does deep down inside. When I was six months old, Guadalupe rode on my back as if I were a pony (so the story goes) while I lay on the floor. It gave me a hernia. It is my only real operation so far. When I looked back at this incident in my twenties and thirties, I believed that the little girl just wanted to truly get rid of me. Early on, in Cincinnati, she'd randomly hit me; I believe it was to see how it felt to hit someone. Violence begets violence. And what is interesting is that at night she'd crawl into my bed to sleep with me and hold my hand. She needed me more than I ever wanted or needed her. She'd tease me more than she slapped, though, which is so much more harmful. She repeated over and over to me for years of how ugly I was and told me of how nobody wanted to be my friend, and later, she'd constantly tell me how fat I was. I struggled for decades with believing her, even after she stopped. It became that internal dialogue that I still hear sometimes. These are words that brainwashed me on what I should believe about myself, and those words never completely go away. They come up sometimes when that guy rejects me or when I'm not feeling good enough for someone or I don't get invited to a certain event a friend is having. And sometimes I've had a hard time looking at myself in the mirror and really seeing what is reflected back. I have forever been so critical about how I look and of my weight. Coming from a background like mine—of abuse and addiction—most would say that my not feeling worthy enough

∞ Evolving to Grace ∞

stemmed from that part of my past. But I believe the majority of my struggle for years of how I felt about myself came from my sister's constant negative words about my image and personality. It has taken a long time to realize the specialness of me and that what she said wasn't all true.

From my parents, especially my mom, I got that I would never get the love I believe I deserved. From Guadalupe, I got that I would never be good enough, pretty enough, or skinny enough. These things are very hard to reprogram within yourself. When I look back now and think of Guadalupe, it's funny and sad to me. I used to cry over many of the things she'd do to me, physically and verbally, but for most of my teenage years, I believed she was out of her mind, which I guess gave me some pleasure for those mere seconds that I thought that way. I can see now that our childhood and the things that went on affected her just like the rest of us. She was just reacting to it differently from the way I did.

I've learned over the years in therapy that there are two main types of individuals—introverted and extroverted—sometimes with a little bit of both. As children, I was almost 100 percent introverted in every way, and she was mostly extroverted. I took everything in on myself, and she lashed out physically or verbally to the outside world—mostly at me, unfortunately, possibly because I was the closest to her.

There is another factor in all this. I believe also something happened to her when she was a baby because of all the medical complications she had. Right after she was born, she was taken back to the hospital because my mother said something was really wrong when she fed her, and she wasn't gaining weight. The doctors found that she was born missing part of her esophagus, and she had surgery to stretch her esophagus to connect it to her stomach. I've heard of a few things that went wrong during this time in the hospital. For one, the nurses had trouble with putting an IV in her, so they thought the best spot was on top of her foot, but actually they didn't get the vein, and Guadalupe's foot enlarged with whatever the fluid was in the IV. It burned her. She has a scar larger than the size of a quarter on her foot because of that. I also heard that her incubator fell and that could have possibly affected her. That happened to a relative of ours, and because of the lack of oxygen he received from it falling, he is mentally handicapped, my mother says. If anyone has ever had an infant go through pain, such as medically—and I saw it firsthand with my son decades later—you are aware that the memory may have forgotten, but the body and soul haven't. We may never know if this trauma at such an early age had an additional effect on Guadalupe. But her outbursts and immediate reactions were so intense that my sisters and I tried so hard to convince our parents that something was wrong with her. It wasn't normal to us that someone would react from zero to one hundred in half a second. I could say now how some of the situations were funny while I roll my eyes. I could also see how sad it was, but now I can say it is okay. She's pretty mellow nowadays, and what I sometimes struggle with because of what she inflicted is minimal now. But I do feel for the child she once was and of how miserable she must have felt to make her do the things she did. She was always the one that was outgoing and made friends easily with everyone, which is one of the positive things about her. She needed attention, though, and would try to find love by having the spotlight on her. I was always her shadow. Even when I became friends with someone, I felt they'd use me to be friends with her. Through the years, I came to learn something that was very precious, which was making a few real friends who were out of Guadalupe's shadow and reach. Finding that they wanted to be my friend, not hers, was very gratifying and genuine to me.

While we lived in Ohio, I was never as close to my sisters Candelaria and Paoletta as I was to Guadalupe. They were much older. In those days, they tell me they spent most of their time away from home. I do recall moments like when their friends from down the street would come over and skateboard and use our roof as a platform to skate off of. I found it so cool and even got my very own first skateboard because of this. Candelaria told me she drank a lot and went to parties. Paoletta always tried to follow just to get away from my parents and what was going on in the house. I can't recall sharing too many moments with Candelaria and Paoletta in those years. I see flashes of them but not necessarily lengths of time with them, except for the moment when Candelaria had to stay home from school and watch me because I was sick and my parents had to work. She had done this on a few occasions, but there was one time that has remained very clear in our memory.

I was still in my pajamas. I must have been around seven years old, and I had a fever. Candelaria was in the kitchen opening those old glass Coke bottles that were about a liter. And because she couldn't get it to open, she tapped the top of the bottle on the kitchen counter, like we all do sometimes. The Coke bottle exploded, she screamed for me, and I walked into the kitchen just seeing blood everywhere. My parents worked too far away to be able to rush home, so I frantically ran around the cul-de-sac in my pajamas to find someone to drive us to the emergency room. Keep in mind that during this time and for many years to come, this was very hard for me, because I was so introverted and extremely shy. I barely ever spoke up, so going outside of my comfort zone to ask someone to do something like drive us to the hospital was huge. I remember not only the panic of seeing all that blood but the panic of going up to someone's door and asking for help. Candelaria to this day has the longest scar on the front of her leg, and we now can laugh at that moment we shared. It was one of those *wow* moments—did that really happen?

We were all having our own ways of dealing and reacting with what was going on. Not only was my mother going through becoming or having become an alcoholic, but there were times of physical abuse. One can say it was the '70s and that was what was going on, but ours was and progressed to something much more. I cannot remember what Guadalupe and I would do wrong except keep our bedroom messy. Maybe Guadalupe would speak back, but I remember a time when my father asked me to choose the belt I'd like to be hit with, and I never remember just being hit once or twice. It was several swats. At the age of six, seven, or eight, could I have done something so wrong to deserve this?

Another form of abuse that arose was neglect. I can't say it happened every day but it happened more than it should have. Within these households that have addiction and a parent that is emotionally broken, it happens. My mother didn't know how to love us and never learned to truly put her children before her emotional needs. When things were going well for her, she did spend some time with us, I'm sure—*I think*. But when things weren't going well or when life was asking too much of her—like being a wife, being part of the workforce, keeping up the house, and then being a mother—she wasn't able to figure out how to keep up with life's expectations. I remember more of being taught that love was materialistic, and our love from our parents, mainly my mother, was bought. We were bought the finest things and given almost anything we wanted. In my teenage years, I'd come to realize how this was done to us. We had mostly chaos and unhappiness in the home, but the lavish Christmases, holidays, or birthdays or nice clothes felt like they were supposed to make up for what they possibly felt guilty for not giving us. An apology goes a long way! Time and good experiences are priceless when it comes to relationships. A lot of us lose this importance in our demanding lives. Money doesn't buy love under any circumstance.

In my first few years of school, I felt out of place but did not know why. My earliest memory was of kindergarten. I had my first crush. He was a cute Caucasian boy with medium-brown hair. His name was Steven, better known within our family as "the kissing boy." I remember that he'd run around during recess and kiss all girls except for me. I even vaguely remember possibly crying about it or being sad. I believed that I was too ugly for him (or maybe I had been told that by Guadalupe at the time). Steven and I would become friends and sit together at lunch, and I'd invite him to my first birthday party that included boys. He was sweet.

During first and second grade, I began learning to read and write English very well. I've been told that Spanish was my first language. It must have been a hard transition for all of us to learn English fluently, except for my mom, who already spoke it well, including several other languages. My mom says I spoke Spanish up until we moved to the States, but I was three. She says that I stopped speaking for three months, and then I started speaking English. To this day, I'm not fluent in Spanish and don't really speak it very much. I like to say my pronunciation is worse than any American trying it for the first time, so I rarely try, just *un poquito*. I can get words across, and when needed on trips to Mexico, I can try to put together some kind of a sentence. At least in somewhere like Cancun, they don't get mad at me like they do sometimes here in California when I cannot fluently speak Spanish. I even had someone here in L.A. say to me, "What kind of Hispanic are you?" *Essh, that was harsh.* I would have loved to answer and say so much to that person, but ignorance has to be sometimes ignored, and even to this day, I don't know how to react to people when they speak to me like that, so I say nothing. Maybe one day, that cashier will venture out of L.A. and see that Hispanics aren't all the same. But I do hope to one day be able to speak Spanish.

My parents, for a short period of time, had been interested about how our education was going. But within time, their schedules with both of them working, making sure the kids were fed and dressed, and possibly her drinking, there was little time to help us with schoolwork or to go to our back-to-school nights and see what progress was taking place. I do recall hearing at times from various family members that my mother's drinking was the issue and that she would show up drunk. And when she drank, it was always apparent. I think it was when I was in the second grade. It would be the last school show my parents saw. I sang and hand signed Debbie Boone's "You Light Up My Life." My mother was very moved, but I believe this was one of too many times that she showed up to our schools having been drinking, and it boiled over into another fight once we got home. My parents did take time to go and see us in our dance recitals, gymnastics competitions, or horseback riding lessons. But all these memories I have of this effort by them is summed by this: if my dad was in town, which he rarely was, or if my mother had been drinking, just the chaos of never being on time and getting everyone out the door determined if we or they showed up at all. This was the beginning of my hate toward chaos and learning to not rely on anyone else. To this day, I fight with and try to control as much as I can. I typically like to be on time and have a schedule, a plan.

When I was in the second grade, I had my first best friend. I can't remember her name, but she was my age, very pretty, and a light-skinned African American girl. Here we were going to school in an upper-middle-class area where it was predominantly white. She didn't stand out to me. Maybe what was running through my mind at that time was that she was just like me. She was fairly close to my skin color. Besides, my older sisters were teaching me to spend lots of time in the sun. We loved tanning; we worshipped the sun. I'm the darkest in the family, holding on to tans much longer than anyone else; it is the native Peruvian in me. I had black hair, not the light-brown locks anymore from when I was littler and that my mom remembers.

One day, I invited my best friend over; it was going to be the first sleepover we had. My father was away on a business trip, and I think my two older sisters were at a high school football game. It must have been around 8:00 p.m. or 9:00 p.m., and my mother and I were waiting on my friend to be dropped off. Her mother and my mother had talked over the phone and were looking forward to meeting one another. My friend arrived, and when my mother opened the door, she came at a standstill. I somewhat remember the awkwardness of the moment. Eventually, my mom asked them to come in, and we sat in the kitchen as my mother came up with an excuse for why we couldn't have my friend over to spend the night. My mother was furious with me when they left. Why hadn't I told her they were black? I cried, confused and upset at my mother, as she ranted and raved on how I could no longer be friends with her. Being only seven years old, I couldn't understand it. Yes, I had realized my friend's mother was much darker than we were, but what did that matter? What was so wrong with these people that had darker skin color than we? I couldn't understand why I couldn't be friends with them. This made a big impression on how I now saw my mother, and I'd question what she thought from then on. It also opened my eyes to see that maybe everyone out in the world felt as she felt. I looked at the world differently and noticed race for the first time in my life. I'd obey my mother's wishes for now, but the following year, I'd develop a crush on someone I knew was forbidden—maybe a subconscious effort on my part to go against the norm?

My forbidden secret was that I had a crush on Billy Dee Williams. I had just seen the movies *Mahogany* and *Lady Sings the Blues*, which he starred in with Diana Ross. I thought I couldn't let anyone know I liked him, because this was what my mother had forbid me from. I'm sure it was not him I liked but the parts he played, but I was aware that he was of color, and I had just been taught to stay away from people like him. My sisters figured out my crush but thankfully never said anything to our parents. It was our first tiny little secret. We all finally had this unspoken language of knowing how our parents felt about certain things, and we kept silent when one of us did something against our parents' wishes. Also at this time because of my admiration for Billy Dee, my sisters would tease me for liking an African American boy who went to my school. But I never liked him. Maybe they just did it because he was one of the only black boys—or maybe the *only* black boy—who went to my school, and they liked to tease me. Neither my family nor I could have ever predicted I'd later have a child who was half-Haitian, who had skin color similar to my very first best friend whom my mom early on had forbidden me to be friends with.

The '70s was a time for a new way of thinking about race. Some people's hearts were awoken by the movie *Roots*. I can't recall if we saw it and if it inherently made an impression on me. All I know was around this time, I began having such a deep empathy for people of that race. Sometime over the next decade, my parents loosened up on their ignorant views. By the time I began openly liking guys who had a darker skin color than mine, my parents' racial views, I believe, were gone, and thankfully, they completely accepted my son and didn't see the color of his skin.

In my late teens and twenties, I'd bounce back and forth between liking guys who were white, black, and for a short stint, half and half. When I had begun liking Billy Dee, I also liked Harrison Ford when they were in *Star Wars*. I couldn't decide which one I thought I liked more. Billy Dee's roles and the character he played with Diana Ross are what I think I liked. It was my first time seeing a man in that way. And with Harrison Ford, it was definitely his looks, because I can still find him as attractive as when I had first seen him.

The incidents I remember of my parents fighting mostly centered on my dad and his business trips. My mother's insecurities, I know now, played as a major factor in this. My feelings toward my dad were that I loved that I had a dad, but I didn't feel close to him. There was some form of attachment there, and I did still like it when he was around. He stepped in sometimes and took care of us when my mother was incapable of doing so. The first memory I have of really wanting him around was on my seventh or eighth birthday. I was having my first slumber party. I recall there was some questioning from friends about my father and if I had one. I was excited when my father made it back from a business trip, but barely in time. It seemed as if he had been gone for a long time, and it meant a lot to me to have him there. My father had arrived pretty late, right as all my friends and I were getting ready for bed, but I was still happy he made it. But not before long, my parents began to fight, and I remember my mother had been drinking. My father was mad because she had been drinking. She was mad at him, I think, because he delayed his return back home. Shortly after my parents started fighting, he left the house, left my party, and didn't return until what seemed the middle of the night. They took all the fun out of this celebration and not only brought me to tears but made such an impact on me that I remember it to this day. I recall that night so vividly because I took a big notice about how extreme their discontent with each other was at times, and I was worried that he was never going to return. I was attached to him in a way, and his presence in our lives did mean a lot to me.

Most of their fighting was initiated by my mother. I remember her drinking somewhat prior to the fights. She'd always throw her accusations of infidelity at him. *Infidelity* is a big word for a child, but I heard it often when I was really young. We all heard of my father having affairs, like spending time with his secretary on the beaches of Rio de Janeiro, where my father would travel sometimes for business. I will never know for sure if this ever truly happened. It may have been a mere figment of my insecure mother's imagination. As an adult, I can see how my mother did spin these types of creations in her head; she did it with me later when I was a teenager and an adult. In my childhood, it seemed like he had multiple affairs. My mother was insecure, and in her eyes, my father was running around with other women. I wouldn't blame him now if he had, because my parents' relationship was awful. But if he had, I do wish he'd have stepped away from the marriage, because it could have saved us from some of my mother's misery. I also don't like how I learned about cheating at such an early age. I heard it so often when my mother was drunk, and I was not able to tell myself that it was nonsense coming out of her mouth but instead had it ingrained in me that it was something that men did and women had to deal with. It made me believe for a long time that every single man would do it, and I know that isn't true.

Loneliness is a void in one's self that everyone feels at some point in their lives. I always felt so alone and at such an early age that it seemed like I was always alone, even when I was playing with Guadalupe or someone. For as long as I can remember, I always felt like I would be alone in this life, and unfortunately, not much has changed about that. I was content with being alone at times. I can be nonsocial for long periods of time. It has always felt natural, but part of me has never been completely happy being so alone *all the time*!

I did have a new best friend in the third grade, Lynda. We were best friends because I had no other friends that I think really wanted to come over and play. I had a hard time making friends because I was so shy and quiet. All my life, I didn't have an abundance of friends—never enough even to count all on one hand. Yes, I knew several people, but I couldn't really call them friends. And because of this, I felt so alone at an early age. I didn't always have someone around to play with. As a matter of fact, it was rare when I had someone to play with besides Guadalupe, and that wasn't always pleasant. She, for the most part, didn't want to play with me, especially if I didn't play by her rules or do what she said to do.

Lynda would later also become very good friends with Guadalupe. She spent a lot of time at our house. She had been adopted and had an older brother, and her parents were much older. It was like she connected more with our environment than her own. After we later moved to Houston, she even came and spent every summer with us, but later, our friendship would end after a blowout of jealously I had about the fact that she was also very tight with Guadalupe all those years. After that, she and Guadalupe became best friends, and later, Guadalupe would move back to Ohio when she graduated from high school in Texas. But their friendship wouldn't last.

There were times in my childhood that I was jealous of Guadalupe. I admired her social ability to make friends easily and behave as if she were comfortable in any situation. Why couldn't I make friends easily? One time in Cincinnati and a few years later in Houston, I found myself so distraught about this that I went to my mother and wept. I wanted to know why no one liked me. What I recall is that I didn't see that anything was wrong with me. My mother just replied something to the effect that everyone liked me and quickly tried to dismiss it.

I had these big moments of comparing myself to my older sister. We were very different—opposites, really. There was no shyness to her. I was extremely shy, almost to the point that I think some people thought there was something wrong with me. She took chances; I was extremely cautious and scared to. My whole life, it seemed everyone gravitated toward her. There were times when I wanted to be like her because it seemed so easy for her to make friends or later have boys like her. I now know nothing ever was wrong with me. I was just very shy, and because of this, it took me a little longer to become friends with people. But when you are young, you don't understand much. You just compare yourself to what you see, and all I saw was that my sister had lots of friends and I didn't, which at times made me feel lonely.

Life at home was normal to me. *Normal?* Was anyone in my family ever going to know what normal felt like, looked like? To me, this was normal. Inside our household, not knowing what was going on in other people's households, this was normal. But it wasn't normal. In these early years of my childhood, I couldn't even understand the alcoholism—much less realize that my mom drank too much. Many don't understand what alcoholism does to the family unit. There is so much focus on the alcoholic, and most alcoholics are very selfish. We don't stop and think of the basic things like child development or other factors that may need to happen for raising a child to become a productive, happy adult. In an addict's home, there is this neglect that goes on for everyone else besides the addict, because everyone is focused either on when the alcoholic is drunk or not doing anything to encourage the alcoholic to get drunk. Many doctors like to use the term "walking on eggshells" to reference this, and they are correct. But stress, anger, resentment, depression, and just being worried about what could happen next are compounded day by day, week by week for the rest of us.

Within our household, my mom's drinking created a family with lots of verbal, mental, and physical abuse by mostly everybody toward everybody else. Both my parents were under a lot of stress and maybe angry because they were raising four girls with no help and were finding it difficult to adjust to our so-called life. Anyone within our household would be affected by this anger, even our two dogs. My father couldn't stand their constant barking and would hit them with such intensity that it was a good thing they ran away before we left Cincinnati in '79. I believe my two older sisters thought my father left them at a shelter. We'll never know. And even when we had not done anything bad, you could see my mother's anger at the stressful, rushed moments of preparing her youngest daughters for school when she'd fiercely wet and brush our hair back into ponytails. That was the worst for me. She'd brush it with such force and harshness that I'd be crying. I think she was relieved when she had my father take me and Guadalupe to the barbershop to cut our hair. But I was the only one to get that horrible boy's haircut. I'm sure it was because I cried the loudest. My mother's alcoholism continued, probably because of all the factors contributing to the life we were leading, like a new social demographic, my parents being on their own, and needing to be true adults; the abuse and violence were just additional components brought on by that alcoholism or unresolved childhood issues.

Abuse and alcoholism usually does go hand in hand in most cases. These two components were truly destroying our well-to-do family that had so much going for it. It'd lay a foundation for all us girls that some are still not aware of. The family dynamic of an addict also changes the dynamics for everyone so that you can accommodate and survive to continue. I remember some winter mornings getting ready for school when my dad would have to make breakfast for Guadalupe and me because my mom was hungover and needed her rest before she went to work. This poor man, being in a hurry and having to go to work himself, would cook us Campbell's Chunky soup. It was a warm and fast breakfast to make. I also don't remember a time when there was anyone there to help us with our homework or a parent who could be our comfort spot when we were hurt or teased or could teach us basic life lessons.

I will not completely blame the alcohol or alcoholism. My mom didn't understand how life really was, and she didn't have many coping or social skills, which I believe was why she may have started drinking. Also, my dad has brought up a few times how, in Cincinnati, they wanted him to sign off on papers to institutionalize her, committing her into a mentally facility. She was that unstable mentally and emotionally. I am still picking up the pieces to this day and learning how to handle myself in certain situations or how to cope when certain things happen to me or go wrong. I'm constantly working on my self-esteem and self-worth, trying to make the right choices and learning discipline to finish things I start. These skills are not something we are born with; they are things we are taught, and unfortunately, this—among other things—I was not taught because there were so many other things taking precedence.

These years, I didn't know we were dysfunctional to the degree we were beginning to be. And who would have thought it would escalate to the degree that it did later in Houston? I don't believe that term *dysfunctional* was used back in those days. For a while there, we'd attend family company picnics. My mom loved photography, which I'd later pick up as a hobby and passion. She used to take plenty of pictures and 8mm films of us playing around the house and backyard. There was one film during a cold winter season in which Lynda and I were running in the backyard playing in the snow. There is no sound, but we were making snow angels, and it looks like I had a wonderful childhood. I never can remember being there, but when I see it or photos of that time, I sometimes look so happy. We all did for the most part.

We celebrated birthdays, Thanksgivings, and Christmases in a big way. Our mom opened us up to more holidays from other countries. We had our Danish shoes in the closets for a holiday and loved to go and wake up to see them filled with candies. All the photos that remain show us having such beautiful moments—and in these early years, we did half of the time ... but for the other half, we'd just try to keep up appearances. That was one thing our family learned to do well: wear disguises, covering up what was really going on behind closed doors. Children can convey this, but only for so long.

Some parents never realize to stop and see what their kids are experiencing while growing up until it's too late. Parents need to realize that their reactions—or nonreactions—sometimes have long-lasting consequences. It is such a fine line, raising children. Everyone is so consumed with education, having their children fed and clothed, and making sure that they are getting to bed on time. A lot of parents don't realize what their children witness is a learned behavior that more than likely the children will follow in their parents' footsteps and repeat. *Family cycles.*

My parents, particularly my mom, knew there were issues, because I recall her dragging us all into family therapy. My mom had been on a lifelong journey with therapy that I think she still continues to this day. I completely believe in therapy, but not as my mom does, because she stops going to see a therapist as soon as she hears something she doesn't like to hear and doesn't want to listen to. Along with the alcoholism, there was an abuse on her part of psychiatric medication for most of her adult life. That, I do not believe in. Maybe for the person that is suicidal, bipolar, or schizophrenic, but my mom was and just is an addict.

I can look back at myself at an early age and see it was apparent that I was hurting so deeply by the things that were going on. I was crying out for help in subtle ways at an early age. I had an obsession with covering my body with Band-Aids in Cincinnati. I always complained of the pain that wasn't apparent to physically see because it was the inner spirit that was being torn down and hurt. Nothing was ever physically wrong with me; it was mental and emotional. I always told my mom, "Mommy, it hurts," but she never understood what hurt. She couldn't understand what she and her husband were really psychologically doing to me and how sad I was because of it. I see now that is when possibly my depression was beginning at a tender age of about eight years old. I had become a child with sad, puppy-dog eyes that I can still see when I'm not wearing makeup, and I don't like to see that. I was extremely shy and insecure, which didn't help. I shut the door for happiness too early on in my life, and I now see I began my struggle with depression there. Yes, some of it could have come from my internal makeup, but no one can deny that my world, my environment, played a role also.

By the time I was in the fourth grade, I was so scared of people I didn't know, and I didn't like crowds. I was so introverted and began to fail assignments that required me to read aloud in front of the class. I didn't and still don't feel comfortable when people look at me or stare at me for very long. As a kid, I felt so ugly that I felt if someone was staring at me, it was because of this. I was proud that I was a pretty good student, and even though oral assignments began to appear, I remained a fairly good student—usually plenty of As and a B or two, which I continued until the middle of sixth grade. My achievement in school and the fact that I knew I was nice was everything about myself I liked.

In the late fall of 1979, my mom and my sisters and I went back to our homeland. I was going to see relatives I didn't remember I had because we had never revisited Lima after leaving, and I was just three years old when we left. When we arrived at the airport in Lima, I remember it being so chaotic with men with large rifles—the *policia*. I had never seen anything like that. This place had so much activity going on that it felt like everyone was frantic. I was scared.

After we left the airport, we arrived to a beautiful place with cousins, aunts, uncles, and especially my grandmother, whom I will never forget because of her tenderness. I remember being in the backseat of a car, seeing this vast land with sand pyramids, and one had a drawing on it—a beautiful, mysterious Nazca drawing. No one really knows to this day how the magnificent Nazca lines and drawings got there. Most of the drawings and lines can only be seen while up in the air looking down. It was a lovely sight for me to see and experience.

While in Peru, we went to the beach and played with cousins, searching for mussels on the rocks. We had fresh seafood like Peruvian ceviche and drank Inca Kola, the national soda. At my maternal grandparents' house, where we also stayed, we'd sit at a large dining room table and have an array of Peruvian dishes, more dishes than we ever had at home, and there were so many to choose from. When you walked into the center of my grandparents' house, where the floors were covered in marble, you got a taste of the privileged life my mom came from. There were two staircases leading up to the two parts—two ends of the house—which we used to call the east wing and west wing. The two staircases wrapped around some of the finest workmanship found in many mansions.

I remember taking a siesta with my grandmother and sleeping in her bed. It was summertime in Peru. We had a light breeze coming in through the open french doors of her bedroom. There is nothing more pleasant than having a large meal with many courses and then retiring up for a catnap in the middle of a sunny day. I wish we did it here in the States. We had the privilege of meeting Lina Medina and her son. I vaguely remember greeting them and just remember how tall her son was.

We were still not very far from tension, though. I completely didn't understand at the time what was wrong, but at any age, you get this gut feeling that something is wrong. We weren't allowed to go to a certain part of the upstairs—something about an uncle. I heard my mom talking about him, and I guess it was a feud that had been going on for a very long time between him and my parents. The things I unfortunately remember. Part of my predisposition was that I had become fearful of doing something wrong, and I was scared of whatever it was going on between them.

After a few weeks, it was unfortunately time to say good-bye to our grandmother and leave this country I still haven't been able to go back and see. For the most part, it was a good time meeting with family members we hadn't seen in over six years, playing with our cousins, and experiencing what our lives would have been if we hadn't moved a continent away.

The trip was really for my mother and her sisters to divvy up the inheritance. My grandmother was getting old. I think they wanted to try to compromise on who was taking what, and my mother probably wanted us to see our grandmother for one last time. There were a lot of material things like paintings, vases, silver, jewelry, and furniture. Mom eventually shipped back her portion, which was a lot; that portion was about 25 percent. But there were also nonmaterialistic things like photographs, books (in the house, my grandfather had a library), and documents my mom grabbed, which may have been more valuable to us.

We returned to Cincinnati to just gather our belongings together, pack up, and wait for the movers to empty out the home I had only come to know. It was December of 1979, and we were moving to a suburb of Houston, Texas, because of my father's job. The company he had been working for in Chicago, Conval International, had been sold off, and he was going to be laid off. My dad was going to start up with a partner and own his own valve distribution company. It was International Controlled Fluids, better known as ICF.

While I had been away in Peru, my best friend, Lynda, had already made really good friends with a girl down the street. As we drove out of our neighborhood, even at the age of nine, I caught myself feeling such loss, not being happy about leaving all that I had ever known, even if it was bad. With tears running down my face, the last thing we'd see was Lynda in front of her new friend's house, waving good-bye.

3

Houston, We Have a Problem!

The first few months after we moved to Houston, life seemed promising, a new start, a do-over. It was exciting when we drove up and saw the house for the very first time. Our new home was a brand-new, two-story house with five bedrooms that had a three-car garage, a game room, and vaulted ceilings. Each of us had our very own bedrooms. The game room was the length of the three-car garage. There were two wet bars, which were really big in the '80s and so inappropriate for our family. Our backyard was not as big as the backyard we had in Ohio, but everything else was bigger. My parents' master bedroom was located on the first floor. Up the stairs, located right above them, was my bedroom, the largest bedroom of all us girls. Back in Cincinnati, my parents came to Houston to look for a house to buy. When they bought this one, they showed us the blueprints, and we were able to choose our bedrooms. I don't think anyone else wanted to live above my parents' bedroom. I liked it because it was so big and had two separate doors that opened to my walk-in closet. I realize now that my bedroom may have been the length of my parents' bedroom in addition to their en suite master bathroom. That was a big room for a girl who was just nine years old.

I was about ten years old when my eyes began to open. I was able to identify that the problems in the house were mainly caused by my mom's drinking. It, along with any disagreements my parents had, would cause so much tension and stress among us all that abuse, bits of rage and anger, and bouts of depression would fester in all of us, and within time, one or a few of us would explode. I don't feel like this type of behavior really happened before, at least not to that degree. As a child, I knew things weren't right, and even at the time, I couldn't verbally say it was alcoholism and abuse. I also didn't have anything to compare it to, but I now knew that it was wrong. It had always been this gut instinct, or maybe it was just me not liking and accepting this as my life. I was always a gentle, soft-spoken girl. I liked niceness. I couldn't understand meanness, whether it be one person who was being cruel to another or a group of people hating another because the other was different. I couldn't understand why people had to suffer or hurt so badly. My sensitivity had me understand and feel the pain and suffering of others as if I were hurting with them. Had I always just been too sensitive? Am I still too sensitive at times? I had always wanted and felt that life should be peace, love, and happiness. I truly was the end product of the '60s.

I can't recall exactly when this new path of destruction for our family began. When I look back now and from everything I heard, it started way before we ever became a family. I've been told of stories about parties my maternal grandparents would have, and my mother would take sips from the drinks that were being served. But by the 1970s, her sips had turned into cases of beer and jugs of wine. Her drinking had begun to partially destroy whatever possibilities of long-term happiness our family would ever have. There are also very brief stories of abuse in both of my parents' upbringings—maybe not direct abuse but possibly seeing some violence done to others. Maybe these stories were so brief because they also have been looked at as discipline or something else. There's no doubt in my mind that both of my parents came out of their childhoods with an incomplete foundation to be well-grounded, whole individuals, much less be great parents and adapt to what life lay before them.

With an inconsistent, unbalance of love, nurturing, and guidance, my sisters and I acted out in the way most children do when there are major problems at home. Nowadays, we can identify that some adolescents who are having problems are acting out for a reason that is more than likely stemming from their home situations or because something bad happened to them, but back in the '70s or '80s, most counselors or authorities didn't see where the root of a troubled teen stemmed from. Back then—and even still a little bit now—people chalked it up to a rebellious, out-of-control teenager.

I began to feel that we were different from other families. I also couldn't imagine that every family had physical and verbal outbursts like ours or that when a child went to bed, he or she would wonder whether his or her parents would drive home safely or not. My mother got in a bad accident once that almost killed her, and her daughters had to go through saying good-bye to her because the doctors were not sure she was going to survive.

Our home was once again in a prominently white suburb, Klein, Texas, about thirty minutes from downtown Houston. Having moved into these white, upper-middle-class American suburbs in

Cincinnati and now Houston, my parents still don't realize what an impact it had on my life. Once I was able to identify the race thing, that we were a different nationality, I understood why some people in these suburbs at the time treated us differently. They didn't like us, and racism was also part of my experience. I think my parents thought their—her money had changed the color of our skin or the nationality that we all are. Even though my parents are very fair skinned, the four of us loved to sunbathe and kept very dark complexions until we moved away from Houston. When most of us were not basking in the sun, we were pretty fair skinned, due to the fact that we have the Irish and German heritage. The darkest out of my family had always been me, and with that, I just looked part native Mexican-Indian as a child. One of my sisters used to call me Injun Joe because of my dark complexion and the straight black hair I used to have as a child. I hated that nickname back then but cherish the beauty now I see in having any exotic features like that.

The prejudice we encountered in Ohio was pretty mild in comparison to Texas. It might have been due to the fact that we were living in a state that was right next to Mexico and because of the history behind that. Guadalupe and I had a good number of friends, though we were teased sometimes, and later, while going to the local junior high, a boy had made up a riddle, teasing us, and he'd sing it down the hallway walking behind us. I can't remember how it went, but I do remember it wasn't nice.

Besides dealing with that on occasion, in the beginning, school was all right; I was in the fourth grade when we moved there. But life at home was getting more terrifying for me, I guess because I had become older and saw more of what was really going on or it was just escalating to another level. Over these years, I dealt with domestic violence that not only came from my mother initiating a fight or father and mother reprimanding us but also us as sisters physically tearing one another apart. It became more violent with the sisters taking out their rage and anger on one another. It was sibling rivalry on a whole other level. A sister who maybe at the time was about five foot five and weighed 130 pounds hitting a sixty-five-pound, four-foot-five girl was just brutal.

The scariest thing, though, was the temper of my father and whether or not he'd hit me or someone else. My father's temperament was usually cool and collected. I can calculate my father losing control maybe once every three or four months, but I assure you, that was enough. I think he kept all his stress contained from the friction the alcoholism was creating in the family and whatever problems he was having financially or with my mother, but everyone eventually explodes if they don't deal with or change their issues. And now, the "discipline" graduated from hitting us with a belt to hitting us with a whip my parents called a *Samalteen*. My mom had brought it from our recent trip to Peru. It is a special whip that is made out there from a certain type of tree, so I was told growing up. People may associate child abuse as daily or weekly events, but that isn't true. It can be anytime by anyone. Mother drank almost every day when she was on her binges, and she took on the violence too, which I can't remember her doing very much in Ohio.

I've heard horror stories about how my two older sisters used to get hit back in Peru and sometimes not even completely remembering what came next. They recall it like everything went black, and they can't remember—complete mental block—which most therapists will tell you that your psyche does this to protect you. But with Guadalupe and me, my father had hit us with belts in Ohio and had now graduated from a belt to a whipping, either with his hand or the Samalteen. There are distinct memories also of metal hangers, but I think those were more threatening than actual hitting.

I recall more of the physical abuse coming from my father, maybe because my mom drank so much that I don't overplay it in my head of her hitting us that much, but she did. I can remember times when she'd hit me, and I remember her chasing Guadalupe up the stairs and possibly hitting her with a hanger and always threatening us with the Samalteen that she hung so proudly in the breakfast room. My dad's hand was so hard that he didn't need to hit us with anything else. Later, a boyfriend of mine in Los Angeles met my father, and after shaking his hand for the very first time, my boyfriend later turned to me and said that there was no way my father ever hit us. He said that my father's hand was too big and strong.

In time, I had gone beyond the point of feeling or recognizing any of the severe pain the hitting would place on my backside. It was as if I had become immune to the pain or my tolerance level was just high. When it did really hurt, I hated giving him the satisfaction of what he was doing to me as if it would make an impact for me to behave. In that sense, I became very strong, and so did my sisters, because in time, when we became old enough, we physically fought back. We'd hide our fear. It'd intensify the situations, but how many children just let it keep continuing and do nothing? We knew how wrong it was, and this was the first thing we fought back against and stood up for. Not that fighting back made them stop hitting us; I just know that it may have deterred us from more abuse.

Violence was very much a part of our household, but now more than ever before. It had always been just our parents disciplining us, but now it became us defending our dad against our mother too. Even though he is much taller than she, she had such strength when she drank, and my father didn't always want to fight and didn't like the fighting that went on.

Our fighting sometimes went beyond our family unit too, involving poor outsiders like Missy. One day, Guadalupe hit her with the telephone while Missy was interrupting Guadalupe while she talked on the phone. Guadalupe just hit her so fast in the head with the phone that no one knew how to react. It was so hard that Missy had the welt of a lifetime on the top of her forehead above her eye. Who knew what Missy's parents thought? It was rare that an outsider would get stuck in the middle of our horror of violence, though. But it did happened or was witnessed.

We all ended up practically raising ourselves, and we never listened to our parents, respect them, or did what they told us to do. No one could have predicted life in Houston was going to tear us apart for many years and significantly change the course of all our lives in so many ways. It was around the age of eleven when I completely recognized that our life as a family was all wrong. We were reaching our peak of financial wealth. Well, let's just say we were living comfortably and as children had a little more than the bare necessities—a five-bedroom home and a game room, the nicest clothes from Sakowitz or Lord & Taylor, money most of the time when we asked for it, a great school, English-style horseback riding lessons, and piano lessons that I hated. And for the most part, I was still doing well in school. But we had two highly dysfunctional adults raising us, teaching us to escape from our problems by drinking and also teaching us violence. Who knew what kind of impact that would have on our lives in the years to come?

Our neighbors started to talk about my mom being a drunk. She'd get wasted at parties and become out of control and make a scene, which then would initiate a fight between my parents when they got home. There were two major things that my dad would fight about with my mom—her spending money as she did and her drinking. He was never happy with those aspects that became part of his life, but who would be?

Nothing was ever spoken between us sisters as far as I can recall about her drinking or that my parents' "discipline" was over the line at times and in fact child abuse. We just knew we all hated it. Alcoholism and violence had always been a way of life for all of us. I wonder if my parents thought it was okay or ever wondered how things had gone so wrong and out of control.

When I was in the sixth grade, Guadalupe and I were attending the same local junior high school where she was two years ahead. I became known only as "Guadalupe's sister." My grades also began to decline, and I began a serious involvement—*relationship*—with depression that would cross over to being suicidal at times. I don't discount the fact that I also hit puberty at this time. Maybe a cocktail of my physical makeup, hormones changing, and the unpredictable chaos I lived in was a great breeding ground for my depressed tendencies.

Toward the last few months of my first year at Kleb, Guadalupe began dropping her friends for mine. I was never jealous of my sister as she may have thought or wanted me to be. I did like her outgoing self and how she made friends easily, but I began disliking the fact that who I thought were my friends would just come up to me in school and ask me where my sister was. It really hit home once when I had been out sick for more than a week. I don't think my friends had realized I had been gone, because they never mentioned it, and one girlfriend just asked, "Where's Guadalupe?" That really hurt.

I was the opposite of Guadalupe. We still weren't the closest of sisters, but we were the closest in age, so we'd sometimes go through these periods of "being friends." None of us were ever really close to Guadalupe. My other two sisters and I always saw her as the bad seed. Around the ages of about six to sixteen, there were constant put-downs. She taught me to see myself as the fat, ugly girl whom nobody ever liked. She was my evil twin and at the same times my savior in some instances. There were those rare times when she'd stand up for me. But I also remember back in Ohio when we were at the bus stop waiting to go to school, when she slapped me all of a sudden for no apparent reason. I may have been only six or seven. I ran back to the house crying and telling her that I was going to tell Mom. She chased after me and asked me what was wrong, acting as if she had never slapped me, or maybe she was just scared to get in trouble. It never made any sense to me what she had done back at the bus stop or now what she was continuing to do to me. This was one of many similar situations.

What I still carry from this behavior is that I learned to accept not-so-loving relationships with many people that came into my life later. I've had many people mistreat me, and I don't do anything about it. I even now sometimes don't immediately recognize when I am being mistreated—and sometimes when I do, I freeze up and just walk away because I don't know yet how else to react, and I fear confrontation, because, in my mind, that leads into violence.

There were days when we were all just pretending like nothing was wrong. From the outside, life looked beautiful, very idealistic. We did have happy times. There were months that my mom would stop drinking, and there were times when there wasn't much fighting going on. Life within an alcoholic home can be very confusing and unpredictable, a roller-coaster ride most of the time. Chaos did happen a lot and not knowing when the other shoe was going to drop. It is that whole walking-on-eggshells syndrome. There can be good times and bad times, and sometimes you just mask the sadness and anger or hide it just to get by and continue on with life before things like drinking and fighting happen again.

The first few years of living in Houston, we continued with activities like the horseback riding lessons, gymnastics, and piano lessons. We'd play outside in the rain. We'd continue our obsessions with the Sun God during the hot Houston summers while tossing some lemon juice in our hair to lighten it. We'd go as a family and sometimes take friends to Galveston, the closest beach to Houston. Once in a while, we'd be fortunate enough to go to AstroWorld, an amusement park about forty-five minutes away. We were just like any normal, suburban kids at times, looking for whose pool we could go take a swim in. We had a really nice home that had a lot of antique paintings hanging from the walls and Baccarat crystal in the living room from my mother's inheritance.

At Kleb, Guadalupe and I began a trend. We began wearing nothing but Ralph Lauren Polo, from shirts and jeans down to our socks and up to our earrings. Yes, there were Polo RL earrings. And, when we and our girlfriends Missy, Misty, Michelle, and Dana went to the mall to go see a movie or hang out, we made sure that there were enough Polo oxfords or T-shirts to go around. I laugh now, but our paternal grandmother would complain later to my father that my mother bought us too many expensive clothes. We did have a lot of top name-brand clothes in our wardrobes, but the main shopping sprees were done only at the beginning of the school year and at Christmastime, along with the few pieces like a new pair of jeans or sneakers in the middle of the school year and on those special occasions like going to see *The Nutcracker*, when my mom also bought us those fancy dresses.

Just because we shopped at Lord & Taylor or Sakowitz didn't mean we were having shopping sprees every weekend. It wasn't like my mother's upbringing was; we weren't able to shop at Bergdorf Goodman, and we never experienced how it was to shop with a personal shopper, but we heard about it. My mom did spend and would teach us how to have expensive taste or have fun spending, but it never seemed like a problem to a teenage girl. What teenage girl wouldn't like to have the expensive clothes my mother bought us? The only problem was that there was this distinct chatter that happened between my parents once in a while at The Galleria for spending too much, which would result sometimes with my father disappearing for a bit. My mom actually did spend money as though her parents were still providing for her. It wasn't in her nature to know or understand the term *budget*.

During the middle of sixth grade, I hit puberty, and life got unmanageable, because I felt I could no longer live this life these two people brought me into. I began hating and having anger toward my parents that would just show as me being distant or having an attitude. I know their intention of having a family was pure, but they had no idea what it took to raise children or to have a good family unit, because they themselves were broken and never took care of their issues prior to meeting and getting married. Toward the end of sixth grade, I began not caring about my grades or doing homework. I thought, what was the point? We had always dressed very clean cut and preppy, but now I turned away from that, as did my two older sisters.

MTV had just aired a few years earlier, and punk and New

Wave music trends were happening across the country, and we loved it. The new British invasion included a band called Duran Duran, and I wrapped myself up in everything that had to do with them. They were my escape from what was going on around me, the only pleasure and happiness I could find. I'd just have to put on one of their albums, lock myself up in my room, and dream of being on tour with them, photographing them, not being in this hellhole. There were a few times later that their music helped me hold on for just one more day and try not to end my life. To this day, I'm so thankful for their music, because it helped me get through very tough times.

Having my own bedroom, I now could really close myself off from the world and my family, which wasn't the best thing for someone who was already having depressive tendencies, though I made an exception for the paw under my door that used to make me cry a little less. There was enough space underneath my bedroom door where my cat, Soccerella, used to wave his paw underneath for me to let him in. He was the only one I felt that truly cared for me in the world at that time. He also used to wait for me outside to get off the school bus. We had our suspicions he was doing this because he was always at the same spot every day, and I believe Candelaria saw him once running up the street. So it was not until one day when I had stayed home from school sick that I looked out my window and saw him running as the school bus came up the street. He'd go and wait for me on our front lawn every school day. We bought him in May of '84 after my sisters and my mom and I went window-shopping at a pet store. I saw something in his face, his eyes, and my mother fell in love. We brought him home late one evening in a shopping bag and presented him to my dad, so that way he would allow us to keep him, which he did. He was my first and last real pet, minus all the goldfish I went through.

My mother's drinking progressed to a dangerous level. There were many times if she wasn't passed out at home or fighting with one or all of us that eventually we'd wonder where she was and if she'd make it home safe. During these years, I remember trying to go to sleep, and all I could do was wonder what would awaken me in the middle of the night—a brutal fight between my parents or officers coming to our door once again. This is how our life was turning out. Her drinking practically got her killed.

It was in October of 1982. I was twelve. I grew up with my

mother drinking and driving. I don't understand why it was ever accepted, though. Didn't my father ever think that it was dangerous? Or was he just in denial? Or did he just get so fed up with her when she was drunk that it was better to have her out of the house? In Houston, she was working as a secretary in a small office. There, sneaking behind her boss's back, she'd drink. Time and time again, she'd already be wasted when she got home from work. And in the fall of '82 after countless times that she'd drive into the long, extended vertical windows of our breakfast room in the back of our house, there was this specific night that really let me know what her drinking could do to the outside world and not just her or us.

After work, like most nights, she'd go and lie down in her room to pass out, but usually she'd awaken a few hours later to have something to eat and to bother us. I remember so many times our father tried his hardest to not have her wake up, but it was hard because their bedroom was downstairs, right next to the family room. We'd have to tiptoe around as we ate dinner and watch television with the volume very low.

I can't always remember what led up to the very critical points and traumas of my life. Maybe that night I was up in my room, listening to Duran Duran, trying to escape and dream away my reality while I tried to fall asleep. As I got the story from my mother in 1992, she may never understand that this was traumatizing to me, even though I told her that this incident was maybe the most heartbreaking thing up until then that I had ever had to experience in my life besides a friend's death in 1991. It was a time when I thought I was going to live without my mother.

My mother is the type of person who holds on to painful situations forever, as I used to, which is probably from whom I got it from. That and the fact that my father bottles everything up and just explodes every so often, which is funny, because I bottle things up also but rarely explode. I just get stressed out, lose sleep, feel irritated, and grind my teeth to the point of almost dislocating my jaw, or I have heart palpitations at times. My mother's lack of coping skills really came to a head this one evening in 1982, though. With no disdain because of the lack of memories from blackouts that evening, she speaks as if it were another person that night. It is amazing how we can disconnect ourselves from either feelings or things we have done to harm others.

From what I am told, it began at the house when one of my sister's friends came over around 7:00 p.m. My mother had already a few drinks. This friend of my sister's that she didn't like and that she didn't want in the house that specific night was there. To my mother, something just was not right about this girl. My mother says the girl smelled like alcohol, but if I know my mom well enough, the drinks she had already drunk brought out the evil spirits in her mind, and it was probably my mom's own breath that she smelled. And even though maybe this friend who came over was a bad influence, my mother just found a new person to fight with or fight about, which is something she did.

My mother went to my father and told him that she wanted this friend to leave, and as he sometimes did, my father ignored her. This always intensified my mother's hostility. My father told my mother to leave him alone, that he didn't know what she was talking about, and that she, my mother, was just being crazy. Maybe he had recognized that she had already been drinking. After not getting her way, she blew up into a wild, alcohol-driven depression.

My mother told me as we sat in a restaurant in Los Angeles while I was interviewing my parents for this book that it was an explosion involving ten years of seeing things around her not going the way she had always dreamed of. Her personal unhappiness was that she believes her children were educated by everyone else, besides her. That the outside immoral world had taken over. She also later told me that she had left the house with the intention of suicide. As an interviewer trying to be impartial, I could not help but being shocked at how she told me this as if she had no care in the world for what that possibly could do to her children. Inside, I cried for the little girl who had to go through this experience of feeling her mommy would be out of her life forever. It is something no child should ever go through.

In the middle of the night, a police officer came and told us not to worry but that our mother had been in a car accident. There had been a few times prior to this that the police had shown up in the middle of the night, but this time, it was an emergency, not a complaint or a suspected DUI. She was in the emergency room suffering from four or five broken ribs and two or three crushed vertebrae. Her car was completely totaled. She had driven into another car before rolling over into a ditch. I could not believe they told us not to worry!

∞ Evolving to Grace ∞
49

When my father went to see her, she was still drunk, and for several hours, the doctors wouldn't treat her because they didn't know what she had done besides drink. She was so far gone that they thought she was on something. My father remembered her head split wide open. "It looked as a piece of tissue totally opening the front of her head," he told me while interrupting her as she told me of the incident. There, she had thirty to forty stitches. She was in ICU for seven days, where her daughters would have to go and see her because in the beginning the doctors didn't know if she was going to survive.

As a child, the smell of hospitals always made me queasy. Even now, if you talk to me about medical problems or needles for too long, I need to lie down. So when I went to see her, I was already shaken up because it might have been the last time I would see her, and I had to go into a hospital of all places! I felt deep down inside this was bad. I don't remember anyone saying that might be the last time I'd possibly see her. Maybe my dad did say something like that, but the way it definitely came across was that those could be her final moments and the end to having a mother that I still did love and felt I needed.

So, in the middle of the night, we got dressed and went to the hospital. Sitting on the bench in the hallway and waiting for my two older sisters to get finished seeing her, I began to feel faint. I think I was in shock. It was extremely hard on a child who was about to see her mother for maybe the last time. We had our problems, but at the time, I still loved her and thought I still needed her as a mother. She was one of my first loves. She did love and care for me as much as she could. I had to be strong.

My father took my hand and walked Guadalupe and me into the room, where there were about five other patients hooked up to machines. She was to the immediate left, and as I came to her bedside in tears, not really understanding why, my father left us to go and join my two older sisters who were in the hallway outside, full of anger.

My mother was partially shaved on the top of her head where her stitches were, and there were still glimpses of glass from the car's windshield in her head and face. I was out of there within a few moments because of her horrible condition; I didn't know what to say to her or how to react. She wasn't coherent or, to my recollection, completely awake. She mumbled. I'm sure they had her highly medicated. I remember Guadalupe dealing with it better than I, because I vaguely remember her at least saying something to our mother.

In 1992, she says I'm one of the two faces she remembered seeing in the ICU, though I wish she remembered it all, because then maybe she'd have realized what she had put her daughters through. When she recalled the story for me, she said it with no feeling, no remorse, and no apologies, which just made it worse over the next few years.

I understand now why my two older sisters felt so much anger toward her when they only went to visit her that one time, even though she was in the hospital for forty days. They saw how selfish she was. It was my second most painful recollection of my childhood, and my mother couldn't even remember most of it because she had drunk so much. Feeling what I still hold on to so dearly, I could never imagine putting my child through the insecurity that he might ever be without his mother. Did she not love us? How could she want to leave her own kids? I suppose the motherly instincts and love just disappear when you are high as a kite. Or maybe they were never really there to begin with. Addiction could have killed any parental instincts she ever had. Addiction becomes the addict's main love, the only true thing he or she really loves.

In the end, my mother was never prosecuted for drunk driving even though she had hurt a woman and her daughter. My father said they weren't that badly hurt, but he was probably just minimizing it all in his mind so that his conscience could be cleared. He saw them in the emergency room. "They were bleeding," he recalls. Hearing this, my mother doesn't flinch, as if it were someone else who had done it. When my parents spoke of it, there seemed to be no realization or care that they may have put their daughters through an intentional feeling of loss that still to this day hurts so deeply.

And after interviewing them, learning more about the details, and writing about this incident twenty years later, I see that my parents' priority was never their children but themselves first and then their relationship. Even though their relationship was extremely convulsive at times, and my mother was self-centered, they were as codependent as they come and loyal to one another. It is clear to me that most of my childhood I felt this way, but this incident, even though I did not know at the time was intentional, solidified that their children were never as important as they should have been and were not put first, which only plays into our own lack of self-worth, which had lifelong lasting effects on me and possibly my sisters.

Children need to feel important, especially to their parents. And even though our mother didn't die, we were taken to the point of feeling the loss anyone could feel when they lose a loved one. In some of my future relationships, I'd relive this feeling of anguish once someone walked out of my life. Maybe this is partially why I also didn't get too close to many people in fear of when that day would come and they would leave me. The heartbreak was too much. It's also amazing to me how she and my father didn't seem to care that life could have been taken away that night, because the drinking and driving continued.

Until the spring of my seventh-grade year, boys didn't like me, or I hadn't heard of any boys liking me. I'd had a crush on a boy since the beginning of the sixth grade, and it lasted until the eighth grade, but I knew I never had a chance with him because he was a preppy jock, and I was becoming different, alternative. In the seventh grade, I found out that a boy by the name of Seth had liked me all through sixth grade. He was in my grade and lived down the street from me, and we'd speak from time to time. He was tall, had brown hair, dressed preppy with a flair of messiness to it, and was good looking. This meant a lot to my self-esteem and how I felt about myself at the time; that a decent-looking guy could like me maybe meant I wasn't ugly, after all, like Guadalupe had always told me. I remember him teasing me sometimes on the school bus, but not in a mean way, kind of like he was trying to get my attention. After I found out he liked me, I gave my number to his friend. We spoke a few times on the phone. We made a plan to hang out during spring break over at my girlfriend Tammy's house, just her, me, him, and his friend Eric. Somehow, Guadalupe got a wind of all this and was excited (supposedly) for me. She invited herself. Even though she was now in high school and had her own friends and we were in junior high, she still wanted to be part of whatever was going on with me. To this day, I don't understand why.

Guadalupe, Tammy, and I were at Tammy's house while Tammy's parents were at work and her sister wasn't home. It was a sunny spring break day, and Guadalupe and I had ridden our bikes over to Tammy's, which was about a five-minute bike ride. While we sat around Tammy's house, we were talking, especially Guadalupe, about what to do. She brought up the idea of drinking, but I had never had a drink before. She mentioned we could play quarters, the game where you bounce the quarter into a cup, and if you make it, you can make anyone drink. We got into Tammy's stepdad's beer, and Eric and Seth showed up. We played quarters at Tammy's round kitchen table. I pretended to drink. Guadalupe, with her loud, outgoing self, brought all the attention to herself as she always did. Within an hour or so, we ran out of beer and just hung out. I sensed by this time Seth's attention gravitating toward Guadalupe. This was pretty much the same thing that would happen with my girl friends, but now it was with boys I liked. Guadalupe didn't do anything to change it. To this day, I believe she pretended to be drunk so that she could blame what she ended up doing on the liquor. I became furious with her as she flirted with Seth.

We had to clean up and leave soon, because Tammy's sister was about to come home. I tried to physically drag Guadalupe, but she wasn't willing or able to leave with me. Someone, possibly Eric, picked her up, took her upstairs, and laid her onto Tammy's sister's bed. The last thing I saw before I left was her and Seth making out on the bed. I cried all the way home. I thought of how she was right all those years—that nobody really liked me or would ever like me.

I'd carry this broken part of my self-esteem with me for more than twenty years and have nightmares when I seriously liked a guy. The incident reoccurred in my dreams when I felt I had fallen for someone. I always thought if Guadalupe wanted to, she could take anybody from me. For months, possibly a year, she and Seth were boyfriend and girlfriend. I'd overhear of him sneaking into her bedroom at night, and even after he moved near downtown Houston, she continued sneaking away to see him. I knew this because Tammy, Guadalupe, Lynda, and I had our parents drive us to the Houston Galleria one summer so that we could just hang out and go window-shopping, but Guadalupe and Lynda had other plans and separated from us. They went off to see Seth. They made up some story and told Tammy and me that they were going to take the bus to Montrose, which was about ten minutes away from the Galleria, but I knew better. She thought this whole time I hadn't known about her and Seth.

As the day went on, I clearly became pissed off and sad. When my father came back to pick us up, he was furious because she was not with us. He was in the dark when it came to the fact that Guadalupe had a boyfriend who lived downtown and was still in junior high. That day at the Houston Galleria, Tammy and my dad and I were waiting around for what seemed like hours for Lynda and Guadalupe to show up. It was on the way home in the car that I blurted out that she had left the Galleria to go see a boy, and because of this, she was grounded for a little bit. That was the only mention I ever made out loud to let Guadalupe know that she hadn't kept it a secret and that I obviously knew all along what she had done to me and was doing to me. I lived with this scar of this incident for a very long time. It is the worst betrayal I'd lived through, but worst of all, I thought it proved that she had been right that I was too ugly or too fat or just that she was prettier, was thinner, or had a better personality than I all along. There was never anything in my future that played itself over and over again like this, even if it only was in my nightmares.

By the eighth grade, I would lock myself up in my room for hours, scarring my wrists over and over again with safety pins, not looking for attention but to overpower the pain I was going through. I had even tried strangling myself with a belt, but I couldn't get that to work. I couldn't figure out where to place the belt so that I could hang myself. Somehow I also knew of overdosing as a way to kill myself. In those days, we didn't have the Internet, so I wonder where I even got the idea. I thought I'd just go to sleep and never wake up. I tried killing myself twice this way, both times with aspirin and Tylenol.

By this time, I was just so hopeless. I knew the bottoms of despair like no other. Faith did not exist in my life. Life had sucked for as long as I could remember. In my mind, it was always going to be this horrible, miserable life. It was too hard to try to live anymore. Yes, I had fun times here and there. Yes, we weren't always fighting. Yes, she wasn't always drinking. Yes, Guadalupe wasn't always a shitty sister. Yes, there may have been glimpses of real love. But the bad outweighed the good by volumes, at least in my mind. I wanted out so badly, and when you saw and felt that nothing would ever change—and somehow, I felt wherever I went it would still be a horrible, miserable, sad life and all I could think is that the only way out is death. I wanted to be free of the pain—the stifling pain I had endured for years, maybe over a decade, even though I was just thirteen.

Suicidal depression is like seeing no other way out, and the darkness runs so deep that almost nothing and no one could tell you anything different about your life, your situation, or how it was going to change. You feel what you feel, the deepest bottom of a sadness that shouldn't even be referred to as sadness. You can't compare it to being blue or sad. Only those who have been suicidal truly understand, and I understood too well because I had been suicidally depressed for more than a year or two. I had the feeling of being done with life, wanting out, but it was just in the last few months that I finally started thinking about how to end my life.

The times I tried to hang myself really ended up being more of me strangling myself, and I'd physically stop at some point. I don't know if human beings can actually strangle themselves. I did get to the point of closing off some circulation because I ended up with hundreds of dots all over my face. It didn't heal for a few days, and somehow I was able to talk my way out of what had happened to my face.

The first time I tried to overdose, I just got very sick to my stomach but was eventually able to lie down, and within a couple of hours, I stopped throwing up but needed a few days to get back to feeling normal. The second time I did it, I almost succeeded; the throwing up was so bad that blood came up, and after a couple of hours of that, I was so tired and then scared—not because of dying but because of the throwing up being so bad for so long. I thought I was going to lie down in this peaceful sleep that I dreamed of and never wake up. Instead, it was this endless vomiting, and I just wanted it to stop. I went to my mom and told her what I had done, and I was rushed to the emergency room. They pumped my stomach, and somehow, my parents talked the doctors out of telling the authorities or having them not commit me for a psychiatric evaluation. I stayed in the hospital for a few days. The doctors said my stomach was bleeding and that I had messed up the lining a bit, but it was not too serious. I was told to monitor or not eat certain foods that would harm it more.

From that point on, my parents catered to me, letting me stay home from school (legally ditching) for days at a time; they'd treat me sometimes to my teenybopper magazines and caramel popcorn from the specialty shop down at the strip mall outside of our subdivision. I wasn't bratty about it. They just kept asking and asking if I wanted this or that, and I was just looking for anything to feel better, which happened to be sweets and my magazines.

Staying home from school made it a little better, because that was another thing that I hated in my life. And for a little while, the focus was on me, which had my parents behaving. I didn't try again to kill myself. I thought it couldn't happen, or at least I couldn't figure out how to do it. Also, I think it really scared me. Maybe part of me from that point forward learned what death truly was, and a small part of me at that point became scared of it.

But the hopelessness remained. The sadness was still there. The wanting out, being done with life, remained. I never spoke up about what was troubling me, even though there was one time my mom came to me and sat at the edge of my bed and asked me. There was no point. Who could change my situation? Who would change our lives on Silver Shadows Lane? And if it wasn't clear enough—because it should have been—there was no point in saying anything.

Our years in Houston (1979–1986) were those with ups and downs. Our downs, for me, were outplayed more. Unfortunately for me, this was the start of many years of my negativity, but fortunately, I believe it was just a way that my psyche wanted to hold on to all those bad moments because they were so wrong. When we made our move to Houston, my parents chose the best schools and a great community. Our life was picturesque. My father's business did well for the first five years. My mother, once again, worked off and on as she had done in Cincinnati. At first, our daily lives consisted of school, work, some extracurricular activities, and trying to make it to church on occasion. My father would usually do laundry and make dinner because my mother would be drunk, which I didn't mind, because he was and is a great cook, and I learned that men could clean also.

Typically, when my mother returned from work, she'd have already been drinking. Sometimes she'd go straight to bed and pass out. Then at about 8:00 p.m. or 9:00 p.m., she'd wake up and start a fight with my father. She'd speak about his infidelities or call him a queer in Spanish. I'd usually go to bed soon after, but I was kept up, depending on how far the fight would go. I could usually hear my mother breaking or throwing things. She even got a kick out of throwing a pitcher of ice over my father's head just to get a reaction. When she was drunk, she would do anything to annoy us. She was vulgar, loud, and in your face. She'd constantly cut the cable cord to the TV so we couldn't have any escape to what was going on around us.

Within time, all us girls became rebellious against our parents. To this day, I never recall once having any respect for them. I grew up seeing my two older sisters physically protect themselves against my father. If he lifted his hand to them, they'd do likewise.

When I was thirteen, they had begun going to downtown Houston and wouldn't show up for a few days, even though one of them was still in high school. In our home, downtown was known as the place where the drug addicts and homosexuals were—at least that was what we heard always coming out of my mother's mouth. My parents tried to get my sisters to stop going there. The last time this happened explains my childhood and how far things had progressed.

My sisters were on their way out, and my parents were trying to stop them. What I recall was my mom at the front door. My father insisted that they weren't going anywhere. On their way to the door, my father went after them. He pulled at one of them. My sister reacted by throwing her bags to hit him. Fists began to fly. I watched one sister being dragged by the hair through the living room in front of the fireplace. I cried and cried, yelling for it to stop. Guadalupe tried to make him leave them alone. She threw a shoe at him, which hit his head but didn't slow him down. Somehow, my two older sisters got away. They ran out the front door with nothing more than their lives. Their purses, bags of clothes for the weekend, and even a shoe one of them was wearing were left behind close to the front door.

By this time, Guadalupe and I knew to run to our rooms. We knew instinctively even though this fight had nothing to do with us that it would affect us. We ran to my bedroom, which was the first room up the stairs. We locked the door. We cried, screaming out my window to my two older sisters who had just fled. We cried out to them to not leave us behind. I visually can still see them running down the street, looking back at us, looking as if several men had attacked them.

Just then, there was banging at my door. It was my father. We shut the window. He yelled at us to open the door. He needed to teach us a lesson, which was that we should never follow in our sisters' footsteps. Because he persisted and said not to make it worse for ourselves, my sister opened the door and ran down the hallway to her room. He chased her. I shut my door and hid under my bed. I could hear her screams and cries. Then it stopped. It was my turn. I then heard him open my door. When he realized where I was, he told me in Spanish that if I didn't come out at that moment, when I did, he'd hit my head between the floor and the bottom of the bed. I came out to receive my punishment just like many times before. It didn't matter to my parents that I had done nothing wrong but watch this spectacle they had created. Years and years of craziness were created by two so-called adults, two so-called parents, our role models. We were not only mirrors of their dysfunction but also their children.

After he was done hitting me, he gathered my sister and me together to go downstairs, and he told us to apologize to my mother. I remember being confused by this. This was and still is the most awful thing someone has ever asked me to do. It completely made no sense in every fiber of my being, but that whole day was the darkest of all my nightmares, the height of the insanity. We went down to my mother, who was in the kitchen cooking. But it wasn't until we apologized that I had realized one thing: she was drunk. I was apologizing for nothing I had done to a drunken lady.

For the following few weeks, for the first time I can ever recall in our lives, we were scared of our parents. After seeing what I had seen, I was scared for my life. We kept quiet, held our heads down, and did as they said. I don't believe my father ever realized that his wife had been drinking that night. To this day, it takes him a very long time to clue in to the fact that she is drunk; as for me, I can tell in less than sixty seconds. That was one thing that magically happened for me that day—to be able to detect in a small amount of time when she was under the influence.

My two older sisters were not heard from for about six months. They snuck phone calls in to Guadalupe and me, checking if we were okay. Somehow, they also knew inherently that their actions might affect us too, and they were concerned. Things had never been this bad. This was the climax of violence in our house and in our upbringing. What I saw was three adult-size people physically fighting, fists flying, throwing any objects they could find, and kicking with all their might. One was trying to restrain, one was fighting in self-defense, and another was trying to protect. And they all supposedly loved one another and called each other *family*.

During the fight, all I could do was cry at the edge of the breakfast room near the fireplace in our living room. I was a child who believed in love most of all. All I saw throughout my life were mixed messages of love and violence intertwined, learning that love was truly a battlefield.

During our lives, we had received tender touches by my mom

at times; all us girls would jump in her bed and have her scratch our backs. We'd have a balance of humor from our dad and actual interaction, like when he'd play with us in the ocean or like that one time we all had a major water fight that went inside and around the outside of the house. All six of us would share beautiful moments like these that we all hold so close, but I would unfortunately, vividly, remember the horrific scenes too, like this brutal fight. What do moments like this fight say to a child, especially a girl? What would be the implications to me and my sisters in the future of learning and experiencing these mixed messages by the ones that were our first loves, our protectors, and the ones who were supposed to love us the most?

Within time, my parents let up, but my life was changed forever. A seed had been planted for a while, but now the soil had been covered and patted forcefully down. This life I had known up until that point was wrong. I hated it! I'd fight against it. The true rebellion in me was born, and the silent "Fuck you" to life, authority, and my parents began.

I continued going through periods of suicidal thoughts. I continued escaping in my room, dreaming of a life other than mine. My grades had fallen drastically. I had been an A/B student, and I was now completely failing. At fifteen, I'd begun my descent of finally dropping out of school. My parents were always those types to be too lenient with exception of their well-overdue violence, which they considered discipline. They did plead with me to go to school but did not force it. I think they knew I had depression, so they'd do anything to please me, thinking that would resolve it.

The four of us went back to being the family we had been before, never mentioning anything that had gone on. We'd try to bury our secrets, hide, and escape from the pain. Guadalupe and I began following in our sisters' footsteps, drinking and partying just to find some kind of pleasure in life. My parents went back to their ways of not enforcing anything. We'd go out and say that we'd be home by midnight but wouldn't show up until after 2:00 a.m. Our parents would tell us we were grounded, but by the following night, we'd want to go out and promise to by home on time, and they'd bend and let us go out again. And we wouldn't make it home on time again. The dysfunctional cycle continued. No rules, no discipline, no respect— just back to being normal.

"Do as I say, not as I do." That saying scares me. I heard it one too many times during my childhood. It was pretty much my parents' slogan as we grew up and the hypocrisy of my existence. My dad would later warn us of how my mother and her drinking didn't start off as what we were then witnessing. He told us time and time again about how she started socially drinking at parties. He was in fear of us picking up on that behavior—that bad trait of hers. But what about teaching a child how to deal with life and not to avoid life? And, most of all, what about the violence? This was beyond disciplining a child. When you love someone, do you on occasion hit that person? My soul told me no. My heart told me no. But the life I had been given told my mind, "Love and pain go hand in hand."

We were being taught to accept violence, but we were also being shown to escape from our problems and learning how not to deal with anything. These two were our teachers of life, and we were just following instinctively in their shoes. Do as I say, not as I do. How do children learn anything more than what they are shown? Did they expect us to guess? Why couldn't they just have shown us how to live differently? It would take decades for me to understand this.

4

Little Girl Lost

High school came around, and now I had broken away from society and my so-called life. I dreaded it, all of it. With the combination of my family and school life, living was torture; it was killing me inside. I had two failed suicide attempts under my belt, I was still shy and introverted, and most of my peers whom I had known for years at one time or another barely communicated with me, because by this time, I was so edgy and they were still so clean-cut that they kept their distance. But I kept close to a few girls whom I had been friends with for about a year or so.

My freshman year went unnoticed. It was amazing how counselors let you fall through the cracks. Guadalupe was repeatedly brought into the counseling office, but she had always had difficulty in school. My failing, not completing assignments, getting grades like 15 percent or 23 percent out of 100 on tests, and lack of attendance went unrecognized for the most part.

During spring break of 1985, my freshman year, a friend of mine's parents were going to be out of town the entire week, which coincided with my birthday. Debbie lived in the upscale, pricier Champions Forest subdivision. Guadalupe somehow convinced Debbie to have a surprise birthday party for me. This party was supposed to be small, just us few girls—Debbie, Tammy, myself, Guadalupe, and another friend, Steph. But as soon as Guadalupe got the green light, it became a real high school party. Guadalupe told so many kids to come. For the most part, she had been part of the in-crowd, with the cheerleaders and jocks.

The first night, which later turned into almost a weeklong birthday celebration, was the first night I ever drank; I was just fifteen. Guadalupe went behind the bar and poured me a cup of Bacardi and Coke. I remember about the first ten minutes of that evening. I was truly my mother's daughter. I'd eventually pass out and throw up. I was told stories of what went on. Supposedly, I kept on trying to do a strip tease show on a picnic table outside. Guadalupe drove Debbie's father's Bentley to go pick someone up. Someone else, at some point, drove a car up on the front lawn and left tire tracks. I have pictures from that night of many of my peers drinking it up, playing quarters, or dancing. I was not the only one who got wasted. There is a picture or two of some other girls passed out, but most of the pictures are of everyone cheering, raising their drinks. It's bittersweet, because it was one of those high school nights that are portrayed in the movies like *Sixteen Candles* that I would have loved to remember. The photos I have are priceless. But reflecting back, it is also sad, because from day one, I obviously had a problem with alcohol and didn't stop there.

This is when the true partying began for me, which really never stopped until my mid-twenties, but for the most part, I was still locking myself up in my room and was still depressed—though my depression was now being expressed differently at times.

I think a lot of individuals who have substance abuse problems, whether it be with alcohol or drugs, are depressed on some level. My friends and I would hang out around our subdivisions late at night, sneaking out, just to hang out or drink or try to drink. Guadalupe and some of our girlfriends and I had been sneaking out of our second-story game room window to go to other people's houses to go swimming, go drinking, or to run around the country club near Champions Forest. It wasn't hard to go to parties. I'm sure our parents asked us where we were going or what we were doing, but like most parents at that time, they were clueless about what we were up to.

I have a picture of Guadalupe and me in our house in the breakfast room having my lobster dinner for my fifteenth birthday. My parents bugged us to come home from Debbie's house (the week we were having parties). They wanted to celebrate my birthday, but in the picture, I look so tired. I am sure I was hungover; if they had only known what we were up to that week. What would they have said? I was unintentionally mimicking my role model. We were rebellious like our two older sisters had been. It wasn't hard at first, because my parents rarely said no, and they really couldn't lay down any rules that they'd stick to. It'd be almost impossible for them to start saying we couldn't do this or that because more than likely we were already getting away with doing what we wanted.

In Klein, like most places, you have your jocks and cheerleaders, your drama kids, the band geeks, and the nerds, and then there was the rest of us—the outsiders. Some of us were what later became the alternative kids or death rockers, skaters, punks, and some of us were just unique, not fitting in any specific category. I like that we couldn't be defined—no label, please. So, every clique mostly did its own thing and had its own parties too. For a while there, we mostly partied at John's.

I can't remember how or when I first met him. He was a tall, somewhat lanky, blond skater boy. John and I met and just clicked and became close friends. He lived in Champions Forest in one of the biggest houses of any of my friends. He hung out with a cool group of guys, one of whom I'd come to have a mad crush on, CAC. I even branded his initials, CAC, on my wrist one day when I was hanging out at my friend Emily's house. She had a branding machine for wood, and I wanted to try it out on my skin like a tattoo.

John had lots of parties at his house. I saw my first porn at his house, and in my drunken state, looking over the balcony of his living room, I couldn't tell at first what I was looking at. My eyes were blurry, and the shots were close up. I leaned over for so long, talking aloud, asking what that was. I still don't think at that time I really knew what sex was. I really was clueless and innocent. I had my first real kiss and made out for the first time at one of John's parties too— and it was with John.

Most of the parties were fun, and some of them I can actually remember. I was a klutz too when I drank. I was that girl that always runs into glass doors or screen doors, which is funny because I always had perfect eyesight. I even still have a scar, a little bump on my lip, from running into John's sliding glass door that led to the backyard. *Priceless.*

But like the roller coaster of my life, the good came with the bad. I was almost gang-raped, but thankfully, an adult intervened. I also was groped by a bunch of boys, which was humiliating, and I had to kick some of them and hit their hands off from touching me as I walked up a staircase to a bedroom to go to sleep one night. They were like a group of wolves.

If we weren't at John's, we more than likely were hanging out somewhere, and by the summertime, Guadalupe and Lynda were now hanging out with us. But when the summer was over and school began again, John and I began to drift apart. I missed him and felt hurt by it, because like he once said to me, "I know you like the back of my hand," and he did know me. We were never close again. He was two years older than I, and I heard years later that after he graduated, he moved to Hollywood with his girlfriend, and after a fight or breakup,

∞ Evolving to Grace ∞

he ended up committing suicide. He was the first person I ever felt my heart fall to the floor for. He was my first real loss. I felt he really knew me and still accepted me. I wished we had remained friends so I could've been there for him in his darkest time. I still tear up when I hear the song "Under the Milky Way," which played after I heard the news of his death. It reminds me of him.

By my sophomore year, I started to drift almost completely away from attending school. It wasn't like before when I'd miss a lot of school and then be good for a month or so. Now, I'd miss days in a row and then, toward the end, weeks in a row. Less than four years prior, I had been receiving mostly As. Now in my sophomore year, it was Fs and maybe a D. In Texas, the law was that you couldn't legally drop out until you were sixteen. But at the age of fifteen, they might as well have changed that, because I was beginning to not show up at all. I'd maybe attend ten days out of each month.

It's not that I didn't love to learn. I used to beg my mom to send me anywhere, even a convent, to continue to go to school. I knew boarding school was out of the question because of finances, even though I asked. I thought anything would have been wiser than to have me end my education and for them to get their youngest child out of the misery she was going through, at least in school. I was being teased and wrongly labeled because of the way I dressed, cut my hair, and possibly also because I wasn't very social outside of my group. I didn't like the way that felt. To them, I looked like someone that smoked pot and took drugs, but I didn't do any of that, yet. I just drank like the rest of them. Even in the high school newspaper, there was once a picture of me where I was quoted as saying that the best time of the day was lunch period so that I could take a smoke. I didn't even smoke at that time!

My parents once took me to see the principal, and she asked me why I wanted to drop out. She tried to educate me about what my life would be without a high school diploma. All I was thinking was I didn't want a life anymore, so it didn't matter. I really just needed to get away from that life I was forced to live. I never saw or wanted a life beyond those years. By that time, I had given up on school, on my family, on me, on life. Nothing mattered.

The oil industry by this time had plummeted in Houston. My father's business hadn't been doing well due to the drought of oil in the Gulf. He couldn't find work at all. A few months before I turned sixteen, my father had already lost his business, and my mother was pawning thousands of dollars of what she had, from pounds of silver to her diamond-and-emerald wedding ring to jewelry (Mikimoto pearl necklaces and other jewelry), diamond earrings, and crystal (Baccarat, mostly), all from her inheritance. Anything and everything to keep our house going was being pawned.

The electricity had already been shut off, and the only thing left was this cold house with its memories of heartbreak and sorrow. My mother selling off her inheritance to pawnshops all over Houston helped pay to turn the utilities back on and keep it going for some weeks or a month. I didn't see it then, the sacrifice my mom was making for us. The material inheritance meant so much to her too. This was probably the biggest thing she has ever done for us, and I'm thankful that she did.

Heat is actually important in the wintertime in Houston, because it can actually get cold, and I'm sure it was costly to keep a five-bedroom house warm. When we didn't have electricity, we layered our clothes and beds; we used gas lanterns, the ones used for camping. I don't believe my two older sisters had ever faced being without heat and electricity for as often or as long as we had. We'd have to take very cold showers. This was a rude awakening to me of how things could be taken away from you so quickly. Vital things like warmth, shelter, and food that we all think we will always have were dissipating. It was hard to keep putting food on the table, and I remember my mom going to a food bank to get some food sometimes. That was tough on her. I'm sure she never imagined her life like that.

Our house was being foreclosed. My two older sisters had moved to Chicago with some friends from downtown Houston. My parents, Candelaria, and Paoletta had reconciled from their vicious fight two and a half years earlier. My father had to eventually leave us and move to California to look for work. In February 1986, my dad moved to California, where most of his immediate family lived. They were willing to help him out while he got back on his feet. My mother was to stay behind to wrap things up with the house before we were officially locked out.

That spring, Guadalupe was graduating from high school, and she was going to move back to Ohio with our longtime childhood friend Lynda. My mother was to rent an apartment with some of the money from the several garage sales she had. And when I turned sixteen, I went to my school, and I officially dropped out, newly shaved head and all with just enough hair on top to appear at times like I really had a bob haircut. It was my final "fuck you"; I was done with that school.

After my father left, my sister and I moved in with a friend of ours, Kim, and I eventually drifted anywhere and everywhere because my friend's mother didn't like the fact that I wasn't going to school anymore, and I'd just stay at their house all day doing nothing.

Another spring break approached. Tammy, Kim, Guadalupe, three other friends—Emily, Hailey, and a friend of Guadalupe's—and I made a plan to go to Galveston. We made a reservation at a hotel on the pier. As a family, we had gone there in the summers. I have sweet memories of those times. I remember being in the warm waters, our father swimming with us, and our friends, Lynda and Jennifer, a friend who lived down the street, joining us sometimes. In those waters in the Gulf, there are flying fish. I recalled being startled by the fish that not only would fly but would swim close to our feet. I'd be startled but would relish in the joy of the warm ocean waters that I'd remain in most of the day, swimming.

Now my sister and I and our friends made a trip to party for a few days during our spring break there. I don't think any of our parents knew. We probably just told our parents that we were going to someone else's house. The drive was a wild one. The last stretches of the freeway leading to Galveston were pretty desolate in the early parts of the afternoon as we sped at excessive speeds. We drove in two separate cars. Some of us hung out of the sunroofs while the driver sped veering in and out of lanes, the *Pretty in Pink* sound track blasting. We all were excited about this trip and adventure.

As soon as we got in our room, we began to drink and fix ourselves up to go walking around out on the boardwalk. We broke off looking for guys to invite over for a party later that night. I remember going with Tammy into this old, grand hotel, Hotel Galvez—the oldest hotel in Galveston. I dragged Tammy in there because I had to go to the bathroom. We were still tipsy; or at least I was.

As we walked into the lobby, the first thing I saw was a guy with a short, sandy-blond Mohawk, combat boots, and a cutoff red-and-black flannel sitting on a couch obviously waiting for someone. I couldn't believe my eyes. I was shocked at this stunning guy and how he was dressed all punk in this classy hotel. I loved it! I don't think I had ever seen anyone like him before. He smiled at us, and all I could do was giggle. As we left the hotel, he had vanished, and I was crushed.

Nighttime came, and all us girls dressed up like we were going to a club. Our hotel room was tiny, and we actually wondered if anyone that any of us had met during the day was going to show up. We just started to drink again, and soon enough, boys came. A very eclectic group of guys showed up, nothing like the guys we went to school with. One was even really tall, skinny, black, and obviously gay. They were the coolest guys I had ever been around. And before I knew it, there he was, the guy from the lobby of the hotel—Johnny. I didn't know what to do with myself. He came up to me and asked me if I was that girl from earlier in the hotel. We spoke for a little bit, and it was obvious that we were interested in one another. But soon enough, our party got broken up by the hotel manager, and we were being thrown out. We hurried to gather our stuff together because the cops were on their way. I wonder whose credit card we used for that hotel reservation, because I remember someone saying something about the patio chairs being thrown over our balcony into the Gulf of Mexico.

We all caught up with one another in a parking lot, and we touched base on what we were going to do. Guadalupe, her friend, and two others had already decided to take off for South Padre, another hot spot for partying during spring break, but it was about four hours south of where we were, and I didn't want to go. The rest of the girls were going to head back home, but it was the middle of the night, and who knew what they told their parents? Tammy and I decided to stay down in Galveston even though we had no place to stay. It was not an option for her to return home.

Tammy had technically run away from home, leaving her mom a note prior to leaving for Galveston. Going to Galveston was a present to herself for having been so misunderstood by her mom and her family for so long. Now she had nowhere to go, and I wasn't about to leave her alone. Johnny and a friend of his hung out with us for a bit before they offered to take us back with them to stay at Johnny's friend's home. His friend lived in an apartment with his mom, and he thought his mom wouldn't mind. We stayed with them for a few days.

Johnny and I danced around the fact that we wanted to make out but didn't. I used to love the way he looked at me, half smile and all. We had Johnny eventually take us back to Galveston because his mom's friend didn't feel comfortable with us staying there any longer. I believe she realized one or both of us were runaways, and she wanted no part in that.

The day after Tammy and I returned, we hung out and smoked pot at the house of some girl that we had met while walking around. We hid all our luggage on the beach against the rocks, where we thought no one could see them. When we returned from being at the beach cottage where the girl lived with her brother, all our suitcases were stolen, and I was walking around with no shoes and stoned out of my mind because that was the first time I smoked pot, and it was just another substance I did to the extreme. I didn't know who to call but Johnny. I tried to tell him what happened, but I was laughing hysterically one moment and then crying the next. He came back and picked us up to at least take us closer to our homes. He left us at one of the nice hotels in downtown Houston, per my sobering-up request.

I finally reached my mother, and she had just been checked out of a hospital for either detoxing or a suicide attempt. At the time, I didn't care what she was going through. I just pleaded for her to pick us up from the Galleria. Tammy and I returned to my family's abandoned house, where my mother was still conducting an ongoing garage sale. Tammy's mom had already brought over a garbage bag full of all of Tammy's stuff and left it at my house. She had given up on her daughter. She came over as soon as we returned and picked up Tammy to just drop her off at the airport. She was sent away to live with her father in Huntington Beach, California. I thought that would be the last time I'd see my friend.

The house that we once used to treasure and despise had become colder and darker than I remembered just one month earlier. The bank had finally foreclosed on the house and locked it, but my mom managed to still find a way in through a window in the back of the house. I spent the next couple of weeks in my room without electricity or heat. There was no playing Duran Duran to help me escape. There was no going down to the family room to watch TV. There was no one and nothing to do in the place I'd refer to as my childhood home. Even with all the tainted memories I had, it was my childhood home, and these final days were going to be the darkest of my memories of "home."

My mom drank herself through the night until the next day

when she'd once again try to sell as many of our belongings as she could. By April of 1986, my mom had sold most of our belongings, and the house was securely closed so no one could jimmy themselves in. We had left my cat, Soccerella, with our next-door neighbor who had cared for him almost as much as we did.

My mom got an apartment. At that time, I tried so hard to be there for her with the little emotional strength I had. All the times I wanted to be so far away from this house on Silver Shadows Lane, I now felt like I still wanted and needed it so badly. I saw it as an end to our family, and we were never the same. Our family unit, dysfunctional or not, was now gone in a sense. We'd never have that family home to go back to or to make better memories to replace the bad ones.

But it wasn't soon after my mom had moved into her apartment that I went to Chicago to stay with my two older sisters. Even though I felt I needed to be there for her because there was no one left, she spiraled more out of control than ever, and I couldn't handle it. I was on my way to my own destruction and needed to run away from hers. My life had been turned upside down seemingly overnight. The years I had endured, especially the recent ones, were too much to handle.

While in Chicago, it was apparent that my two older sisters partied a lot but were still somehow managing to go to work. While I lived there, things were tough. Even though they wanted and offered for me to live with them, they were in no position to take care of me. They were barely taking care of themselves. There was barely and rarely any food, much less toilet paper sometimes. I had enough of living like that, so after a month, I returned to Houston.

I was living a life of which I was so independent, trying to take care of myself, but not by choice. I was sixteen and dying inside to still be taken care of. Even when everything was stable years earlier, I now somewhat subconsciously felt like I needed to be cradled and cared for more than ever, just a little while longer. I was crying inside for it. I just wanted to be back home and crawl into my bed. I hadn't had enough years of being treated as a child whom others should look after. I felt abandoned in a sense like an orphan would feel. Now the child in me had to ignore the fact that I was still a child and the feelings that came with that, and somehow I needed to take on a role as an adult. It was another pivotal time when I had to live in the reality of what life was giving me, whether I liked it or not and to ignore any feelings that came with that.

Being back in Houston, I'd do anything to be out of my mother's apartment. I just needed to escape the cramped quarters my mom and I were living in. It was nice to be back, but we had our problems; her drinking was bad, and I was all alone to deal with her alcoholic behavior. We were sharing a one-bedroom apartment. It wasn't an easy emotional transition to go from having a huge house where we all had our own bedrooms and could escape within them to the new circumstances. My mother was on a continuous binge, and I was running wild and it seemed like this entire downfall was only affecting she and I. Everyone had moved away, and they didn't have to face the reality of really losing everything and still being so very close to where it all was.

We were still scrambling at times to pay rent and to find money for gas and food. Going from having so much for my first fifteen years to suddenly living with the fear of being on the streets, not knowing how I'd eat again, was traumatizing, and it made a lasting impression on me that would always play out in my future. The time my mom and I spent together brought us so much closer than we would ever be. Though we were violent with one another, and she still drank most of the time, we had a bond because we were surviving the biggest tragedy thus far in our lives. We were definitely in shock. My mom and I were suffering together. No one else would share memories of having nothing in the refrigerator and counting pennies for me to get a chocolate bar and for my mother to get a pack of cigarettes.

Guadalupe was still living with our friend Kim that May when she graduated from high school. She was planning to move to Ohio with Lynda. Lynda had come out to Houston for one last trip and for Guadalupe's graduation. Lynda and I were back on speaking terms after our fight the summer before, but our friendship was no longer the same. She was now really Guadalupe's friend.

It was a sunny, warm day on Guadalupe's graduation. I remember feeling something I had never felt before, like I could just breathe and feel a sense of freedom, and I felt I was going to be okay. I was so happy she was moving away. I'd no longer be under her thumb, shackled to her. I'd no longer have to fear her. The physical attacks that had been there since I can remember—and that included her chasing me down our hallway with scissors a year or so earlier or when she beat me up in the streets of downtown a month earlier, punching, choking, and biting me, from which I still have a scar—would never happen again. In her graduation pictures, I look happy for her, but I was happy for myself. From that point forward, I felt as if I could come into my own, and at that point, I knew I didn't need her in my life. She left about a week or so later, and I felt blessed.

Once again, I felt as I needed to flee or I'd die. That was how my life was panning out. I wouldn't be able to deal emotionally with my surroundings, my life, so I'd take off and run, thinking it'd be better somewhere else. At the end of May, I moved to California to live with my dad and his brother's family. There was that hidden notion that my mother would hint about my father's family, either them not liking us or maybe just her. I felt unwelcome by my dad's brother almost immediately after meeting him. He'd make remarks and look at me in a certain way. Who knows what his family heard in the beginning of my parents' relationship or all those years that we had not seen them? I was an unwelcome guest from the beginning, but I was family, and he was doing this for his brother. My uncle would be mean toward me, subtly. He'd talk about how I needed to do something about my weight. I was chubby, but still only 112 pounds. But maybe this was just him being him, because I wasn't the only one he was criticizing about weight; he was talking to his then wife about hers, also. Dinnertime wasn't fun in that household.

Within a month and a half, I begged and cried for my father to allow me to return to Houston. I thought I could deal with what I knew rather than deal with this stranger's meanness. My dad wasn't happy, and I think he was embarrassed, but he finally bought me a plane ticket out of there. His intentions for me were to get me back into school, but I wasn't ready.

I returned to Houston to only stay for about another month before I ran off to Chicago again. I just felt I couldn't deal with my mom and that reality. Candelaria, Paoletta, and I had always been very close. I was their little sister. Both of them, especially Candelaria, always wanted to take care of me and protect me, and they did really want to try to be there for me. It was like them to offer for me to stay again with them. I went to work at a retail store, Beauty and the Beast, because there was no money to even feed me.

As soon as I returned to Chicago, Guadalupe came to visit from Cincinnati. In Chicago, I was living as if I were an adult, but I was only a very naive sixteen-year-old. After work or on the weekends, I used to hang out on the front porch with Paoletta and their friends, doing "front porch action"—drinking and hanging out. Candelaria and Paoletta used to fight over this, because Candelaria thought I was too young. We used to buy a suitcase or two of beer, and we'd sit on the porch steps, around the block from Wrigley Field, drinking all afternoon. Back then, all four of us girls were heavily drinking. For me, it was so bad that I was constantly passing out and throwing up almost every time. There was even one time I almost fell out of the second-story window of their brownstone. I had been sitting on the windowsill, looking out, but the window was completely open. At some point, I passed out, and just as I was slipping out, Paoletta walked in screaming at me to wake up, and she grabbed me. I was alarmed for half a second, and then I ran to the bathroom to start throwing up. Our drinking had become an ongoing daily routine, our new way of life as we had learned.

I had become friends with some kids who were around my age and a little older. We used to hang out around the city, drinking. There was a boy in the group who liked me and asked me out. We began dating but hanging out in groups. We made out a lot but nothing more because I was still a virgin. I'd get loaded but never that drunk to go all the way. He tried and tried, but the last night I went out with him, it became such an issue that I stormed into the brownstone after our date, very upset, saying how I was never going to see him again. Candelaria, Paoletta, and their roommates were having a party. I went straight to the back bedroom, which I was sharing with Paoletta. I had been drinking that night. A little time later after passing out, I got up to see if there was actually anything in the refrigerator to drink or eat before I threw up, and as usual, there was nothing.

While staying in Chicago, I really learned to fend for myself. Yes, my sisters provided a place for me to stay, but they didn't usually have the means to feed me with the exception of when I'd visit Candelaria at Houlihan's, where she worked. I learned that mustard sandwiches could be tasty. Just a slice of bread and mustard in between was all you needed.

That night was no different. There was nothing in the refrigerator to counter my feeling sick from the alcohol. When I was still in the kitchen, somehow I was told or overheard that Paoletta was on the rooftop with the boy I had just been out with and that they were making out or something else that I'd rather not say. This was the moment that my relationship with Paoletta changed.

I shake my head while I share this story and look back at me as if it wasn't me. I can't believe two sisters of mine did that to me. Betrayal and lack of boundaries is so ugly. I was developing as a young girl, and those were not helpful situations for the normal development of my self-esteem, much less how family was supposed to treat one another. And unfortunately, it also helped me solidify my distrust in people. Also, my perception of what I saw when I looked in the mirror was greatly affected. It left me very confused. It all started the first time Guadalupe told me I was ugly, but the two of them getting the guy in the end really left me puzzled, because I didn't see my sisters as these gorgeous creatures. So this happening to me once again helped me not trust what I saw looking back at me in the mirror at times or trusting anyone.

When Paoletta hurt me like that, I didn't know how to react or really process what I was going through. I just ignored it like most things that had happened to me. I learned to know there was nothing I could do about it, so why even try?

Maybe at that point in my life, I also felt as if I didn't matter. I don't think I ever really said anything about it, though I recall Paoletta writing a letter to me months later, mentioning that he was the first real boyfriend who took her out on dates. It's amazing how I bottle things up, bite my lip, and face people who have hurt me so much, and even though many things were in the past, they were never addressed and resolved. After all these years, I never lashed out at them for the harm they had inflicted. This was just another major thing that happened in my life that would teach me to never react in stressful, in-your-face situations that I might encounter, which isn't good all the time. You must get angry sometimes, and I'd like to be able to at least speak up when things arise. I still carry myself as I did then—shocked, walking away from situations, not knowing what to say or believe what just happened.

A little over a week later, I lost my virginity, technically. I was raped. It is mind-boggling what paths my journey took me on when I didn't make good choices. I never stopped to even think of what I was doing. I shouldn't have ever had a drink. I shouldn't have been at that get-together. I shouldn't have been in Chicago. I shouldn't have bottled things up that hurt me. I should have been in school trying to do the best thing for myself, getting my education. So many should-not-haves or should-haves play over and over in my mind. If I could have only pressed rewind, this might not have happened to me, but maybe like most things in our lives, they are destined and meant to happen for a reason.

I began drinking a year earlier. I drank until I threw up, blacked out, and passed out next to my new friend, Potty, the toilet. And even though I'd go to the extent that I had seen my mom go to and hated it, I was now doing it a lot of the time. Here I was at sixteen, still drinking, bottling up my emotions—escaping from my life and only facing my reality through depressed feelings, scarring my wrists with safety pins, and drinking to excess. At a get-together across the street at a neighbor's brownstone in Chicago, Paoletta, Guadalupe, and I drank. Paoletta was there with her new boyfriend, the boy I had been dating! I had to have felt uncomfortable. I was still so confused about what had happened to me again, or maybe I was just trying to ignore my feelings. I believe by that time in my life, I was trying to push down my feelings, because to everyone besides me, my feelings didn't matter. People, especially family, had done so many hurtful things and with no apology. My feelings didn't matter. I didn't matter.

I can only recall about the first few minutes of that evening. We were at the guy's place that had a tall, blue mohawk. Mr. Mohawk was a guy that I use to have a crush on that lived across the street from us. I was excited because any chance to see him would put a smile on my face for the rest of the day. I don't remember why he and his roommate had us all over because we were just friendly neighbors that just said "hi" to one another when we'd see each other. I kind of remember trying to go over there as cute as I could. I couldn't be pretty or even pretty enough to get Mr. Mohawk's attention, because I still had not bloomed into the prettiness that would come years later, but it didn't stop me from getting excited from going over there. I walked into this guy's place that evening with happiness and with a profound innocence that I still had. I was sixteen going on twelve. I didn't know really what happened during sex. I had never seen a boy naked except for the *Playgirl* magazines that Guadalupe would sneak and show us. I had only made out with two guys in my life, and that was just heavy-duty kissing. Guadalupe mentioned later that I had gotten so drunk I began to throw up all over the place. At some point, like I always had, I had time to take pictures. It's funny how I could continue doing what I love to do despite never remember doing it.

Guadalupe later told me she stuck me in the bathtub to clean me up and then later put me into the roommate's (not Mr. Mohawk's) bed to sleep it off. I passed out. My sisters left me there. Guadalupe had to leave me there because she was catching a plane back to Cincinnati. She had only come and stayed for a few weeks. I believe Mr. Mohawk went with her to the airport.

It was only decades later that I spoke to Paoletta about that night, but it was brief, and we only spoke about the rape. She felt bad hearing what I had gone through, and she didn't want to talk any further about it, so I was never able to find out why she left me there. I cannot blame her, though, because for so long, we all had been only watching out for ourselves. I was blacked out the whole night. I do recall a moment, though. The pain of him trying to enter me woke me up. I remember seeing his outlined figure in the dark on top of me, and I was trying to push him off. I moaned in agony because of what he was trying to do. It hurt, but I just passed out again.

In the morning, I woke up to find myself half-naked, lying next to this dude who was completely naked. I quietly went out to the living room trying to find my clothes, which Guadalupe had partially cleaned of vomit in the bathroom. I made small talk with Mr. Mohawk.

My best time spent on Sheffield Avenue was watching this tall, skinny white guy with a blue mohawk skate up and down the street. This moment in the morning was embarrassing. I acted as nothing happened, like I always did—nothing affecting me—but it had to be written all over my face because I was so uncomfortable. I'd no longer look at Mr. Mohawk the same or his roommate. I pretended that all was good, even to the point that a few days later when I left to go back to Houston, they both rode the subway with me to the airport like we were all friends or something. As a young girl, you don't know how to behave when things like this happen, because you really can't understand what happened and you are probably in shock.

I'd later find out that I'd gotten a STD. I had my virginity taken from me. I felt ashamed and confused, not knowing what to do but get out of there. I walked in as a happy, innocent girl and walked out snatched of everything that was pure of me, forever changed. It took me decades to realize how devastating that night truly was. It took me twenty-six years to finally cry about it. For so many years, I used to say that, thankfully, I was passed out for most it, and that was why it never really affected me. But I see now, it did affect me. My childhood laid a foundation for me to let men use me and possibly lead me into selling myself for sex, but this incident may have played more of a role than my childhood. After the rape, I didn't have sex again for another year, but that time, it was my choice.

My days back again in Houston were spent around the apartment most of the time because my friends were back in school. I'd go to bed late and wake up late. Sometimes during the week and on the weekends, I'd steal my mom's car, even though I didn't have a driver's license. I'd drive thirty minutes to downtown to hang out at the clubs, meeting up with Johnny and some of his friends. I remember the first time I stole the car. My mom and I had gotten into a fight, and after she passed out, I took it. It was such a high but at the same time scary because I remember driving back on the freeway and driving alongside semis. Our parents had taught us years earlier how to drive, but in undeveloped areas of our subdivision. Now I seriously got some experience behind the wheel.

My mom wasn't okay with me taking her car. Once she had awoken and realized that I took it, she locked me out. When I got back, I banged on the door until she opened it. It wasn't the right thing to do, but it wasn't the last time I took the car.

One time, I was driving back with Johnny and a few of his friends, the same group of guys we had first met in Galveston. I can't recall why I was driving these guys back with me to my part of town. They lived closer to downtown. Maybe I was taking them to a party I had heard of. That night was memorable, because when we stopped at a gas station close to my place, a cop stopped us. The cop said to me that he was worried for me because I was this girl with a bunch of guys. Thankfully, he didn't cite me for driving without a license, but he did give me a warning and followed us to my mom's apartment, where all of us had to stay the night until the next morning when she was supposed to drive them back to Baytown where they lived. I hung out with them, used poppers, laughing for a while in the bedroom until it was time to go to bed. My mom slept on the couch, and I slept on the living room floor. I made breakfast for everyone in the morning. Johnny had found my poetry book, which I had starting writing at about the age of eleven. He read some poems that were more recent and asked me who they were about. He knew they were about him. I was so embarrassed and fumbled my words. He just gave me that look that he always did. I drove them back to Baytown after breakfast.

Having taken pictures so often since about the age of six, I wish I had pictures of us from that night.

My mother's alcoholism was now the worst I had ever witnessed. Her moral compass was nonexistent, because she was making steak dinners with my father's money to feed a guy she was either romancing or keeping company with. He'd come by the apartment, and it totally grossed me out. He was homeless and living in the woods next to our apartment complex, and he was half her age. One night, I came home to find her in her panties, drunk on the couch, crying and saying his name and saying my father's name. I couldn't make sense of what I was seeing. This woman who had come from generations of wealthy, educated, successful people had gone to an exclusive women's college in Briarcliff, traveled throughout Europe and Japan, and at some point spoke five languages, was now disgusting to me. She, in my eyes, had hit the lowest point in her life.

I still didn't know how to process the downfall I was witnessing. How could there be any comprehension in a sixteen-year-old's mind? Maybe this was just adding on to a life that never made sense. But our family's lives now more than ever seemed crazy, spiraling out of control, especially my mother's and mine. All I learned to do at this point was to run and leave again. I was lost, looking for something—stability, sobriety, sanity, maybe just to be taken care of like a child should be. I felt I wasn't able to stay in one city for more than a few weeks or a month or so. It felt as if I didn't run, I'd die or suffocate. This time was definitely no exception. I felt bad once again for leaving my mom, but the grief of my life as it was then was too much to bear. I loved being in Houston because my friends were there, all I had ever really come to know was there, and Johnny was there. But I felt I had to run for my life.

After a few weeks, not seeing much of Johnny again and diving more into my drinking and misery, I'd hear the song "California Dreamin" by the Mamas and the Papas on the radio a lot, and I'd just cry, wanting to be back in Cali. There was always sunshine. I loved the beach, the ocean.

By November, I decided to go back to California to see if I could stay with my dad again. He had two conditions, though: I had to go to school and stay put. I decided then it was time to go back to school. I had nothing to lose, except possibly never seeing my friends and Johnny again. The last night I went out with my girlfriends to

Numbers, a club in downtown, I sobbed as we left. Good-byes are never easy. I saw Johnny and most of my friends that night, and they knew I was leaving yet once again, but who knew that would be the last time? I remember not even saying good-bye to Johnny one last time. I went to Cali where my dad was now standing on his own two feet. He had gotten his own apartment in Oxnard, about twenty minutes north from his brother's place. That was the only reason I thought I'd give a go at life again. It'd just be us two.

March to November 1986 was such a lonely, out-of-control, and horrific period of time for me. So many things happened, and for many years, I wouldn't realize their true impact. I don't think my parents really discussed where their youngest child, their baby, was going to end up. Or maybe they did. My father's denial to this day of my mother's alcoholism and mental state baffles me. They had hopes for me to return to school at Klein, but how could he believe that would happen while living with my mother's drinking? What ended up happening to me was that I searched for a home. In less than a year, I had gone from Houston to Chicago, Chicago to Houston, Houston to California, back to Houston, and then to Chicago, and back again to Houston, and then ended up in California for the last time. Each and every time, with the exception of the airline ticket my father would pay, I had to fend for myself.

While in Chicago, I worked to pay for my transportation and food and chip in money for beer and toiletries. In Houston, my mom did feed me, but we went through our struggles of sometimes trying to find out how to get money for food by counting change and going to the food banks. She also put a roof over my head, but I came up with gas money, found someone to pay for me to get into the clubs, and chipped in money for drinking. This was the start of me learning to financially take care of myself. I couldn't rely on anyone else.

I learned what it was to be hungry, to really wonder how I was going to get my next meal. I learned how hard it was to put a roof over one's head, much less pay for the basic things like shampoo and toilet paper. Losing the house and the financial security would make such an impact on me that I'd later come to realize that I'd practically do anything to have a roof over my head, and there were times I'd feel such a sense of despair because of this experience. I learned to value money in a different way. I saw how important it was for our livelihood. We had lost everything—the big house, the nice clothes, and whatever inheritance that could have been passed on to us. I came to realize all those things hadn't ever really mattered, because our family relationship was so damaged over the years. I valued love and felt I never had it as I had pictured or wanted it to be. I was brought up to have expensive tastes, but materialism was unimportant to me now. When I was sixteen, there was no one to count on but myself. Everyone in my family was taking care of themselves, surviving, but everyone forgot I was sixteen years old. I had never felt so lost and so alone in my life.

5

Far from Grace

Just about two weeks before Thanksgiving, I was living in Oxnard, California, with my dad in a one-bedroom apartment. I enrolled myself into Oxnard High School, where I was placed back as a freshman, even though I should've been in my sophomore year. I guess with the style of wearing all black, shaved head except for my bangs, and a long string of hair on one side, even there, I definitely stood out.

I made friends very quickly. I was the new girl. Unlike Klein, lots of people wanted to be friends with me; they liked my style. By the second day, I sneaked away from lunch period with two girls I had made friends with, Allison and Kylie, and we went to go smoke pot. Though I was back in school and I was studying like I hadn't done in a couple of years, I was still going through a wild streak, which was a result of everything that had gone wrong in my life until then. I liked having total control of my life. I felt I was making better decisions because I was in a better environment; the problem was that I was still messed up from all the years before.

I went to school as I had promised to do, but there was no guarantee that I'd stop living on the edge. I did eventually take the car even though I still didn't have a driver's license, but it didn't matter. I ran my life. With everything I had been through, I felt like I could make my own decisions. No one had been there to tell me what to do or teach me differently. I was going to do whatever the hell I wanted to do. It was a little too late to take control or discipline me, especially when it really hadn't been a constant thing in my life. But the fact was, I was still a teenager, maybe even more immature in some ways, though I had experienced a lot in my sixteen years.

My parents had tried throughout our childhood to have us be obedient and do the right thing, but we rarely did. I think we felt since they could live their lives the way they were living that we shouldn't have to listen to them and definitely not respect them. Maybe we were trying to get back at them. Since they did bad things to us and one another, we'd be bad children. We were doing as they did, not as they said. There is a lot to be said about learned behavior and being good role models. Kids mimic their parents or their surroundings.

Most of my life, I was friends with mostly Caucasian kids because they were the majority. Now I found myself in a city where Hispanics and blacks were the majority, with whites coming in third, and then a mixture of other ethnicities also. Growing up in Caucasian communities prior, we'd cringe when our parents spoke Spanish to us out in public, and we'd tell them, "English," so they'd stop speaking in Spanish and start speaking in English. They'd stick us in these areas where the last thing we wanted to be or feel was different. It was bad enough that we didn't look like everyone else.

I don't remember our home as being very ethnic, either. Yes, my parents would play Vicki Carr or some other Spanish-speaking singer, but it was rare that they would. The only Peruvian thing I really felt I was raised with was our food sometimes, and that was about the one thing that tied me into the ethnicity that I was born into. Kids just always want to fit in, and I so desperately wanted to be like everyone else when I was growing up. The foundation of my upbringing was that I lived in ultra-white communities. My race and how I was molded for the future was this. I was open to other races because I was of another race, but I grew up like every other white girl in my community. When I moved to Oxnard, I was friends with everyone. I did have a couple of girlfriends who were Hispanic, but possibly because of my upbringing I still felt more comfortable or could relate better to—white girls. I grew up in the '70s and '80s in white, middle-class, suburbia in America ... that was my experience.

In Oxnard, I fell in with an edgy group of friends immediately, and I got a mad crush on a boy named Logan who looked like a skinhead, with the shaved head, combat boots, and bomber jacket, but he wasn't a racist. Everyone wanted us to happen, even before anything happened. It was so cute; he was cute and our so-called fling lasted for a second. I'd come to have fun going to the punk shows in Oxnard. I first went with Allison and Kylie, but I'd later go with Melanie and then eventually take Guadalupe when she'd come and stay with my dad and me from taking a break from following the Grateful Dead.

The punk shows were held at what I remember being like gymnasiums or auditoriums. Most of the crowd consisted of skinheads, even the girls, but they didn't look like me. They looked and dressed like skinheads, with combat boots and all. I'd wear my boots but with my pretty, long Macy's skirts. It seemed that most of the crowd wasn't from our school or the area. Within our group, with the exception of some of the boys, Logan and his friends, I was the only girl with a shaved head, but I was starting to let it grow out. All the shows had mosh pits, and this was my first introduction to real punk angst. I had a thrill with the mosh pit, even though I stood at five foot one and weighed about 110 pounds. I remember taking Guadalupe into the pit. She had always been so tough, but she had a hard time with other people pouncing and pushing her around. I found this funny and was amused.

These were the fun times of my early part of California living. I did well in school, even though I was continuing to have a social life and still drinking a lot. My father worked as a car salesman in Santa Monica, about an hour south of where we lived. He was barely home because of the long hours they wanted him to stay on the lot, hoping to ring in a customer. This man who had done so well with his career was now selling used cars. Sadly enough, when he came to California to stay with his brother, his brother's career was in selling cars. My father just jumped into that business and stayed in it for almost ten years. I believe it was the hardest job that he has ever had.

These years were also when I began doing more than drinking. Besides drinking and smoking pot a few times, I had only also done "poppers," which is something you sniff and just get high off of and laugh so hard that you'd fall off of your chair or bed. I had done it a few times in Houston with my friends and tried hash only once in Galveston when some of us girls were partying there after Guadalupe's graduation. Now I was drinking just as heavily as I had been the last year or so, but I was introduced to LSD. I'd take a tab of acid in school and would still be tripping when I got home.

Most of my friends lived down near the beach, about a ten-minute drive from where I lived near Route 101, more inland. They lived in Silver Strand, Hollywood Beach, and Mandalay Bay. Our high school was right in the middle of where they lived and where I lived. Sometimes after school, I'd just go straight down to the beach and hang out. I was very tight at first with Allison and Kylie; they even had a birthday party for me at someone's house a few months after I had moved there. But within time, that friendship started to strain. They were into the band the Cure and hung out with some boys that dressed up exactly like the guys from the band. I found it stupid that these guys dressed up like them. I vaguely remember making remarks about them when I'd drink.

And there was a time I was out with some other friends of mine, and from what I heard, I ran into some of these guys at a party and did or said something that had gotten back to Allison and Kylie. Our friendship ended after that, and I'm sure I probably did or said whatever I was being blamed for because, once again, I blacked out, and I couldn't even remember the whole evening mentioned. When I drank, I'd sometimes talk shit and just blurt out anything. I had no filter. I was being like my mom.

I was hanging out with Melanie quite a bit. Melanie and I had become friends through a girl I briefly hung out with, Katy. Katy was part of our clique at school, but not really. Half of the time, she did her own thing—and I don't know if anyone knew what that was. But after staying the night once at Katy's, Melanie came over the next morning to watch the TV show *Fame* with us. I gravitated more toward Melanie. Katy was just a little bit too much energy and too outspoken for me.

Melanie was this cute, stylish girl. She dressed trendy, like the rest of us, but she had her own unique style. She and I hung out down at the beach sometimes after school with some guys in their garage, maybe drinking some beer. At first, it was just to hang out, but almost instantly, we were introduced to sniffing Freon and I think paint thinner. We'd spray it onto a cloth and take a deep breath. It was a high I had never felt before. It was kind of like poppers to the tenth degree. Melanie was into it at first, but at some point, she backed off. It must have scared her. I, though, couldn't get enough. I liked the way it made me feel. It was obvious I had a problem with alcohol, because once the evening started, I couldn't stop drinking. But this and later cocaine were the things that I'd fiend for. A true addict was there. I loved that particular high. I never felt like I could get enough, and I never wanted it to stop.

Candelaria and Paoletta were still living in Chicago. Guadalupe had completely changed while living in Cincinnati over the last few months. She had always looked clean-cut, wearing lots of makeup, with her hair always curled; her hair was now turning into dreadlocks, she smoked pot a lot, and she looked like she never showered. She also became a Deadhead—a fan that follows the Grateful Dead from concert to concert. We considered Guadalupe at that time as a new version of a hippie. We'd hear from her periodically, and sometimes she'd come and visit while taking a break from seeing shows or when she needed something. She did this once while I was living in Oxnard with my dad, and I didn't like the fact that she was coming to stay.

I remember shunning her immediately when she arrived. I had finally broken away from being that weak, nonsocial little sister of hers and finally had a life of my own. She arrived while my dad was still at work. I was making plans with Melanie and some other girls to go to a club in Ventura, the next town over. She wanted to come out with me and my friends, but I wasn't having any part of it. I finally had my own friends, and I wasn't about to let her sink her claws into them. I was also scared of any fighting between the two of us. She got pissed that I didn't want her to go. She flew off the handle, like so many times before, and began to physically attack me. Our physical fights really were her attacking me and me defending myself.

The worst fight we ever had was in Houston in '86. Kim, Emily, Guadalupe, and I were in downtown Houston for a laser show. We all had been drinking, and I made a remark about how Guadalupe was making a spectacle of herself, throwing herself at some guy. She went after me, chasing me down as I tried to run away from her through the streets of Montrose. The punches were thrown, and the hair was pulled, but the worst part was when she had her hands around my neck, choking me, and had me up against a white picket fence. She was attacking me so violently that I fell over backward, breaking the fence while she took a bite out of me. I still have that scar. She finished that night by leaving me in downtown Houston all alone. I had to go and stay the night in an upscale hotel bathroom until I could get ahold of my mother the next morning to pick me up.

So here she was once again in a fit of rage, though this time was different. She did attack me, and I did fight back, but she went after a large knife in the kitchen, threatening me. It reminded me of how she once chased me with scissors down our hallway on the second floor of our house in Houston. This time, after lunging at me with the knife a few times, she then turned, went into the bathroom, got into the bathtub, and threatened to cut herself. Right then, my dad called, and I told him of what had happened. He spoke to her, she cried to him, and then the phone was given back to me. He insisted that I take my sister out with me and my friends.

That was just another mental, crazy situation that was accepted and swept under the rug. Like always, I didn't understand how the craziness happened or why it was tolerated. I felt like no one else around me saw how crazy it was. I had to take her out with me, and thankfully, nothing else happened that night. Within a matter of days, as crazy as it was, I also went back to having a somewhat okay few days with her. This was just how our family learned to operate, to cope. No matter what, we were family. She was gone in a matter of a week or two after that.

About a year after I moved to California permanently, my dad went to Houston to pick up my mom. He was having her finally come out and move in with us. Everything had been going pretty well. I partied and hung out with friends, but I went to school and was doing well. I took care of making dinner when my dad worked, because he worked long, late hours in Santa Monica, and it took him a long time to get home. I took care of paying the bills and kept the apartment clean. And despite the fact that all along my dad had been sending my mom money while he had been in California, we had actual savings in his bank account, because we were budgeting, which was a first I think in our family. In 2010, my dad and I spoke about this time. He said that he had a conversation with me about whether or not to go and get my mom from Houston. He says that he asked me if it was okay, and even though I said no, for some reason, he went, anyway.

Almost immediately after my mother moved in with us, our life went back to "normal." She began drinking and fighting with us again. Even though I drank and partied with my friends on the outside, I couldn't emotionally and mentally function with the chaos my mom brought. I needed my home to be quiet, peaceful, and definitely with less craziness than she brought to the table. Every time I'd come home, just like I used to in Houston when she wasn't working, I once again was worried about what scene I'd walk into.

I remember one day after school I came home to find her drunk, lying down on the couch, and rambling. All I had wanted to do was to come home and do my homework, but instead, I had to deal with this woman talking about how I was raped by my uncle. What happened was that she had found the medical records of when I first came back to California. I had gotten my STD from my actual rape in Chicago taken care of. She made up in her crazy mind that my uncle, the one I stayed with the first time I came to California, had forced himself upon me. This was always going on in my mom's crazy, drunken mind—making up stories, sometimes really bizarre ones. It was very hard to deal with her like that in such a confined space, because that one-bedroom apartment actually didn't even have a bedroom door that closed. I had to deal with her for hours before my father got home. With her on those binges, I didn't have the luxury I'd had before she came—having the apartment mostly to myself. It was too hard, yet again, to stay focused on school, much less do my homework. I dropped out of high school again, never finishing the tenth grade, never going to a dance, and never going to my prom.

When my parents wouldn't allow me to have the car, I used to hitchhike sometimes to get to the beach to hang out or go to a party. The last time I hitchhiked scared me. It was late, possibly after hanging out drinking at the beach. My buzz had worn off. A Hispanic man, possibly field-worker, picked me up in an old pickup truck. He barely spoke English. He was saying some things to me in Spanish, asking me if I wanted to go somewhere and have a good time. I tried to speak so that he could understand that I just wanted to go home. He then started to grab me, and I started yelling at him to stop his truck and let me out. He wouldn't pull over. I began not being afraid anymore and instead put up my defenses to show that I was ready to fight. I yelled at him to stop and I told him I'd jump out. I had my hand on the door handle, and I was ready to jump. My crazy self probably would have. He understood what I was about to do, so he finally stopped, and I got out and walked all the way home. It must have been around seven miles. I never hitchhiked again. Why did I hitchhike in the first place? Normal, well-adjusted people don't do things like that and don't even think about doing things like that. I did it because I didn't want to be home, and I didn't fear anything, because I thought everything bad that could have happened to me already had. Besides, there wasn't anywhere for me to hide away and have my peace, so I'd do *anything* to get out of that apartment. Hitchhiking was one of those stupid little things I did and some people do, and sometimes people disappear and are never heard from again. I was naive up until that last time.

By the age of eighteen, I had changed my circle of friends. On occasion at parties or hotel rooms where we'd party, I'd see some of my old friends, because Oxnard is a small town. By this time, my hair had grown out. I stayed with mostly wearing black, but I was a little bit dressier than before. My edgy, alternative style was overrun by a more grown-up style. I was still that open-minded, alternative person inside, but if you didn't know me, you would have never guessed that I once had a shaved head and had always wished to have my hair dyed fuchsia. I did keep in touch with Melanie, but we weren't hanging out as much. I was now friends with a girl named Leah. She was tall, white, and looked like she could pass for twenty-five years old. She didn't need ID to buy liquor, so we'd start off the night by going to a liquor store and getting two bottles of Boone's Farm Strawberry Hill for each of us and maybe a six pack of beer. This was not everything we'd drink, but this was how we got the evening started.

We were hanging out with a group of guys. We all were a very tight group. They looked like gang members, but they really weren't, I don't think. Some of them were actually drug dealers, though, which at the time made no difference to me. It would later matter to my mom when she worked at the probation office in Ventura and realized who I was hanging out with and that most of my guy friends were on all the local authorities' radar. They were good people to me, and besides what they did, I thought they weren't any different from you and me. Some of the other people outside of our clique who popped up occasionally were bad seeds though. They just had a violent streak to them that I noticed and didn't like. One thing good about my upbringing was that I could notice bad situations and bad people. I tried to stay clear of violent ones, but sometimes it was hard because they partied with us.

My drinking got more out of hand after I dropped out of school for good. It actually had eased up there for a little while before my mom moved in with us. Some of the new friends whom I hung out with would introduce me later to cocaine and ecstasy. It was the party scene, and I fell right in. I had already been using acid. There were a lot of nights we'd drink and do at least two of these drugs at the same time. At my hardest point, my nights usually consisted of two bottles of wine, a forty or two, maybe some regular bottles of beer or shots of tequila, ecstasy or acid, finished off with some lines of coke. For a little girl like me, I built up a tolerance to some extent. My body could take it, but I'd usually black out, and I'd throw up at some point. We partied like this four or five days a week, pulling all-nighters. I did this at first without having to use coke, but it was sometime around the age of nineteen that I finally did coke.

It was one of those nights after being asked for almost a year to try it that I just said, "Why not?" Nowadays, I can think of many reasons why not to try something like coke. For some reason, I was never scared of dropping acid or even doing ecstasy, maybe because I had never heard too much about them before, but coke and heroin (I never did heroin, thank God!) were so taboo. I was always fearful that if I tried either drug, I'd become addicted, become a junkie, and die.

But I accepted trying coke like I did everything else, without any care of the worst-case scenario. I was partying so much during this time that I don't recall ever not getting sick. Most of the time, I'd just come home the next day and throw up for hours or do the same if I was going straight into work. Leah had gotten me a job at Orange Julius (a fast-food chain typically in malls) as the assistant manager, where she was the manager. We partied all night and would sometimes go straight in. I think of it now. It was so gross!

But it wasn't like we were junkies. Those were times like a lot of us had. We went to parties. We had fun and drank. I always had my camera with me, so I was always taking pictures, even standing on top of kitchen counters to get the right angle or to fit everyone in. If there weren't any parties going on, there wasn't somewhere low key to hang out, or a party broke up because of the police, we rented a motel room. It wasn't until later, toward the end of the evening that we concluded at someone's house, just the few of us continuing until the wee hours of the morning.

Until I got too drunk, they were good times. Once I went over that limit, which I did 90 percent of the time, the fun stopped. Since the time I started drinking up until I was about twenty-three, my stomach was usually too weak to hold my liquor, so I threw up a lot. Maybe it was the damage I had done when I tried killing myself. Or maybe I drank way too much! I had a problem since the beginning. It's very surprising that all my friends and I survived doing what we did to the extent that we did toward the height of our drug use. I guess I didn't see it as a problem, because I wasn't on a street corner trying to buy it or trying to steal to get high or exchange anything else to get my hands on coke or ecstasy. It was already being supplied by our friends. And besides, I could still get myself to work and knew if it wasn't around one evening that it was okay; I didn't *need* it, so no problem, right? Who knows what internal damage it did to me?

For the next few months, all I did was hang out with my friends. I recovered during the day and was ready to go out the following evening to see what we could get ourselves into. My parents lived in several different areas of Oxnard, mostly due to the fact that they'd get evicted. Even before our downfall of losing everything in Houston, my parents typically lived paycheck to paycheck. My mother's spending behavior since childhood, I believe, has not really changed. You would have thought that eventually she would learn to budget and save just a little, but she never has been able to. So where they lived, I typically followed. Once, we were living in a nicer apartment complex close to a residential area on the outskirts of some farms near Victoria Boulevard. We were within walking distance of a main intersection.

Another problem my mom had even with having a good source of income was that she'd run up the phone bills. Usually this happened because she would call Peru when she had been drinking. I remember the phone being turned off a few times back in Houston because the bills would be too high to pay, but this also went on in Oxnard. One night, I wanted to go out and meet up with my friends, but our phone was shut off. I believe it had been more than a week or so since I had gone out. I decided to walk to the gas station about a block away and around the corner to use the payphone. It was around 6:00 p.m. or 7:00 p.m. I don't remember getting ahold of anyone on the phone, but as I was leaving, I noticed this white man who was acting odd. He seemed to be checking me out in a creepy way.

I left to go back to our apartment, and in the less-than-five-minute walk, I noticed from the get-go that he was more than likely following me. Just to make sure I wasn't being paranoid, I'd slow down and speed up to see if he was doing the same. He was. As I was coming to the end of the block and could see the apartment complex's parking area, I began to sprint. As soon as I realized he was running after me, I began to scream for help. As soon as he touched me, trying to cover my mouth, I started throwing punches. He had one hand trying to cover my mouth and the other trying to grab me and pull me away. Thankfully that I kept screaming at the top of my lungs and was fighting as I did, and lights began to go on, and people began to come out of their apartments. He fled. I had a torn blouse; I was bleeding from my mouth and had a few scrapes on me. But I was safe.

The police were called, and we filed a police report, but he was never found.

I think back at all the things that have happened to me in my lifetime and how amazing it is that I've lived and survived, at least on the outside. What is interesting also is that this incident or the hitchhiking incident didn't seem to affect me much, at least no more than half an hour or so after they happened. Was I just immune to reacting or being stunned anymore? Or was it so easy for me to bury traumatic events? Did at some point my psyche go into survival mode where I could act as if nothing was wrong? ACOA (adult child of alcoholics) are good at covering up what is really going. I did this very well and even fooled myself, maybe.

For the most part, I lived with my parents, with the exception of one summer that I moved into an area that seemed like just cottages in a housing community. That was one great summer. Every day, it seemed we barbecued, had fun at the pool, and partied. There were two girls who shared this cottage. The cottage had just two rooms—a really small living room with a tiny kitchen and a bedroom. Leah and the guys and I all started going over there to party, but within what seemed like a week or so, one of the girls moved out. Leah moved in, and then I think I followed. My mom was horrified when they were helping me move some of my stuff over there. I remember that day.

My parents never went in, but some of our guy friends were hanging around outside. There was this specific guy who was interested in me, though we were just friends. He was standing in front of our place, and he looked like he was straight out of Compton, like a member of the rap group NWA. How shocking that must have been for both of my parents. I thought it was hilarious, which was probably just the rebellious side of me throwing something like that in their faces to hurt them.

This was also where I met Mark. He was what I thought was one of the best-looking guys around. He was the first guy that I really liked who was mixed. I was surprised when he first approached me, said a few words to me, and then kissed me. We began seeing one another, but he and his friends weren't in our inner circle; they just partied with us sometimes. It was obvious that I wanted more from our relationship, but he was young and just having fun. I knew I wasn't the only one, but at the time, I really wanted to be his girlfriend. This was the first guy who I hooked up with more than just a few drunken times.

We only went on one date. I had never really learned how that all worked. I never went to school dances. I was never asked out before on dates, except for in Chicago. I had only been with two other guys, not counting the creep who raped me. This was the first guy who I was constantly running into at parties and leaving with each and every time. It sounds so pathetic now, but this was one of my downfalls that took me a long time to learn—what happens when a boy really likes a girl. They call them, date them, and really get to know them. This didn't happen between Mark and me. I fell hard for Mark and saw him for over two years.

In the fall of 1989, something in me changed. Every once in a while, I'd get ahold of my life and take it head-on, trying to control it and perfect it. Somehow, I'd find this motivation to do what "normal" people did. I wanted so desperately to be okay. I had my first job at fourteen, working at McDonald's. I only worked there for about three weeks, because I could no longer lie about my age. Now I began a new quest: to finish my education. I wanted to prove to myself also that I could complete a task, unlike my mother. I knew education was important; that's how we were raised. Before Orange Julius, it had been very hard for me to get a job because I couldn't find it in myself to lie about not graduating from high school, and I didn't want to have a struggle with that. So I enrolled myself into the local community college in Ventura. I worked full-time and went to school full-time. I was still working at Orange Julius. But as soon as I started school, I cut back on going out with my friends. I wanted to do the right thing for myself, and that was to focus on school and work.

After working almost a year, I wanted to leave Orange Julius. I felt I was doing all the work for Leah. She took a lot of cigarette breaks, and I thought that she was taking advantage of me because I was her friend and that maybe she just wanted to kick back, because after her shift there, she'd go to work at another job. Whatever was the case, I tried to quit, but the regional manager begged me to stay. She had known that Leah was doing a poor job, and she had wanted to fire her. She fired my friend, and I became manager. This was one of the first shitty things I did to someone. I knew it, but at the time, I justified it as just being business.

I excelled at work and at school. I rarely went out. Almost a month and a half passed by where I didn't see anyone. I heard that Mark was seeing some girl who lived down at Silver Strand and was possibly staying with her. One night, I treated myself to going out. Like most nights, we wouldn't be confined to partying at one place. Sometimes police would break up a party, or we'd hear of another party and would want to go and check it out. A bunch of us went out and ended up at the tiny beach house of the girl whom Mark was seeing. The funny thing that happened was, like most of the times before, he left with me and without me even asking him to. We went to his best friend's. That was the end of them, I think, but we picked up our relationship again. Things were really good between us. But within a month or so, he ended up having to move in with his sister, who lived over three hours away. I think he had nowhere else to live. Yet again, I plunged myself back into my studies and work.

In the summer of 1990, I felt as if I had nothing left in Oxnard. School and work were keeping me busy, but it wasn't fulfilling yet. I felt empty inside and was desperately lonely because Mark had left. Also at that time, I wasn't hanging out anymore, and I was still feeling like I couldn't handle living with my parents while I was trying to focus on work and school. Even a therapist whom I had seen about a year earlier told me that it was difficult to treat me and help me heal because I was still living in that environment with my parents, so I decided to move to Huntington Beach, where Tammy from Houston was living.

HB is a seaside city in Orange County. It's known for its long stretches of beach and is one of the premier spots in Southern Cali for surfing. Tammy's dad set her up in an apartment just as long as she'd attend school. I transferred from my job in Oxnard to an Orange Julius in a mall in HB and signed up for my third semester in college. Tammy and I had been through so much together in Houston, but now after moving in with her, I found out how much we had grown apart. Or maybe I had never noticed that although we cared for each other as best friends and we liked some of the same things, we thought very differently about most things.

At that time, I also felt that I had matured extremely just in the previous year, trying to put some order in my life and trying not to be angry or hurt by my past. I felt that she was still living in a world that said, "Fuck it. Nothing matters."

I was trying to just be happy and have fun. I had stopped taking drugs as soon as I entered college. It would have been impossible for me to party like I had been and also work full-time and go to school full-time while also doing lines or dropping acid. That would have been crazy if I tried. I don't know why exactly I felt so many miles away from her, but I just did. I felt sorry for her because I knew her past, and I loved and cared about her, and here she was living her life with no family around. Somewhere, deep down inside, I felt cared for by my parents—at least they were physically there, but her parents were nowhere around. Maybe her mom couldn't deal with her and her dad was off with his girlfriend, but I felt they should have really been there for her more than they were. She deserved that. I had always cared for her and valued her. She was so smart and worthy of more than that.

Living in Huntington Beach was okay. I was just working, I began partying a little, and I attended school. Besides Tammy, I didn't have any friends. I'd go out a few times with Tammy and her friends but really didn't mesh with her or anybody else. Tammy hung out with a bunch of professional BMX riders, whom I liked, but I felt out of place around them. Not many people spoke to me. They weren't anything like my scene. I did hook up with one boy once, which brought me back full circle to still liking white boys. That hadn't been lost, just buried because of circumstance.

I went back to Oxnard a few times but stopped going back, because every time I went back, I'd hear rumors that I was saying this or saying that, but while I lived in HB, I really didn't talk to or about anyone in Oxnard; I just worked and went to school. I'd also later hear rumors that Melanie and I had become strippers and were living in the Valley after we moved away from Oxnard. It was so made up. I never lived in the Valley, and I could never be naked on a stage while people stared at me. Yes, I've done worse things in my life than what was said; I just always had a problem with people making up lies about me.

When I visited Oxnard, it seemed like someone always wanted to start a fight with me. The last time I went to Oxnard, I was at a friend's house, and a girl that I never met tried to fight me. She confronted me as I had just gotten into my car, trying to take a friend home. She tried unsuccessfully to get me out of my car. She pulled me by the hair, threw punches, and finally kneed me in the eye. I had a black eye for about a week. And this was because someone was listening in on a phone conversation that I was having with Mark one night. I was trying to defend some of my closest friends' actions because he had called them "easy." This girl that was trying to fight me didn't even know me. She was just asked by some guy to jump me because he misconstrued my conversation with Mark as me talking shit.

I was glad at that time to cut ties with Oxnard, because I didn't like being in that negative, hostile world. It wasn't fun for me anymore. Some of the guys that we hung out with left Oxnard, but the ones who remained, except for a few, were in and out of jail for a while. Hopefully, they got their lives together. Leah would eventually leave there too. I'm happy to have reconnected with some of my old friends from there that had nothing to do with these last dark times there.

While I was living with Tammy, Guadalupe had come off the Deadhead tour again and came and stayed with us for a while. I wasn't too happy with this, but I couldn't stop it from happening. Even at the age of twenty, I didn't feel like I could speak up for myself. I was too scared to, because to me that linked up with confrontation, and confrontation always resulted in violence. I knew what her reaction could possibly be if she heard something from me that she didn't like, so I kept my mouth shut.

I kept in touch with Mark, and he came to visit me in HB once or twice. I remember going to see him the night that girl tried to fight me. Well, technically, she did fight me; I just didn't make it easy for her to completely maul me. Mark was very sweet and came back to HB with me for a few days, which was really cool, but everyone looked at us and my black eye. Poor Mark. I knew what people on the street thought. And even though we were now only living about forty-five minutes apart, he kept it casual like always. There'd never be a future for us.

My parents were having a tough time again financially and left Saticoy, a town on the outskirts of Oxnard. They moved in with one of my father's sisters in Santa Ana, another city in Orange County but more inland, about fifteen minutes from where I lived. Eventually, they'd get their own place in Tustin, five minutes away. This was about the same time my mother sold her property in Philadelphia, one of the ones that had been bought with the selling of the Atlantic City property. I was working as an assistant manager at Orange Julius because even though I was manager in Oxnard, HB already had a manager. After a few months living in Huntington Beach, though, the manager was leaving, and I was up for the position. The regional manager, Kris, wanted to review other candidates for this position. She thought it was the right thing to do. Guadalupe jumped right in, trying to go after the position I wanted. One other thing there is to know about her is that she sells herself like no one else I have ever met. She was the type of girl who could go in asking for an application (like she did in Chicago) and walk out with the job, even though she clearly never had the qualifications or experience.

By this time, I knew Guadalupe too well and her competition toward me. Once she gave her application and had her interview set up, I backed out of possibly being the new manager, and I also resigned from my job. I explained my situation with my sister to Kris and let her know that I didn't have any bad feelings toward her or any decision she was going to make but that I wouldn't work with my sister, whether it was above her or under her. She hired Guadalupe and made her manager.

Guadalupe is a good seller but not a good closer. She couldn't do the job and eventually quit or was fired.

I eventually found a new job at a car wash, and I moved into my own studio apartment about a block and a half away from the beach, near Main Street. Guadalupe left Huntington Beach and went back on the road with the other Deadheads.

One day, I drove to Long Beach, about fifteen minutes from HB. I had to pay a late jewelry store bill. I went there because I didn't want to pay the late charges. I didn't know the area. I parked, and unsure that I was at the right place, I asked the first person I saw. A man was also getting out of his car, and I asked if this was the mall I was looking for. He said yes, but right as I was saying thanks and walking away, he said, "You are beautiful." I was amused, smiled, and walked into the mall.

When I was done paying my bill, I stepped out of the mall and saw that man there waiting for me. He was tall, dark, and pretty handsome. I was startled but not creeped out. He tried making small talk, but also asked me to have dinner or coffee with him sometime. "No, no, no," I said. "I can't." It was weird—flattering, but weird. *Who goes out with someone that they meet in a parking lot?* I thought. Besides, he seemed twice my age. He then proceeded to offer me $100 for my time—coffee, tea, anything, he said.

I was living in HB. I wasn't using drugs anymore. I drank half of what I used to drink, if I drank at all. I went to school full-time and had a full-time job. From outside appearances, I would probably look like a normal girl, working hard and doing the right things. But I was anything but normal. I ended up taking him up on his offer but also ended up having sex with him, which was probably the only thing he really wanted from me. I can't answer why I did what I did. Not only do situations of my life baffle me but I've at times looked back on my decisions and I am baffled by myself. Was I crazy? Who did something like that? All I can say is that only someone who has no self-esteem, no self-worth, no self-love, and is a little screwed up can and will do things like that, and I was all of those.

Brian stayed in my life for a few months, and he helped me financially. It seemed like every time we saw one another, there was an exchange of money. We celebrated my twenty-first birthday together at a very ritzy restaurant in downtown Long Beach. I thought I liked him a lot, but deep down inside, I liked the money, the attention, and the validation that the money and attention brought. I don't know where my thinking came into play. Was I ever using my brain? What I thought was that I couldn't be ugly if someone wanted to give me money, right? It was a warped sense of my own self-worth. And, obviously, I had none. At the time, it felt like this experience was validating my self-worth and my beauty. I was worthy of being so wanted that a man would give me money like that for doing something I probably would have done, anyway.

One night, I visited him at his job and found out that he was married. I left there. At the time, it was a line I wouldn't have crossed if I'd known. I was pissed. I felt at the time that I actually wanted more from him. I felt I could have more, or maybe deep down inside, I knew I deserved more. I never saw him again, but that set down the foundation for what was yet to come.

6

City of Broken Dreams and Mr. Haiti

My lowest point when I look back upon my life was in my early twenties and the decision I made to move to L.A. and do what I thought I needed to do to survive. For years, I had taken over the reins of victimization. For most of my childhood, I was a victim, and I was bound to my family. After I left home, I took over, and I was victimizing myself—unknowingly allowing the passing of the torch. I was so lost, so broken, and yet I was no longer a child. I never had hope or faith that my life was going to be a beautiful, peaceful, happy one.

By the age of twenty-one, I found myself living in Los Angeles, and I remember one crisp October night when I was with my friends Morgan and Kris. It was 1992, and we were at a club in the VIP section, which had been reserved for a birthday party for Jim Hill. He was and still is a sports anchor for a local television station here in L.A. Everyone who was anyone was there, from Magic Johnson to other pro athletes to people in the entertainment industry—producers, agents, models, and actresses. My friends and I were of the mere few who weren't involved in the industry, though we were at the parties and at lots of the social events. I hadn't been out in about three weeks. It was Sunday, and I had to be at school the next morning. I was glad to be out at that party, though, and hanging out with my girlfriends.

Even though I had lived there for several months, the Hollywood scene was still foreign to me. I supposed it would always feel like that, because I didn't want to lose myself in it. It's a fast-paced lifestyle that I never wanted to join in completely, because I knew I could never keep up and didn't really want to. One thing I did hate, though, was that I felt like a little fish in a big pond. And when these parties came around, I felt out of the inner circle. I wasn't an aspiring actress or model, and I didn't want to be. It seems if you live in L.A. that you are aspiring to be someone in the industry. Film or photography was my dream or anything close to it, but not the Hollywood scene, per se.

As Morgan and I were standing there talking to one another and Kris was reliving memories with one of the older Wayans brothers, I glanced over to the entrance of the VIP lounge. People were making their way in, and just then, I saw someone I never wanted to see again in my life. It was Mike, and for more than seven months of my life, you could say he was my pimp.

As I stood there starting to tremble on the inside and Morgan made it obvious that I felt uncomfortable by his presence, Kris noticed and turned to me, asking me how I knew him. I didn't know what to say. Many women that I came across knew what he was all about, and most likely, even Kris knew. She had been introduced to him by Morgan, but it came as a big surprise to her that I knew him also. She probably thought there was no way in hell that I could be a part of that whole scene—that scene being the escort business. I didn't fit the part. So how did I know him? I didn't meet him through Morgan, but rather a year and a half earlier, before I had moved to the bright lights of Hollywood. I met him one night on an adventure from Orange County to the hottest nightspot on the Sunset Strip in West Hollywood, the Roxbury.

It was 1991, and I was living with my parents in Tustin, a very small community where people were happy with not having their names in bright lights. I never really spent much time there. I was still working at the car wash in HB and still going to Orange Coast College. It had been a few months that Guadalupe and I had been going to that trendy club, the Roxbury (*Roxburys*). One night in July after Guadalupe had returned to Cincinnati to visit and help out a friend, I decided to take along my friend Lily from work into Hollywood to go to Roxburys with me.

When I met Mike, it was a night just like any other. It was packed, and lots of people were trying to get into the VIP room. The Roxbury was comprised of three levels. On the first floor was a small lounge with a dance floor and bar, on the second level was an upscale restaurant, and on the third level was the club with the VIP room toward the back, with booths and windows overlooking Sunset Boulevard.

As Lily and I entered the VIP, within not even two minutes of standing there, I was approached by an elderly gentleman. He appeared to be in his fifties, and he was pointing at another distinguished man sitting at a booth. He said his friend wanted me to join him for a drink. Usually, I would have passed, but as tipsy as I had already gotten, I happily accepted, because he was decent looking enough.

I sat down next to him. He must have been in his early forties, looking very nice in his suit. I was only twenty-one. It wasn't a far stretch from Brian, whom I had been seeing a few months earlier. Out of the blue, I had become attracted to the older business-type men—men in suits. Maybe I thought that they'd be more grounded, as in wanting to settle down, and had their priorities straight, which I wasn't but wanted to be. Little did I know, I was so wrong.

Lily and I introduced ourselves, and I thought very highly of the way he was so courteous and of the way he conducted himself. Throughout our conversation, I had come to the conclusion that he was a producer, because that was what he was suggesting. Looking back now, I realize how he never gave a straight answer, and if he did, it was something you should never listen to. So thinking he was a producer and seeing that he was friends with a lot of these successful men, I thought it'd be okay to leave with him to go to get a bite to eat. While we talked at Roxburys, he had told me if I had ever wanted to move to L.A. and make some real money to let him know. God, I was so naive to not catch on to what he meant.

We left the club. I thought I was following him to a restaurant; instead, he was taking us straight to his house up on the ever-so-grand Mount Olympus, a section of the Hollywood Hills. As Lily and I entered his house, I joked politely that I had assumed that we were going to get a bite to eat. He took my hand, walked me into his kitchen, and opened up the refrigerator. If it had been anyone else and he had the nerve to do that to me, I would have left. But I was so in awe with the way he appeared, the nice cars in the driveway, and his house on the hill that I let it pass.

We got a tour of the house. It was beautiful. I went with him up to the gazebo, which connected to his bedroom, and looked down. I looked at Lily, feeling the water temperature of the pool, and as she looked up at me, her eyes were so big trying to grasp the luxury that could be bought. I don't believe she had ever seen anything like it before.

Mike led me into his bedroom, where we sat on his sofa and talked more about me. It wasn't too long before he picked me up, kissed me, and took me and laid me onto his bed. Within seconds, he was inside of me, and Lily was knocking at the door. I pushed him off of me, because I didn't know what Lily would have thought of me. I felt so ashamed and kind of disgusted with myself at that moment. I straightened myself out to allow Lily to come in. She was trying to get away from Mike's friend Rob. (She would later nickname Rob "Grandpa" because he was at least thirty years older than she.) She plopped onto Mike's bed with me as I was bragging of how big and cushiony it was. The three of us fell asleep in his bed, and Rob passed out in one of Mike's guest rooms. All I thought I knew about this man was that he was some kind of producer and friends with Arsenio Hall because they had spoken at the club, he had a son (from a previous marriage, I thought), he dressed well, and he had nice cars and a fancy, big house in the Hollywood Hills.

Lily woke me up around 6:00 a.m., only about three hours after we had fallen asleep. I was still drunk, but we had to leave, because she had to be at work at 7:30 a.m. at the car wash where we worked together. We got our things together and began to leave when I realized we couldn't without waking Mike up to turn off his house alarm.

As I retreated back up the stairs, he was seated up at the top of the stairs. He probably had been there watching us running back and forth, wondering of how to sneak out. He disarmed the alarm and asked me to write out my full name and telephone number at work and at home. It sounded awkward at the time, because who asked for someone's full name? But I wrote all my information down. He probably had to check out if I was for real. Could anyone be so naive? I ran up the stairs like a child, all cheerfully, and kissed him good-bye. On the way home, I wondered if I'd ever hear from him.

We drove up to the car wash on Beach Boulevard. Lily and I ran into the boutique, dressed up in our club clothes from the night before. We must have looked awful having had only three hours of sleep, especially me looking as hungover as I was.

Soon, Monday came, and I hadn't heard from Mike. Lily was working with me that day as a cashier. Five minutes after we had closed, Lily was counting the money when the phone rang. She picked it up, and knowing I still hadn't heard from him, she handed the phone to me with a smile. It was him. He asked me to come over later that evening. I did. I think I must have been really drunk the night I met him, though, because as he opened his front door, I hesitated because I didn't recognize him. Our evening consisted of me lying on his bed in the guest bedroom, watching television as he sat and worked on his computer, which was next to the TV. The man had no romantic vibes at all, but throughout all my encounters with guys, serious or not, I couldn't remember one guy who was that kind of romantic fairy-tale prince every woman dreams about.

That night, he kept talking to me about moving to Los Angeles. It made me think that he must have really been into me the instant he saw me. It was crazy. He seemed to be so well adjusted that I was sure plenty of women would have jumped at the chance to be with him. I wondered what was wrong with him that he would want me.

For the next couple of weeks, I continued going to Mike's house. But within time, like every other guy in my life, he stepped away and stopped asking me over. The reason, as I found out months later, was because I had no intention to move to L.A. and because of that, I was no use to him.

I began dating a guy, Jake, whom I had met in a club in Orange County while I was with another guy who had come down from L.A. to visit me. Previously, I hadn't been asked out on too many dates. Within the next few months, I'd date a lot. Before, I was solely committed only to liking one guy at a time, but I had been hurt so much by guys that I didn't want to become so attached for the fear of being hurt again. So I was dating two, maybe three guys. But, then I met Jake. Jake, a guy I was seeing at the time, became very special to me after a while, because he was about the healthiest relationship I had ever had; in better terms, he was just a normal guy. We became really close really fast. I was over at his place most of my nights.

Even though I was dating these other guys, I was still thinking of Mike. I think I had attached myself to Jake so I could get my mind off of Mike. I told myself to let things go with Mike, but I thought he had been the best catch yet. Usually, up until then, I had dated guys who didn't have jobs or much less try to even get jobs or further their education—losers, basically, except for Jake, but he struggled to make ends meet. One thing I learned later is that you could be a loser and be financially successful, even having a big house in the hills.

One night in September (Friday the thirteenth), Lily called me up to say that we should take a friend of hers to the Roxbury, but there was one problem: Lily didn't have an ID. She had previously been using a paper ID of Guadalupe's, but it was getting harder and harder to use. The bouncers were getting impatient with us because it was not a valid ID. I had told her a few times to get a fake ID. I had just come to find out that she was only sixteen years old. She called again, and I told my mom to tell her that I'd call her back. I really wasn't up to going out that evening and dealing with trying to get her and her underage friend in, but I did want to see her, because she was no longer working at the car wash, and it had been a few weeks since I had been out with her. My other friend Susie had returned to working at the car wash in Lily's place.

I had only seen Lily that previous Wednesday when she came by the car wash to visit me. Some say and it had also been said in the newspapers that she had a feeling something bad was going to happen. Maybe this was her chance to see me one last time. We talked for about fifteen minutes, and I handed her my sister's paper ID so we'd no longer have problems at the door with the bouncers at the club. I told her to go to DMV and get herself an ID. It had been about three weeks since I had seen her, and it made me so happy because, besides Susie, I hadn't made any other friends in Orange County since moving there a year and a half earlier. Little did I know that it was going to be the last time I would see my "Lee Lee" alive.

After Lily called and I told her I'd call her back, I had an idea. Since she hadn't gone to get an ID like I had told her to do, I thought we could try to use Guadalupe's copy of her passport to get into the Roxbury, but it was too late; she didn't pick up the phone. I left a message on her answering machine that Friday night. I was never to speak to her again.

The following day, my mother gave me a message that Lily's best friend, Dolores, called me but left Lily's number for me to call her back. Dolores and I didn't get along, so I laughed and wondered to myself why the hell she was calling me. I never would have thought that something was wrong, that something would have happened to Lily.

Monday afternoon, I returned to work, and as I was walking through the parking lot of the car wash, I received unusual stares from the guys who dried the cars. Usually, the guys would whistle jokingly or say hi. I entered the boutique, and Stephanie, another coworker, was working on the cash register. The managers of the car wash were there. Stephanie immediately said, "Did you hear what happened to Lily?" They were all shocked that I didn't know what they were talking about.

I.D., one of the managers, asked, "Hadn't you been with her?"

Stephanie then said Lily had been shot and was dead.

I cracked a laugh as if they were trying to make a cruel joke. Once I realized they weren't joking, I asked what had happened, and I.D. once again asked, "You didn't go out with her on Friday night?"

I told them the whole story of how she wanted to go to Hollywood but didn't have ID. I began to cry and pace back and forth in the store, thinking if only I would have told her, "Let's go to Roxburys and try to get in," she wouldn't be dead. No one close to me that I was in touch with had ever died before. I wished I would have never had to go through experiencing a death that I felt was my fault.

In tears and gasping to catch my breath, I continued to do what I had to do at work. I left early, having Susie come in to work on the cash register for me. I just spent two or three hours there working in the office on the balances and deposits from the weekend. They must have been all wrong, because I wouldn't stop sobbing and couldn't think straight.

The following day, I went to Jake's apartment in L.A. He lived near the USC campus, right off of Hoover. I had called him and told him that I needed somewhere to go to collect my thoughts and be alone. I didn't want to be at my parents' apartment. All I said to him was that something bad had happened. I told him that I would tell him what happened later when he got home from work. He went home during his lunch break to leave his apartment key where he usually left it for me. While I sat around in his apartment, I read about the shooting in all the newspaper articles that I had picked up before I left Orange County. Something inside me told me to turn to Mike for comfort. He had met her months before with me.

I called him and left him a message on his answering machine. I hadn't talked to him in a few weeks. I just thought that he'd be there for me. He immediately called me back to ask me what was wrong, when I began crying again. I told him of how Lily had died and that she was accidentally shot at a party, that it had been intended for a boy she had gone to the party with, that her friend had been arguing with some other guys, and how the other boys followed them as they were leaving and shot at the vehicle she and her friend were in. This poor, innocent, beautiful, full-of-life sixteen-year-old that had been living a life as a high school dropout, abandoned by her mother at an early age, being raised by her grandmother, was now dead. Mike asked me to come over.

I arrived at his house feeling that he was the only one left in the world. I was shaking. He gave me a glass of wine to relax. I wanted him to help me get away from that way of life. I felt like just running. I felt in such despair. I thought I had nothing worthwhile to live for if things like that could happen. I had been so close to guns in the past with my friends in Oxnard. I hung out with guys who were always trying to prove how "hard" they were through having guns. I even had pictures of friends of mine holding guns to my head as we posed at parties. I thought it was cool at the time.

I stayed with him that night, and in turn, I only kept us both awake. I had woken up about 2:00 a.m., and I was in such a state of shock that I began throwing up. I went downstairs to have some juice. I had become so dehydrated. He came down to the living room where I was. We sat on the couch in silence. We then began to watch the movie *Ghost*. We were both trying to keep my mind on something else other than what had happened. Toward the end of the movie when Demi Moore finally gets to say good-bye to Patrick Swayze's ghost, I began to fill up with tears and heartache again. It was almost like I couldn't breathe. I raced back upstairs. I needed to get away from viewing that movie. It brought me back to uncontrollable crying. I needed to rest. Lily's funeral was in the morning.

I hadn't shown up to work. I didn't bother to call. I'm sure they didn't expect me, either. I met up with Tony and his wife, a couple who had lived next door to Lily. Tony worked with us at the car wash. We went to the funeral. I tried so hard to keep myself together. I wanted to see the little bastard that the bullet was intended for. I wanted to see the guy who had started the argument with the boys that killed my Lily.

As I walked up to the open casket, she lay there with her hair looking messy and dry, and I thought to myself how she would have wanted her lips made up, full and a rich red. It was always important to her that her lips were outlined to perfection. At least they were burying her with her whistle. She wore it around her neck, blowing it while she danced.

Before I left the funeral home, I ripped off a bullet that was on my key chain. I had bought it in Chicago years before. I gave it to Tony. From that day forward, my mind changed on what I thought about regarding the possession of weapons. I thought no one should have one, no matter what, because this is what happens. Innocence is lost.

I went home that evening to try to piece together what had just happened. The sudden impact this was having on me was indescribable. It had felt like weeks had just passed, when in reality, it had only been a few days. I had slept alone most of my life and even lived by myself on and off for the last year and a half, but now I was scared to fall asleep and be alone. I was scared of Lily, or maybe it was death I was scared of. I carried the guilt of her death for more than twelve years. If only. If only I had told her, "Yes, let's go to Hollywood," that night, then she wouldn't have gone to that party in Santa Ana. She wouldn't have been shot and killed. It was my fault she was dead. The night of her funeral, I stayed at my parents, and that night, my mom had to stay by my side until I fell asleep.

I tried to return to work, but through it all, I was making plans with Mike for me to move to L.A. It's obvious that there is more crime and murder in a city like L.A., but where I thought I was going to live seemed like there was none. It had been the night of Lily's funeral that I had made my decision. I told Mike the evening of her funeral that I was going to move to the City of Angels.

That Thursday, I made the move. I thought I'd be moving into the house, but he said he had a place for me to stay. I didn't care as long as I was getting away, running away. I thought I'd room with a girl he knew, Melanie, because he told me to meet up with her. The day I met her, she led me to the apartment; I was so naive about what was really going on. I met her at a Burger King parking lot on the corner of La Brea and Sunset Boulevard, in the heart of Hollywood. I followed her to an apartment complex. I remember asking her on the way up in the elevator to the apartment what she did for a living. Her response to me was "The same thing you do," and she kind of laughed as she said it, maybe out of confusion or disbelief that I asked. I'm sure I gave her this weird look, because it made no sense to me.

In just minutes, I came to find out that this man who was "helping me out" was not a producer but a pimp, and Melanie was one of his high-priced call girls. She had taken me to the apartment the girls worked out of.

I left in a total panic after they tried talking me into it. I cried all the way home as I drove back down the 405 freeway. Really? Why did my life offer me such bad things or bad people? How did I keep getting in worse circumstances than ever before? I felt as if life was always testing or pushing me to the edge, waiting for me to just take that final leap into the darkest of places or tempt me to give up. That black cloud was always following me.

I was shocked at first, but then for a few days, I looked at my life and my surroundings. I felt at the time as if my life couldn't get any worse. What was so wrong with doing something I had done for years and then I'd get paid for it? At least I'd get out of where I was, escape my reality and my memory of what just occurred. It was nonsense, but my state of mind was worse than it had ever been. I did say to myself that where I had been living was a more dangerous area than where I was moving to. It was dumb of me. Yes, maybe you can get shot at a party in Santa Ana, but you can get shot in Hollywood or Los Angeles just as easily.

I rationalized everything. Yes, the guys in my life hadn't treated me so great, so why would it be so bad to be in a discreet, twenty-year-old business where I'd do successful men—actors, producers, lawyers, businessmen, doctors, even rich college kids—and then get paid for it? My decision was to go back to L.A. and be with Mike. I was so distraught over Lily's death, and even before then, I couldn't make good decisions for myself. I knew right from wrong, and that was probably why I hightailed it out of Hollywood the first time. But like most situations, I inherently said, "Fuck it." Plus, I thought my only other option at the time was to continue to live with my parents, and I hated that more than anything. I viewed it as picking one hell over another, and I chose the new hell.

I packed my clothes and moved into a two-bedroom apartment in Hollywood, where two other girls and I worked out of. After my first encounter with a client who was a real producer, I thought of the things life had given me. I had now gotten to the worst times in my life, but with a few shots of tequila, I managed. I was totally isolated from my family for a while, because they couldn't come over to the "business apartment." After a month, I had bought some nice clothes and rented a top-floor apartment in a cool building in West Hollywood. Mike had it furnished while I'd work back in the business apartment up to twelve hours a day, six days a week, most of the time just making calls and appointments or just sitting around waiting for clients to come over.

At first, I'd only receive 30 percent and later 40 percent of what the client would pay, which generally was between $150 and

$3000 for a visit. A visit could be ten minutes with the guy not even touching me to a $3,000 overnight stay. The percentages were so unfair, but in the beginning, I didn't care, because I was still making more money than I had ever made. I had no debt and no bills, so to me, it was a lot of money. I had my own place, my own refuge. I finally got a home of my own, but it was at a price. I had my peace, but I had to live in the silence that allowed my mind sometimes to ponder my life. Was this how my life was meant to be? No longer was I a victim of my parents. Now, by my own choices that I didn't realize at the time I was making, I had handed the torch over to myself and was letting life and people victimize me.

Night after night, I'd cry myself to sleep. I was distraught at times about how this could be. Was this truly my life and all I was good for? It wasn't fair, I thought. Life sucked, but at times, I didn't want to die. The times I did want to die were just thoughts, bouts of my suicidal depression again. It came back during this time, but not the thought of how to kill myself, just the thought of how I wanted my life to be over.

Mike and I kept a distance from each other for a while, which at times made me very sad, but then again, I didn't want to be intimate with him because I knew that, since day one, he was so kind to me only because he wanted to use me for business. At times, I was angry with him. I was so conflicted and confused. I knew I was nothing to him but a way to make him lots of money and to spread my legs open when he wanted me to. He'd usually show me some attention when he thought I was slipping away from the business, and then he'd force himself upon me to make me feel like he was interested in me again, therefore getting me to want to stay with him and work for him.

I still went to community college in Costa Mesa. I told Mike I wouldn't give that up. I'd commute every Tuesday and Thursday but would have to go straight to work after a couple of hours at school. The only day I had free were Sundays. Mike liked us working long hours, because then we wouldn't have any time to go around and have a social life or, heaven help us, get involved with a guy. A boyfriend would definitely draw a girl away from the business. He always had to keep us in line and create motivation to make that money.

By Christmas, he and I barely spent five minutes together. He gave me a cell phone for Christmas, and as I went over to pick it up, I rushed in and out of there because I didn't want to be in a situation where he'd make me have sex with him. When we did have sex, it'd put me in a trance because I was so vulnerable and felt so alone; it filled those needs temporarily. I needed the attention. He knew that I'd confuse sex with love like many women do. I suppose I thought I was falling for him, but it hurts to think that someone you think you like could do what he did to me. He may think of it as giving me the opportunity to make money, where I wouldn't have been able to do so anywhere else without having an education. But it seems funny to me also because he'd act all lovey-dovey for a few days after we'd be together. It wouldn't last for more than a couple of days though. After that, I'd be left feeling the loneliness and depression I was going through. I knew it was better for me to not have sex with him so then I wouldn't confuse his intentions.

At the end of January, I went out with one of the girls I worked with, Melanie, not the same Melanie from Oxnard but the one that I met at the Burger King parking lot. There at Sushi on Sunset was where I met Isaac. He was far from my type. I had stopped going out with those absolutely gorgeous types. For some reason, I hit on him. I had just been so deprived of a real guy and real attention. I was so alone, and my life was much emptier than ever before. We began seeing one another regularly.

I had wanted for a while to leave the business but was scared that I couldn't survive with a real, legitimate job while going to school, and my first priority was my education. I couldn't get by being a high school dropout. Besides, I was paying for an apartment, and I was having some of the finest things in life again as I had growing up.

Within a few weeks' time and after hearing Isaac's name one too many times at work, Mike returned to my life. He came over one night in February about a month after Isaac and I had been seeing each other. It was 2:00 a.m.; mind you, in the business, you can't have an outsider as a boyfriend. Your pimp is your man in your life, even if you hadn't slept with him in months as I hadn't. An outsider would endanger the business and the pimp's livelihood. A girl could get too wrapped up and fall in love or lust and want to leave the business to become committed to her newfound love or infatuation. Mike wasn't about to let that happen with me. I had too many regulars—the same men that I saw on a regular basis, usually weekly.

He came over, and we talked for a couple of hours, which always led us back into a compromising position. Once again, I was in a daze of what I thought was infatuation, and he achieved what he wanted—control over my life. I began to let go of my relationship with Isaac up until I got a grip on what Mike had done to me once again. I could only be fooled so many times, and my brain really knew who Mike was and who I was to him.

I resumed my relationship with Isaac. A week later after going out to see two guys from France with my business partner Tina, I got into bed, and Melanie (from the business) called me. It was really late. We began to talk about my outing with Tina, and then Melanie asked me about Isaac. Isaac was friends with a guy whom Melanie had been dating off and on, a pro baseball player for the White Sox. I wondered what Isaac was up to. I clicked over to my three-way line and called him. He didn't want me to come over; it was too late, so I thought I'd let him go. I clicked back over to Melanie. Thinking I had hung up on him, Melanie and I began to talk about the business again, those two gentlemen Tina and I had gone out with, and even about Isaac.

The following morning, I was awoken by a phone call from Isaac. He was insisting that I tell him what line of work I really was in. I wanted to cry at that moment, because I knew I had been caught, but I had to play stupid, trying to hurry him off the phone. I had to find out how he had found out about me. After running around hysterically, trying to figure out how he found out, I realized that it had been my fault because I had not used the three-way calling correctly; I never hung up on him when I got back on the line with Melanie. It brought tears to my eyes when I finally admitted it to him. He said he understood to a certain degree and said it didn't make that much of a difference. He would begin spending less and less time with me.

The next day, I had a barbeque. It was my twenty-second birthday. We began drinking at noon, and it was to lead into a night at Roxburys. Isaac didn't show up until we were finishing dinner, around 9:00 p.m., and he only stayed for half an hour or so. Everyone who couldn't make it during the day was joining up at the club. I got so drunk that night I couldn't remember half of what went on.

After dinner, we all went up to the VIP room. We had a corner booth. The booths at the Roxbury were generally reserved for guests spending $100 or more. We had spent over $500 at dinner. I felt that I had been a bitch toward Isaac. We didn't leave the club together. I wanted him to spend the night, but he didn't.

On the way home in the limo a client had given me for the

night, I got on the phone to call Mike, and I finally stopped denying my feelings toward him and also cried about the situation he got me in. I told him how I was sad that he had just wanted me for the business. For months, Mike had always tried to get me to say that I cared about him, but every time, I'd tell him it was his imagination. I was so depressed this whole time. I cried to him. I thought he was the only one there for me because he was always there for me to lean on, but it was actually an act. He did it because he knew I needed someone in my life, and he filled that gap. I needed so badly to feel like someone cared for me and that is what pimps do. He sang me "Happy Birthday," and I went home and passed out.

I blacked out after talking to Mike, maybe even a little bit during because I didn't remember fully the whole phone conversation. I didn't even remember Isaac coming over until he told me the next morning. He hadn't stayed the night because I obviously said or did something. A few days went by, and I hadn't heard from Isaac. Something told me that I had said something I shouldn't have the evening of my birthday party. I had already apologized for being mean to him inside the club, but I knew myself well enough that I had probably said something more than just being a bitch to him out in public. I felt like I told him he wasn't important to me because all this time I had feelings for someone else. Part of me wanted to hold on to Isaac because there could be no future with Mike because of the reality. Isaac and I never got back to being as close as we had been, but we remained being somewhat friends for a while.

By that time, the business was tearing me apart, emotionally and mentally. My brokenness had me return, after ten years, to church. I needed some guidance, something or someone to lean on. I saw that I had become such a different person. I had always been the girl in school who was shy and a prude, but now I was a person who could be with a total stranger for money. I became harder and colder toward life. I was more lost than ever before, maybe even almost to the point of no return.

But in May, the fight inside of me appeared again. I knew what I wanted out of life. I told Mike enough was enough. In a split second, like my internal angel was speaking to me, I knew what I had to do to accomplish my dreams and to live a better life than I had been given.

The business was killing my spirit, and I knew it would eventually kill my dreams. There were times again that I wanted to die, kill myself, and end it all. I remembered how Lily no longer had a chance, but I did. A surge to fight for myself was reborn. It wouldn't have mattered to me if I had to move back in with my parents. Mike always thought he could keep me in this business because he thought I'd never go back and live with them. And he thought I was crazy about him. I wanted a commitment, a relationship, and to be loved. That's all I ever wanted from anyone. Mike couldn't provide that.

I went to his house and told him I was done. In tears, I left out of fear of what I was going to do but knowing I was doing what was best for me. For years, I'd also wanted a child, and being in this business, I'd be kept away from getting too involved with anyone, much less having a committed relationship, so I had to break free.

All along, Mike had the wrong girl for this business. Yes, I was desperate at the time Lily died. And it felt good making all that money and having gotten all the things I did, but the price was too high. My health and emotional well-being were deteriorating. Finally, my emotional self and my future meant too much to me. Life dealt me another bad hand to show me if money was everything, and it wasn't; I should have learned that by growing up and seeing what I saw in our family. I've had everything and more, from the nicest possessions to the opportunity of life, which Lily no longer had.

Life is too short to waste time on the unimportant. You can have love even if you don't have two dollars to your name. You will love yourself, and no one can love you better. This business was making me hate myself and hate my life. You can only depend on yourself and will be the only one you can turn to when things get too rough. The fight for my life was back on.

From being such a negative person most of my life, positivity and optimism began to stem from this experience. I realized that my life and my solitude within myself had to happen. At first, I felt like I was treating myself well, because I could dine and shop like a rock star, but that isn't what I craved. What the business told me subconsciously was that I wasn't worthy of a good relationship, and all I was good for was my pretty looks and that I could spread my legs for the right amount. I had to treat myself better, and I had an intuition that life would be better when I left.

About a year after I left the business, I began talking to Mike again. I don't remember why. I don't believe in hating people. I can dislike who a person is or dislike what he or she does, but never hate.

Sometimes I think this is a stupid quality of mine, because in the past, it has kept that door ajar for the undesirables. But I do remember that my funds were running low, so maybe that is why we spoke again. For a short period of time, I went back to work for Mike just to make calls and set up appointments only. That was our agreement. All the other girls I had worked with were now gone at that point, and he was having problems training the newbies on how to really lure men into seeing them. I only worked for him for a couple of weeks, because he really wanted to get me back to seeing clients, and I wouldn't. We butted heads as he tried to control the situation, and I wouldn't budge. His frustration over this led us to have a minor verbal altercation in his car, which I knew was the first time he wanted to hit me but didn't. I again cut business ties with him, knowing that if we worked like that anymore, he'd just get annoyed because he couldn't convince me to sell myself for him again.

But one day he asked me over to one of the business apartments, and at that time, I didn't mind keeping in touch with him. Because of that day, I'd learn to keep my distance; he had asked me over that day to threaten me to keep my mouth shut.

"You talk too much," he said. "You should learn by listening, not by running your mouth." This was being told to me because some guy had overheard what I had done for a living. One night at the club this guy was questioning me about whether or not I saw men for money. I totally denied it. She was a girl who was also a part-time madam and with us that night at the club, overheard. She later went and told Mike that I was saying she was a call girl. Why, if I was denying it, would I turn around and say that the girl who was at the club with us was one? This was a scary, stressful, and very paranoid time for all of us. The Hollywood Madam was all over the news, and everyone who was in the business, had been in the business, or was somehow linked to the business was on edge. I tried at first to defend myself, but he wouldn't listen to me. I didn't want to risk my life or be hurt in any way because he was so mad and threatening, so I kept my mouth shut.

In this business, some women have been hurt or killed; let us not forget where he came from. He was from the streets and had begun his business as a street pimp, and sometimes that trait doesn't fully go away. Women can die or lose so much of their lives in the process of making men like him wealthy. He had never been so cold toward me until I left that day after he threatened me. I had once seen him slap Tina, and he told me of how he beat the shit out of one of his other girls, Lisa. He always wanted his girls to know that he had a dark side to him so we wouldn't cross him. I was trying not to cross him.

I was never really too frightened of him even though I had also seen him lose his temper when a girl disrespected his changes in the business, but now for the first time I reconsidered his dark side. After being abused as a child, I tended to not fear being hit, because as I got bigger, I learned to fight back. And even though he could beat the living daylights out of me, at least I knew I'd go down fighting back, which most women don't; they just take it. With all this mayhem, you ask yourself, how could someone put themselves in situations like this? Some people think they gotta do what they gotta do, but I think it is all about fear. We have fear of not succeeding, we are scared to try, or we just don't know any better. Other people are in tough situations where they must take care of a child or have a drug addiction, but me, like I had done for several years, I had to take care of myself, and at the time, I thought there was no other choice. I also was caught at a vulnerable—maybe the most vulnerable—time in my life.

He might tell me that people got killed for running their mouths, but they could get into serious trouble by being too close to him also. I had many problems with the girls being jealous over Mike and me. He had told me that they knew we liked one another. He did treat me differently from the other girls. We would have long, deep conversations where we both shared our past. Every woman who came and went while I was there would try desperately to sink her claws into him. At times, I felt sorry for him, because the only reason most of these women were into him or wanted him was not because of him but the image he represented. This was probably why I fell for him too, until I knew who he was and what he did. He was a street pimp, making money off of women; a Rolls-Royce and a fancy, big house in the Hollywood Hills would not change that. I am thankful that I got out of that situation with nothing more than injuring my mental and emotional state a little more. I could work on that and recover, but I might have never come back from a beating.

After this, I tried to make sense of my life. I had these moments when I'd like to reflect. Why had I let this man in September of 1991, when I needed someone the most, take me to a place where I would do things that hurt myself so much? Could you call me naive or say that I was desperate, or was I just so lost and broken that I couldn't see or think straight? He took me from a heartless situation to another heartless situation—to the cold, corrupt world he'd been living in for decades. I was just another innocent soul and was sold off for 225 days. In that time, I was used mentally, emotionally, and physically. He possessed my mind.

In some cases, pimps, or whatever you prefer to call them, possess you in a violent way, which is a scare tactic where they can empower themselves over you into fear of leaving them. But I was emotionally played with, which is another tactic some pimps use if they are smart. My first problem was that I was in such a vulnerable state, and then I thought I was important to him. He took care of me and showered me with a gift here and there, which all along I thought he had been doing for all his girls; I found out later that I had been the only one in a very long time. It made me believe I was something special to him. But later and facing up to reality, as I had tried so many times, I knew I was far from special. I knew these kinds of people only cared about themselves and their money. They were more damaged souls than I ever was because all this was okay to them.

I stayed in Hollywood. I didn't have a plan for what I was going to do to support myself, but I knew I could no longer afford my apartment. I was smart enough to save some money. I moved in with Guadalupe for a bit after I left the business so I could continue saving my money and figure out what I was going to do to support myself. She had just moved to Hollywood. I only stayed with her for a few weeks. I think she had had enough of L.A. in the whole six weeks she lived there. Also, the cost of living was too much for her, because she wasn't getting paid enough at her new job, and just like most jobs she had ever gotten, she sold them a box of goods that she couldn't live up to.

Again, I still thought that I was left with really no options or quite less than I thought. One thing I've learned over the years is that we all have many options, choices in everything we do. But once I started to think about choices, I thought I had only two: live with my parents (they would always take me in) or do what I knew—see men for money. It was once again me rationalizing the situation. At least I wouldn't be working for someone else. Getting a job like a regular person wasn't an option. I was still a high school dropout, and I wouldn't lie about it.

L.A. is one of the most expensive cities to live in, and there was no way I could support myself in a city like L.A. without having a high school diploma and some experience in the corporate world. So I reached out to three of my regulars. During the time I was a call girl, it wasn't as if I saw hundreds of guys—not even a hundred. While I was with Mike, I think I was one of the top girls who had the most regulars, thankfully! So I reached out to some of my main regulars and let them know I had left the business.

It was a risk I was taking, because one of the rules we were taught since we started the business is that you don't steal clients. I knew if Mike found out that I could be seriously hurt, so I tried to make sure my clients knew this. I was back to living on the edge of danger, but had I ever really been far away from putting myself in dangerous situations?

I saw three clients weekly, but within months, it reduced to one. By the end of the year, it was just John. He wanted to take care of me. Here was another person like so many in the world who just want to be loved and feel special, and he unfortunately thought he had to buy someone to do that. He wanted to be the only one, and he paid for it. I moved into another apartment just right above Hollywood Boulevard, west of La Brea, and I only saw him once a week.

I continued to make and save lots of money. I continued with school, I continued with alcohol, and I continued with my depression, but I had been in therapy for a few years. After leaving the business with Mike, I reached out to the very first therapist I had as a teenager for a few weeks, all the way back to the days of when I lived in Oxnard. I made the trek an hour away to see him once a week. I knew my drinking had always been a problem since the very first time I drank, but I was now trying to do something about it. I couldn't keep getting as drunk as I did—driving and not remembering, not remembering most of the evenings or things that I said or did, or not remembering bringing home Isaac's best friend one night. I was hurt that night by what Isaac did to me, but did I think that was a way to get back at him? Waking up and seeing someone next to you whom you'd never think of sleeping with, not remembering how it happened but slightly recalling falling into a ditch while getting out of your car when he drove us to my place, I knew I had a problem.

I'd stop drinking for weeks at a time, and then I'd start again at a slow pace, but it would escalate to the drinking that had haunted me all my life, when I drank so heavily that I'd throw up, black out, and not remember where I was the next morning or what exactly had happened the night before. Alcohol had caused so much sadness in my childhood, and now it was causing me more pain, because it put me in dangerous, disrespectful, demoralizing situations. I knew my drinking wasn't as many addicts, where their body has taken over and they *need it*. I was more of the depressed person who, when and if she drank while she didn't have her shit together, couldn't stop until the night was over once she started. I needed to do something about it before it got me seriously hurt or killed; it had already gotten me raped and had me give up my dignity on a few occasions. I couldn't allow it to do much more.

So my therapy and a real, definite shift had begun, because I had read Suzanne Somers's book *Keeping Secrets*. It changed my life. In the book, her childhood closely resembled mine. And even though her family had all chosen recovery, I could see a glimpse of me having a different life, a better one. After seeing her and her family on *Donahue* and reading the book, I was hopeful for the very first time in my life. I wanted to die fighting the disease of alcoholism and violence rather to succumb to it.

Over the next few years, I struggled with more bad choices in my life. I urged my family to help themselves. All of them were now living in San Diego. They were still drinking heavily, and some were still using drugs. They didn't see that there was a problem. I think they wanted (and want) to think that everything was in the past and that we should let it go—to get over it—but it was not. Nothing had changed. At the time, my mother laughed at the fact that I was referencing a sitcom star like Suzanne Somers. It doesn't matter where or from whom you find that crutch to hold on and make a change in your life, just as long as you find it.

After leaving the grips of Mike's business, I leaped further into the L.A.-Hollywood scene. I was an attractive twenty-two-year-old girl in Hollywood, living in a city where dreams can come true. It was a good time to be young and single. I had my problems, like my drinking and depression, which I reflected on from time to time, but I also was having fun and taking in as much as I could out of this town.

L.A. could be amusing, and it was definitely an experience. You could find yourself being followed in your car by someone in a famous band wanting you to pull over just to get to know you and ask you out. But L.A. could also be scary. I once found myself in a club and some random girl tried to get me to go to someone's house. She told me that if she didn't get me to go there that she'd get in trouble. I saw the panic in her eyes, and she frightened me. She was probably in the prostitution world but in a bad way; she was forced into it and also forced to recruit. I hope nothing bad ever happened to her.

I continued with my education, attending LACC, which I felt so proud for doing because I knew of its importance. But, I was still going to the clubs, like Bar One and the Roxbury with Morgan. I went to parties up in the Hollywood Hills hosted at basketball players' or music producers' homes. My girlfriends and I would have dinners at places like Georgia's, an upscale Southern restaurant on Melrose Boulevard opened by Norm Nixon, a former basketball player and several celebrity investors that included Denzel Washington, Eddie Murphy, and Connie Stevens. On any given night, there were quite a few celebrities dining alongside our table.

Morgan and I also attended a lot of Lakers games. She'd get us tickets from various connections that also included a trip after the game into the VIP Forum Club. Morgan knew so many people, so it was not uncommon to be introduced to an NBA player, a Wayans brother, or someone like Mike Tyson. Going to a Lakers game was nothing new to me by then. I had gone to a few with Melanie before I had moved to L.A. At the time, she had her own connection with a Lakers player, and my very first game was seeing Michael Jordan playing in the playoffs, with the Lakers playing the Chicago Bulls.

Looking back now, it seems like getting free tickets to a Lakers game wasn't that difficult to do. We even got into the clubs for free and never had to wait in line. There was always someone you or your girlfriend seemed to know. I also later would be able to manage getting tickets to either Lakers or Clippers games through a player here and there who would like me.

For about a month, I was talking to one of the guys who played on the Clippers team after a night when he hit on me at the Century Club in Century City. He came over to my place one night, and we just talked for hours, but we never went any further than that, because he made it quite clear that he only wanted to sleep with me. Strange to believe, but I wasn't a groupie or a gold digger. So just because he or anyone else was a ballplayer or had lots of cash didn't seal the deal for me. I may have had some girlfriends who were all about that, but that was them. I was never starry eyed, which is a good thing in L.A. because you cannot get caught up in the hype that celebrities are better or different from the rest of us.

At the same time, I still had minor contact with some friends from Oxnard. None of them knew of my life in L.A., except for Melanie, who was just about the only one from my teenage years that I saw on a somewhat regular basis. I did see the whole crew and much of Oxnard one time when Melanie and I went to my friend Mike's funeral.

Mike had been basically my first, after the rape. I somehow caught his eye when we were going to Oxnard High School, and I still had my shaved head. I found it amusing at first because he looked so clean-cut and kind of hung out with the jocks, and I hung out with all the death rockers and skinheads. After hooking up a few times at parties, we went our separate ways. We'd find our way back to becoming good friends when I starting hanging out with "da boyz" and Leah during my later part of Oxnard.

Mike was gunned down in his home after a disagreement with a guy who used to hang out with us. Supposedly, the fight was over money, and from what I also heard, this guy was strung out on meth or something, which was probably true, because he seemed more like a junkie and would disappear for periods of time, not looking great when we'd see him again.

At Mike's funeral, I had to deal with one more person in my life being gone. I remember the last time I spoke to him; he tried to come out to L.A. for one of my birthday parties. His death was tragic and senseless, but I am fortunate to have had closure with him, because one time he wrote to me and apologized for how badly he had treated me when we first met. It was a push-and-pull relationship. He pulled me in and treated me nicely, and then at times he pushed me away and was mean. After his apology letter, we had a newfound friendship. He was a good guy and one of those types of people whom everyone knew and loved. To this day, he's still missed.

By the summer of 1993, the Roxbury was still going strong, and it was then when I met Joshua. I was at the Roxbury with two guy friends of mine, Shane and Paul. I liked just hanging out with my guy friends because I could dress how I wanted and just float around the club, socializing without any agenda. Morgan would have disapproved if I ever wore jeans to the club, even though they were black jeans.

That night, we were there early, and I was at the bar ordering a drink and talking to Juan, my Peruvian bartender brother, when I saw Paul right next to me talking to some guy. All I told Paul was that his friend was cute, but that was all I meant. There was nothing at that time behind what I said. I didn't want to meet him, much less go home with him. Paul got excited and introduced us. We said hi, he shook my hand, and that was it. I moved on, walking around for a bit, as it was still early, and there were just about ten people in the VIP room.

There were actual times in L.A. when the pretentiousness went out the window. I liked it when it was like that, and it was like that that night. I was standing in front of the bar, and I noticed three guys at the bar, and one pulled down his pants, revealing his boxers. It was just then that I realized it was Marky Mark, a.k.a. Mark Wahlberg. He was still big at the time for doing his Calvin Klein ad, among other things. I just laughed and moved on.

The evening went on like that. Maybe it was a relaxed, fun atmosphere because I wasn't out with the girls, and guys typically didn't care about looking and acting a certain way. I just spent most of my night observing and chitchatting with a few people. As far as Joshua, I didn't really see him or put much focus on him the entire evening.

It was "last call." Juan and I were taking a last shot for the night and cheering being Peruvians. As I went outside to find Paul and Shane, Joshua grabbed me and all of a sudden was hitting on me. I was pretty drunk at that point. We sat on the trunk of his classic Mercedes and talked, me about how I wasn't coming over and Joshua about how he wanted me to come over. I was drunk, and most times after one too many drinks, I didn't think and I didn't care what happened to me or what I did. If I'm too wasted, I never question anything. My rational mind, for what it is, stops working.

When he first started talking to me, I was still able to think, but maybe that last shot Juan and I took was hitting me. After about half an hour of going back and forth, I caved in. Who knew that night would forever make the impact in my life that it has. *Choices.* Sometimes good, sometimes bad, sometimes meaningful, and sometimes what you are supposed to do to have a certain life experience.

We spent the next several months seeing each other—hooking up. I wanted more, but it was just us seeing each other after the club and him either spending the night or me spending the night over at his place. We'd take turns paying for Denny's after the club. One of his best friends was always with us. We'd all hang out in the mornings sometimes, just chatting and getting to know one another. After the first time we slept together, we stopped using protection, because I was convinced I couldn't get pregnant, though I was taking birth control pills. There had been times when I wasn't taking birth control regularly, like with Mark from Oxnard, and I never got pregnant, so I just thought I couldn't get pregnant. I guess I thought this also because it seemed everyone around me in my life—girlfriends, sisters—had gotten pregnant accidentally. I was falling for Joshua. I wanted him to really like me. But I knew after a while that I wasn't the only one he was seeing. It was just that womanly instinct I had.

One evening in mid-December, I went out with Morgan to a newer club that we were going to on Wednesday nights—the Gate. It was situated on La Cienega Boulevard near the Beverly Center in West Hollywood. As we got in, I was looking around and said to Morgan, "I wonder if Joshua is here." Just then, our girlfriend Michelle caught wind of what I said. She was taken aback and asked if I was speaking of the same Joshua she knew—the same Joshua that she and her then boyfriend and club promoter, Julian, had gone out to dinner with many times; the same Joshua who was Haitian and had a girlfriend that Michelle said he was pretty much engaged to.

Michelle wondered and asked how I knew him. I just said I knew him. She told me to let it go, because he wasn't about to leave his girlfriend; her mother had just died, and she was coming into a big inheritance.

I drank so much that night. I went home and cried like I hadn't in such a long time. I wanted to throw in the towel to my life. Thankfully, I just cried myself to sleep, and the next morning, I was still upset but not as much as I had been the night before. Alcohol makes you feel like things are so much worse than they really are. Out of days of sadness burst out this light of hate—hate for me being lost and feeling wounded again. I was not going to let myself be knocked down because of that! I had to get back up again.

I spent the next two months getting control of my emotions, my health, and my problems like my depression and using alcohol and cocaine. I wanted so desperately to stop getting into stupid situations where I devalued myself. I wanted more from life and wanted more for me. I realized that my life was off track—again! I fought back. I needed to keep fighting. I was going to do the opposite of everything I had seen growing up, letting horrible situations win and affect me in a negative way.

I took back control of my life, full throttle. I stopped drinking. I stopped using coke, which I had begun using the last few months and which was starting to really become a problem, because I even sometimes bought it. It was stupid that I had even started using it again, because none of my L.A. girlfriends did it. It had been just one of those nights being out with a girl whom I had just met, and the guy she was with had it. We did it all night long. I am thankful that moment gave me the reason to stop, because I was truly becoming addicted to cocaine. I craved for years after to just have some dripping down through my nose and down my throat or to be able to place a little bit on my gums; the taste and feeling it gave me, haunted me. A true addiction was forming, and I caught it in time before I couldn't stop on my own.

I rarely went out unless it was to do Sunday brunch at Le Petit Four on Sunset Plaza. I went to the gym five to six days a week, cut out soda and sugar, and ate lots of salads. I was in the best shape and health of my life. I felt good about the choices I was making to change my life.

In January, I went to Cancun for the very first time and by myself. I wanted to cleanse myself of any emotional attachment of Joshua that I thought I might still have and just prove to myself that I was done with him. It was therapeutic. It was better than cutting off all my hair, which was what I'd usually do under those circumstances. We hadn't seen each other since I had found out about his girlfriend, but that hadn't stopped him from calling me.

When I returned from Mexico, I had over fifty missed calls and messages from him, and I had only been away for five days. I didn't return his calls, but by late February and with my birthday being right around the corner, I began to get sentimental and didn't like that I didn't have anyone in my life. I called Joshua on a whim, out of a second or two of mental malfunction. He came over. We had sex twice, and right after the second time, I pushed him off of me and went to the bathroom. I was sick to my stomach because I was disgusted with what had just happened. I was disgusted that I had sex with him but worse because I had sex with someone who had never really liked me—he was with someone else, and I knew it. I had crossed the line and most of all hurt myself in the process. I wanted more for me and loved myself better than this. Two steps forward, one step back. I knew definitely then that any feelings toward him were dead. I never was with him again, but little did I know what role he'd play in my life.

7

Hollywood, Tupac, Mr. Laker Guy, and the Single Pregnant Female

On my birthday, Melanie from Oxnard came to Hollywood so that we could celebrate our birthdays together as we had done several times before. I loved it when she came and visited me. She was just about the only thing in my life at that time that was real, genuine, and had no agenda.

We went to Roxburys. We had invited just a few girlfriends to celebrate with us. It was very cool, even though it ended up being just the two of us. We could have a blast when it was just us two. We had fun together always. There was never any judgment from her, and she was always down with just about anything, which could be a little dangerous at times because we'd get ourselves into the most adventurous of things.

She had been living in Ventura with a boyfriend. She'd come sometimes to hang out with me in L.A. and a few months prior, we had gone to see the movie *Poetic Justice* at the Cinerama Dome, a legendary movie theater on Sunset Boulevard. The movie had been out for a while. As we left the movie theater, we were in awe over the rapper on the big screen, Tupac Shakur, whom I just hadn't paid much attention to before seeing *Poetic Justice*. We were both intrigued the night of our celebration when we realized that Tupac was there. There were always celebrities and pro athletes there, but this was the first time I had seen him there. After a while, Melanie said to forget it and that he wouldn't notice either one of us because he was talking to some girl. So we went on with our night.

Melanie is a dancer at heart, and I found it funny sometimes because she'd accept dancing requests from just about anyone just so she could get down on the dance floor. I, on the other hand, wouldn't and still won't take random requests. There was one night we were at the Mayan in downtown L.A., and she danced with a random guy. Let's just say he could've been voted the worst dancer of the year. He made such a scene while he danced that a large circle formed and watch him in disbelief. It was so sad but hilarious at the same time.

Melanie hadn't even been aware of it for a while because she was doing her own thing, but as soon as she noticed his dancing and that everyone was staring, she stopped dancing and grabbed my hand, and we walked away quickly. The expression on her face was priceless.

So at Roxburys that night, some random guy walked up to her and asked her to dance. I stood at the edge of the dance floor, watching her and sipping on one of my first drinks in months. I eventually saw that Melanie and her guy were dancing right next to Tupac and his crew. The girl he had been talking to and dancing with earlier was gone. Without much thought or hesitation, I took a deep breath and went for it.

I usually never had this bravery or confidence to go after something or someone. I had let a few guys in my past move on because they wanted me to come out of my shell and make the first move, but I never really could; it just wasn't me. So I pretended to dance with Melanie, and within less than a minute, Tupac was grabbing me by the waist dancing with me. We introduced ourselves, talked as we danced to Snoop Dogg's "Gin and Juice."

After dancing with him to two more songs, he asked me if I wanted to leave. I said yes. He grabbed my hand, I grabbed Melanie's, and we headed out of the club. As we were walking out, some guy that Tupac didn't know started some beef with him. After some yelling, I eventually grabbed the back of Tupac's shirt and pulled him away to leave. We left in his Lexus, with Melanie and me squeezed into the front passenger seat and a friend of his in the back.

Melanie laughs about it today. She says she had no idea at first where we were going or with whom until we were outside and getting in his car. She says how she remembers sitting in the front near the window and Tupac was driving with one hand on the steering wheel and the other hand on my leg.

We went back to the apartment in Hollywood where Tupac was staying, which was actually a block away from my place. After some small talk, he and I got together that night. I look back at this, and I think it was really the most scandalous thing I've ever done. It was one of those legendary "Top 3" nights I had with Melanie, maybe even number one. I laugh because many who know me could never imagine me doing something like that; others would judge me and say that I was a groupie or a slut, but all I do is smile and think that I did have some fun when I was young and just went for it. It isn't like I went around fucking stars. And he used a condom that night, just to put it out there.

Tupac did try to get Melanie to join in on the fun, but she had a boyfriend and wouldn't. She just sat in the room, watched us, and tried to take pictures with my camera. It's not like she's into that kind of thing, but I think she was probably having an Andy Warhol moment from what I could see. We were drunk and young, and it was about the most amusing event out of our Hollywood nights. Besides, she didn't want to be in the other room with Tupac's friend or bodyguard, whoever he was.

After he and I were done, he grabbed her as he had to pee, and they talked in the bathroom for a second. She told me she touched his chest and tattoos while he smoked a blunt, but she didn't cave in and have sex with him.

We eventually left and went back to Roxburys to try to pick up my car, but the valet was already closed, so Tupac drove us back to my place.

The next morning, Melanie went home and stupidly told her boyfriend everything. She was a good girlfriend and wanted to be honest with him, but what guy wants to hear about a tryst like that, even if you didn't have sex with Tupac Shakur? They got into a big fight, and she packed up her things and hightailed it to Arizona, where she had family. I didn't hear from her for a couple of weeks until she got settled in Phoenix.

In the meantime, I hung out with Tupac. I'd just walk over to his place where he was staying, and we'd just really hang out, talk, drink beer, or watch the Lakers on TV. One of these nights when a friend of his was there, he said out loud how things were going great in his life and how all of a sudden these beautiful women are coming around, and he grabbed my hand, smiling. That was the second time someone had called me beautiful. It touched me. We continued to have sex together, and let's just say it got better and even a little romantic.

I don't know if I was really into him or just sold on the character of who we had seen on the silver screen a month or two prior. That first night together, I was disillusioned after we had sex. Maybe it is what happens to guys once they conquer a woman too quickly; the "wow" disappears. Maybe I realized he was just an average guy like the rest of them. Maybe I continued to hang out with him because I was not involved with anyone and I was just keeping myself occupied. I had already passed the hurdle by sleeping with him and there was no one else. He was a good guy for this moment.

Don't get me wrong, Tupac was nice, funny, and had this personality that reflected to me that he was so happy, but there was no chemistry or passion there. I had to fake that after our first encounter. Maybe he really wasn't my type. He was very thin, even though he had muscles, and he wasn't as tall as I liked them. He also thankfully wasn't the thug that had been portrayed so much in the media; at least that was not the side he showed me. People who never met him probably picture guns lying around and picture him walking around swearing and being all loud, but that was not what I got to experience. He did have a vibrant, happy, excited personality at times. He also had a sense of how big his career could possibly be, and it seemed to me that he was appreciative and felt lucky about it and everything he had accomplished and gotten so far. He had a sweet demeanor and made me giggle, and we talked a lot, even about Peru and his name. He even wanted to know that I was thinking about him, like after I left him and he went to go on *The Arsenio Hall Show*. He wanted me to page him, which made him seem a little insecure about himself or that he needed reassurance that I was thinking about him also.

You'd think he'd be confident or even cocky about women wanting him, but he needed to be reassured that I was interested in him. Maybe that was the vibe he was reading from me. Maybe he was used to girls not leaving him alone, and he still pursued me, even after I gave him the goods the first night. Vulnerability like that is rare and made him more real of a person to me.

So I was learning to make the shift from the person I had seen in a movie to getting to know a real person. But it was all casual. How serious could we take it? We hooked up after a club. We had nothing in common. He was a rapper and movie star. I was a college student who wore suits because I still wanted to portray myself as classy, even though I had and still was being scandalous on the down low seeing a married man for money. Around three weeks after we met, he had to go to Atlanta. He called a few times, but we wouldn't see each other like that anymore, because by the time he got back, I had met someone else.

I went to Roxburys with Morgan while Tupac was away. Inside the VIP room toward the front, Morgan and I stood there. She was talking to a Laker, either a guy she had hooked up with or one that she wanted to hook up with. As they were leaving me to head out of the VIP room to go and dance, Morgan's Laker guy told a friend of his who was sitting down with two other guys nearby to watch over me. His friend, another Laker, came over, and suddenly, I knew who this was. I had met him six months earlier at Roxburys, but he gave me the weirdest, cheesiest line that time—*how does a pretty girl like you end up in a place like this?* Since then, I was unimpressed. This time, though, he came over and was very nice and normal. Before I had met him six months earlier, I remember being at a Lakers game one night, looking at the Lakers bench and asking myself if anyone on that bench was cute. There was only one guy, and it was him.

We talked for a little while, and then we sat down at a table. We had a few drinks and hit it off the rest of the evening. Here was just a normal, decent guy. He was tall, dark, and handsome, had a great smile, and had what I was into—a sweet look and that fun, funny personality.

After the club, we decided to follow each other to a diner on Beverly Boulevard in Beverly Hills to grab a bite to eat. We parked on Beverly, and he came over to my car to walk over with me. The diner, always loud at 2:00 a.m., was packed, and we decided that we weren't that hungry, so we left to go back to his place. We decided to take one car, and I hopped through the driver's side of his Mercedes, and we went to his place on the Wilshire Corridor where all the high-rise condos in Westwood are. After a few months of being sober, I was back to getting wasted again, but thankfully, I didn't black out. This was a night to remember.

I woke up the next morning feeling like throwing up and took one look at myself in his bathroom mirror; I thought I looked puke green. He said, "You look beautiful," though. Within a few weeks' time, here was another guy in my life who was saying I was beautiful. It made me feel beautiful, and it made me feel really noticed for the first time in my life. He drove me back to my car in his Porsche. We swiveled and swerved through the curvy streets of Sunset Boulevard, and all the while, I tried to keep my stomach down.

Mr. Laker Guy was taken by me, or at least he acted like it. He was very excited to see me and wanted to see me pretty much every day. I'd go to his place, or he'd come to mine. He'd leave Morgan and me tickets to go see him play. I was as close to being on cloud nine as I could possibly be. You'd think I was head-over-heels crazy about him, but I wasn't, at least not like he was with me. I was excited and into him, but I held back. I'd get a little lost in my feelings because he was a little too intense with his. Did I have a fear of commitment? Or was I just use to guys not being that into me? Maybe I was subconsciously thinking that as soon as he really got to know me, he'd see that I was not worthy of being loved.

I had never truly felt loved, at least love that lasted and didn't hurt, so maybe it wasn't possible for me, and I didn't want to completely allow myself to be vulnerable to it because it was never going to happen, right? And really deep down inside, I still didn't want to be serious, because then that next step would be marriage, and I was in fear of marriage since my childhood. I longed for a long, committed, monogamous relationship, but never marriage.

About a week and a half after we met, he was over, and we were sleeping, or at least he was. I hadn't been feeling well for a few days. I was waking up in the middle of the night feeling sick. I wasn't throwing up; I just felt like I was catching the stomach flu. In the middle of the night after waking him up, he said, "Maybe you're pregnant."

I told him, "I can't get pregnant."

I thought with all my being that I couldn't get pregnant. I had never accidentally gotten pregnant. I recently accepted the fact that I couldn't have children. I had been sexually active for over six years, since I was seventeen and that one time when I was sixteen. All that time, I had unprotected sex with most of the guys I was with, including Mark, which lasted over two years, Joshua for more than six months, and now with Mr. Laker Guy. I had always used protection with my clients because, thankfully, that was how business was.

Tupac and I had used protection also, but one night still haunts me. I remember him saying, "Wait a second," and the next thing I think I felt was a condom pass and hit me on the leg on its way to the floor. I never forgot that. I would have at least liked to know who I had unprotected sex with, so if that was what I thought it was, I would have liked to know for sure. So, in my mind, there should have been an accidental pregnancy at least once, right? Mr. Laker Guy and I spent another night together, and then he had to go out of town.

A few days later, on April 1st, April Fool's Day, I finally threw up. With how I had been feeling and now finally throwing up, I told myself I was either dying or pregnant; it was no flu. I opened up the yellow pages and found a clinic in Santa Monica that would take walk-ins for pregnancy tests. I got tested, and it was positive. I say that this was the very first joke my son, the comedian, gave me.

I came home and fell to my knees, crying. I had always wanted a child and for some reason always wanted to be a single mother, but now I felt for that baby. I knew somehow it wasn't going to have a father in its life or to have the life that it deserved. Knowing I was keeping my baby, I apologized to my unborn child as I touched my belly, crying. I also asked myself if I was ready to let go of my single life and put the child first. That was the easiest and quickest thing I've answered—"Yes!"

The following day after much thought, I told Joshua. I wasn't sure if I was going to tell him. All I did want was a picture of him so that later this child could see the other half of where it came from. I knew in my heart it was his because of the timing of my period. If I thought it could've been anyone else's, I would have definitely checked it out, because I knew then at least I would have had a lot of child support and possibly there could be a dad for my child. With Joshua, something told my gut that he'd be out of the picture.

We sat in his bedroom as I nervously beat around the bush. He gave me a picture of him in a suit, holding a rose. I was so nervous that he blurted out, "It seems like you are trying to tell me you're pregnant." *Well, yes, Joshua, I am pregnant*, I thought. All I could do was begin to cry. He said how he wasn't mature enough or ready to take care of a child. I loved that he was mature enough to recognize that about himself, instead of maybe being one of those fathers who said okay and then vanished later. I had already made my decision when I went to get tested to see if I was pregnant. There was no doubt in my heart that I was having my baby and keeping it. I didn't know how, I didn't think of how, I just was going to do it, even if it was all by myself.

I left Joshua's, throwing his picture back at him in the hallway of his apartment complex as he followed me to the elevator. He said he'd see me in a few days.

He came over to my place two days later. He buzzed my door and called me repeatedly for more than two hours. I hid in my apartment, scared and crying.

In the following weeks, I dropped out of school at LACC and moved in with my sister Paoletta in San Diego. She had promised me that she'd take care of me and be there for me.

My son would push me forward toward living a life I had only dreamed about at times. It was a new beginning; things had to be different for the both of us. I look back and notice for years that I did want a change from the life I had been dealt. I had been making baby steps toward that, but it was because of becoming a mother I was jolted even further to go after that dream—to have a better life.

As soon as I got to San Diego, Guadalupe and my dad ambushed me into doing an intervention on Paoletta. At that point, the whole family was still living in San Diego. Guadalupe and my dad said that Paoletta's drinking was out of control. I had known that for a long time. I was three months pregnant, and she and her husband were offering me to have wine, telling me how one glass wouldn't hurt the baby. I thought they were out of their minds. Why would I even want to chance it?

Guadalupe and my dad had been waiting for me to move down there so the three of us could tell Paoletta that she needed to get help. My mother's drinking was still the same, off and on for periods at a time. Candelaria was addicted to crystal meth, and she was almost entirely homeless. Why they wanted to address the issue about Paoletta, I don't know. In my mind, we all needed interventions.

About three weeks after I was in San Diego, Guadalupe was over at Paoletta's. We hadn't had the intervention yet, but Guadalupe and Paoletta got into a fight, and Guadalupe spilled the beans about it. Paoletta threw back at her how she was a pothead. Guadalupe left, and Paoletta began yelling at me. She looked at me as the culprit. She said that I had spied on her and made up stories to them about her drinking.

After she was done yelling at me with me trying to tell her how I was confronted as soon as I moved there, I left and went over to Guadalupe's. Paoletta then called over to Guadalupe's and told Guadalupe that I'd better come back over before anyone stole all my clothes, which she had thrown all over the sidewalk. I was pissed because I had just moved my entire life to San Diego instead of Phoenix, like Melanie had wanted me to. I had stupidly convinced myself to trust a family member, and she kicked me out and threw all my expensive clothes out, down the hill to her sidewalk, *and* I was four months pregnant with no job and no baby daddy!

I stayed with Guadalupe, but that didn't last long. She said I was welcome to stay but that she wouldn't stop her pot smoking around me. It wasn't me I was concerned about; it was my unborn child. I ended up at my parents in less than a week, because at that point, yet again, I felt I was out of options for me and my pregnancy. I knew that was the last place I wanted to end up, but I also thought I could handle it. It had only been a few years, so I had not forgotten how living with them sometimes was, but I knew I'd have my own bed to sleep in (that they would give up their bed for me) and that I wouldn't have to worry about food.

It was fine at first. I spent a lot of time roaming the malls or going to the gym, just to be out of the apartment. My parents lived near the old baseball stadium on Friars Road and walking distance to the first mission in California—Mission Basilica San Diego de Alcalá. For the most part, I had an easy pregnancy. I had completely stopped drinking alcohol. I had also completely cut out my coffee, soda, candy, which I love so much, and fast food. I worked out often. The first time I had ever been on a stair-climber was when I was seven months pregnant.

I heard from Mr. Laker Guy a lot for a while after I had written to him, letting him know how I had found out that I was pregnant and then made the decision to move to San Diego with family. He left me quite a few messages, but it took me a few weeks to get settled and decide how I was going to deal with him and me or if that there was anything really to say. The little and most important bit I did forget though to mention in the letter was that he wasn't the father. *Duh!* He called and asked what I wanted to do, that was when I realized I left that part out. "Oh my God. Sorry, it's not yours," I said.

He called often to talk and ask, "Do you or the baby need anything?"

My mom started to believe he wanted to marry me, but the fact that I was having somebody else's baby eventually got to him, though. He called continuously and would ask me to come up and see him. I wouldn't for a while.

I did go to L.A. a few times to see my girlfriends, and I eventually saw him. Morgan, Guadalupe, and I went over to his house that he was now living in on the Westside. Morgan hung out while Guadalupe got stoned with a few of his friends. Mr. Laker Guy and I went to talk in the living room. It was great to see him but also awkward because he was all over me, and I just didn't feel like that single girl anymore. It is a hard thing to express, but I almost felt pure and clean again, not like some girl who went home with someone on a first encounter or second or third. I was going to be someone's mother. I felt worthy of being respected for the first time in my life. He wanted me to stay the night, but there was no way I was going to. I still liked him and wanted to see him, but I deserved a little more at the time than a hookup.

When I returned home, he'd tell me during some of our conversations over the phone that he couldn't handle it. "How can I be with you when you are having someone else's baby? You'll go back to him," he said. He was sure that the father and I would get back together. I tried to convince him that it was never going to happen, but he was just too insecure about it. He'd even call me drunk about it, almost sounding like he was about to cry.

We stopped talking for a bit during the summer. But as October rolled around, he called me. The Lakers were playing a preseason game in San Diego, and he wanted to see me. I went to his hotel, and we had lunch. He couldn't keep his hands off my belly. He talked to the baby. It seemed like he was finally okay with everything and that possibly we would try to keep in touch and see what happened. I went to the game with my dad later that evening, but it would be a while before I'd hear from Mr. Laker Guy again.

On November 24, 1994, Thanksgiving Day, at 6:45 a.m., after not being able to sleep all night, I knew it was time to go to the hospital. The pain was a hundred times worse than the worst cramps ever. I woke up my parents and Melanie. I had been having contractions for days, and I finally threw up. I had read somewhere, possibly in *What to Expect When You're Expecting*, that if that happened, you were in labor. The contractions hurt, and I just wanted to be done with the pain!

My mom had started sobering up two to three days prior. We arrived at the hospital at 10:00 a.m. Melanie, who had disappeared for a while, had called me the night before and was going to come and spend Thanksgiving with me. I hadn't seen her since the night that we hung out with Tupac, and we hadn't spoken since I moved to San Diego. It was a perfect time to see her.

My mom, Paoletta, Guadalupe, Guadalupe's then fiancé, and Melanie were in the delivery room with me. My dad was at the hospital, but he stayed out of the delivery room because he couldn't stomach medical things like that. He would have fainted. Melanie videotaped my son's birth. It was a great moment. We listened to the ethereal music of Enya playing in the background. Everyone was getting along, talking softly, and joking a bit. But Candelaria kept calling, and Mom and Paoletta eventually were fighting with her over the phone. Would it ever stop? It seemed like any good moment always had to have something. Candelaria wasn't calling for me; she was just concerned if she and her boyfriend at the time could go over to Paoletta's for Thanksgiving dinner. Candelaria had been homeless already for a while and was strung out. Paoletta wasn't having any part of it and told her to stop calling.

Besides those few interruptions, it was pretty peaceful. It took me an hour and nineteen minutes of pushing before my baby came to this world and welcomed us with his skinniness and big knees. I will never forget one moment while I was pushing. Someone said something or maybe I did and everyone laughed, but I got the giggles, and I couldn't stop for a while. I think back now and wonder if it felt like I was tickling my baby for the first time.

At 5:19 p.m., my turkey came out. Everyone left me about twenty minutes later to go have Thanksgiving dinner at Paoletta's. I was surprised when the phone rang; it was Mr. Laker Guy. I was shocked that it was he. I thought it was Morgan; she had called before and now had obviously called him to let him know I was having the baby. He congratulated me, and we chitchatted for a while; he said he'd call me back, but he never did.

I kept my baby in the nursery half of the time because I didn't know what to do. I had never been around babies. I had taken Lamaze by myself; Guadalupe had promised me that she'd go to all my classes with me but only went to one. So I learned what to do and expect, but I guess my instinct didn't kick in automatically.

For the first day, my behavior signaled that I wasn't ready for this. I loved the fact that I had my child—*my long awaited child*, that I had always wanted, but I knew nothing about babies except what I had learned in Lamaze class and books. I had never held a baby and had never been around a newborn before. All this was foreign to me. The nurse found me one of the last turkey dinners in the hospital. I was starving because I hadn't had anything since the day before, and I wasn't about to pass up turkey, gravy, and mashed potatoes.

After my dinner, I asked the nurse to bring my son to me. I stood there staring at him for a bit while he lay in the hospital's plastic bassinet. I'd go and touch his fingers and cheek. I tried several times to reach for him, but I was scared to pick him up, scared to do it incorrectly. At that time, like so many times before, I still felt like a child. Even though I was twenty-four, I felt like a little girl doing grown-up things. At some point, the nurse came in and placed him in my arms. The following day, I took him home and had warmed up to the idea that I wasn't going to drop him or pick him up incorrectly.

After giving birth to Oliver, my life and I felt forever changed. Nothing mattered, or no one was more sacred to me than he and I. I had infatuations in my past, what I thought were loves at times, but having love for a child, your child, is the real deal. It cannot be broken; no other love outside of your child or children can be greater. At least, this is in most of the cases when parents have children. I unfortunately cannot say all human beings that bear children experience this. We'd be quite a different world if 100 percent of us did feel this love for our own. I am just thankful that it happened to me toward him.

The first few months of my son's life weren't the easiest. He was born with a health problem that was found during an ultrasound while he was still in my belly. He had ureteropelvic junction obstruction. Ureteropelvic junction obstruction is a condition where blockage can occur. My son's case was that the tube that extended from his kidney to the bladder on the left side was really thin and because of that the flow in it slowed down. Sometimes this condition needs an operation, and sometimes when it is congenital (the patient is born with it), as in my son's case, children's bodies grow and correct the problems on their own. The doctors wanted to just keep an eye on it, but the way this was done was really hard for my baby and me. They began several tests on Oliver when he was just a week or so old. He had to be x-rayed several times while also having a catheter fill radioactive fluid in him. Since he was a newborn, they didn't want to put him to sleep and use any sedation. They had to strap him down over and over and over again with thick white tape, kind of like masking tape, onto a hard wooden board that lay on top of the table so that he wouldn't be able to move during his x-ray. There was so much tape that it covered his tiny twenty-inch-long body. He cried and cried, choking up, sobbing for some relief and air until he'd pass out. It was so hard to not be able to do anything more but stroke his head and speak to him softly. I feel in my heart that his dislike to have covers or sheets on his bed while he slept was a result of this. Growing up, he was eventually able to deal with a blanket while he slept but never learned to be really okay with anything that confined him tightly, like a bedsheet.

Besides that, my son also had a hard time latching on to breast-feed. It took him about three weeks to learn. I'd have to hold him to my chest while pumping formula through a syringe that was connected to a tube that somehow I'd have to also place and hold close to my breast so that he could try to latch on. I obviously needed more hands than I had to really do that, but I tried with using part of my leg as an extra limb while he lay on a pillow. I was adamant about breast-feeding, and so was my doctor. When I'd be trying to do this at times in the bedroom, unfortunately at the same time, I'd be yelling at my mother to leave me alone or throwing something toward her to shut the door and not come in. She had only sobered up a day or two before Oliver was born on Thanksgiving Day, but within another day or two after he was born, she was back to being the lousy, loud, get-in-your-face drunk I had always known her to be. It's obvious that her maternal instincts, if she ever had them, were taken from her by her addiction, because she showed she couldn't be there when her baby had a baby and needed some help.

My dad, on the other hand, was very helpful with Oliver's colic, which came a few weeks later. He'd spend hours with him trying to soothe him down from crying when I couldn't anymore.

Around this time, Candelaria came to stay with us for a while. The last time I had heard from her was when I delivered my son. She had been homeless, living in a tent with her boyfriend. She had dropped over what looked like at least eighty pounds, maybe even a hundred. She wanted to get clean, because she was afraid for her health. She didn't think her heart could handle much more. She only stayed with us for a few days. She had hoped that my parents would also allow her boyfriend, who was also strung out, to stay at my parents', but my parents said no. We lived in a small apartment, but I don't think that was why my parents said no. I believe they thought he was the bad influence and that maybe she'd get clean if she'd just stay with us.

That didn't happen. Candelaria went back on the streets. She later got arrested for lifting a candy bar at a store and thankfully got clean and sober.

My mom's drinking got so bad that on New Year's Eve, she told my dad that something was wrong. She had been trying to sober up from her five-to-six-week binge. She was complaining about chest pains. My dad took her to the emergency room. She had suffered a mild heart attack, which the doctor had said was more than likely brought on by the drinking.

While she was in the hospital, my dad and I had found at least forty various-sized bottles of vodka. This wasn't the first time we had witnessed this before, but I think we were really shocked because we both thought these more than forty bottles were just from the recent binge, not others before. When my mother drank, she barely ate, kind of slept during the day, keeping us up at night, and drank pretty much with that intensity for weeks nonstop.

She went to a sober house a few days after she got out of the hospital, but after a month or so, she showed up at the apartment and ran to her bedroom. She was back at it. Obviously, that heart attack didn't stop her or scare her.

Coincidently, someone from the sober house had just called after mom walked in and asked my dad if she was there. The doorbell rang almost immediately after she came in. My dad's face and mine were priceless. I wondered, *What did she do now?* Two San Diego policemen were at our door asking for her. The story was that she was driving on the wrong side of the freeway. A couple saw this and followed her while also calling 911. She was arrested and placed in handcuffs at the apartment. My dad went to pick her up hours later. She didn't completely sober up, and she didn't go back to the sober house.

Less than a week later, I was in the parking lot of our apartment complex with my son asleep in his car seat. We had just come back from the mall, and I was waiting for him to wake up. I had been there for only about ten minutes when I saw my mother drive up. I looked in my rearview mirror as she passed by. She stopped behind my car and waved. Oliver woke up just then, and I gathered our things and got him out of the car. I found it curious that my mom had chosen to park so far away when there were open spaces near where I had parked, which was near the entrance to get into the complex. Something told me to wait for her as she walked to us. That was her big mistake—to park so far away. She zigzagged all the way as she walked toward us. I couldn't believe I had just gotten off the road with my son, her grandson, and here she was drinking and driving again so soon!

She had always done it, though. Drinking and driving came with the territory I grew up in. It was accepted. It was tolerated. I even did it when I had a drinking problem. It seemed like it was something that could never harm, much less kill somebody. We had never learned anything, even after her first car accident in Houston that almost killed her. She was never scared enough to stop doing it. But I was, now that I was a mother.

I went upstairs and called the city attorney who was working on her case from her previous incident just a week earlier. He told me to call the police. I had her arrested again, a citizen's arrest. It was the first time in our family history that I know of that any one of us took a stand like that against her and this selfish disease. Even though the police hadn't seen her drinking and driving, there was enough evidence to have her arrested. Her car engine was still warm and the fact that I'd testify that I had seen her driving while she was still drunk was enough to do it.

At her trial, three of her daughters wrote letters to the judge about her history behind the wheel while she drank. She ended up spending more than sixty days in jail, where she supposedly made friends and knitted. Nothing changed.

At the time she was getting out of jail, I made plans to move back to L.A. with a little help from an old client I had kept seeing after I left Mike's business. He wanted to help me again. But this time, he said that it wouldn't even matter if I didn't want to see him on a sexual level. I had to go. I couldn't live with my mother any longer.

When I was seven and a half months pregnant, I was physically fighting with her while she was intoxicated. She wanted to be in our faces, verbally attacking us, sometimes even throwing stuff at my father. I wanted peace, tranquility, and for her to stay in her room. So the fights were more of her pushing to stay in our space and me pushing her to go back to her room and leave us in peace, but it was still fighting. I didn't want my child to see stuff like that or hear her ranting and raving and being vulgar. No child should be witness to that. I wish I hadn't and had someone who would have loved me enough to keep me away from things like that.

A few weeks later, I had Oliver baptized at the mission up the street. Leah from Oxnard came; she was to be his Godmother. There was commotion over Candelaria and Mom attending, because even though everyone didn't speak of what went on, they did get angry with one another at times about it. Nothing happened at his baptism, and Oliver was baptized just in case this religion thing had it all right in the end. I wanted to make sure I had our bases covered. I didn't and still don't follow any organized religion. I just sometimes like to be careful, because I don't know what is going to happen in the end or who we will meet when our time is up. Oliver has faith, is spiritual, and has love for humankind. Isn't that all we all could ask for from our children?

Emilio Manuel Montero-
Meyerhuber, Great Grandfather.
Owner of the Hacienda in
Caucato Alto and Mayor of
Pisco.
Married to Dolores Marie
Messler.
Portrayed with Samurai armor,
part of the Collection of Arms in
Peru's Gold Museum. Photo
taken approx. in 1924 at the
Hacienda in Caucato Alto.

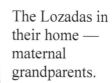

The Lozadas in
their home —
maternal
grandparents.

Maternal grandmother.

Me and my maternal grandmother in Peru in front of her house.

Me, Christmas in Ohio.

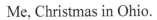

One of my birthdays in Ohio. Birthdays and Christmases were important in our family.

In my bedroom in Houston.
Nothing but wall-to-wall
Duran Duran wallpaper.

Ninth grade school pic.
Still going back and forth between being
clean-cut and not. Wearing my pearls.

At my sister's graduation, with
my partially shaved head.

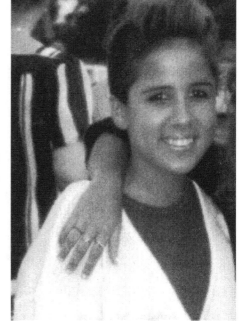

My Oxnard days.

The days in the biz.

A night at Roxburys.

Up in the Hollywood Hills at a party, 5 ½ months pregnant.

One Love
Kiki ♡
It's been a long time but
I'm glad 2 have regained
contact with u.
Keep YA HEAD UP!
You'll be a great mother
I have No doubt
about it ☺!

CRAZ

I'd like to be the sort of friend
That you have been to me;
I'd like to be the help
That you've been always glad to be;
I'd like to mean as much to you
Each minute of the day
As you have meant, old friend of mine,
To me along the way.
— Guest

It is written, Man shall not live by
bread alone, but by every word that
proceedeth out of the mouth of God.
Matthew 4:4

2Pac's card that was with the letter he sent me while he was at Clinton Correctional Facility.

8

Changes

We moved to Los Angeles into a clean, airy, bright studio apartment on the Westside. Oliver was five and a half months old. Guadalupe had just gotten married, and during her honeymoon, she found out she was pregnant. A few months later, she set a restraining order against my parents. She had finally gotten into therapy, and she didn't like how things were still going on. Why such a drastic measure, cutting ties with her parents? I understood where she was coming from. Mom and Dad had always made us feel a life of uncertainty. It felt like they had no bounds on what they would do to us. Guadalupe had it in her mind that if my parents wanted to, they could take her to court, say she was a pot smoker and so on, to take her unborn child from her.

Guadalupe wrote a letter to our parents explaining why she was doing what she was doing and sent each of us a copy. Paoletta didn't understand the letter and why Guadalupe was cutting ties with Mom and Dad. I'm not sure if it ever reached Candelaria at that point because she might not have been sober yet. But I felt that my sisters didn't understand where Guadalupe was coming from, and they were then making up their minds to trust our parents. And one thing life should have taught us was that we could never trust our parents. If we felt we could at times, we'd be sadly disappointed. It wasn't that they lied to us; they just could never follow through on things they said or put the welfare of their children—and now grandchildren—first.

Guadalupe and her husband ended up moving out of state because they couldn't be where my parents were. I understood. I don't think Guadalupe spoke to our parents for about eight years and even longer to Paoletta, because Paoletta took it personally and cut ties with Guadalupe after the letter. *Crazy drama.*

A week before I moved back to L.A., Mr. Laker Guy called Morgan looking for me and asked her to have me call him. I hadn't spoken to him since the day I had Oliver and he called me in the hospital to congratulate me. I thought I'd just wait to call him when I moved up there. Looking back, I wonder why he wouldn't stop giving me hope on us working it out.

By the time I got around to calling him, his phone number had been changed. I wrote him a letter. He somehow received it the next day and called me at 8:00 the next morning. He came over within thirty minutes. That was it. We talked about getting back together. *Yes!* But I never heard from him again.

I was shattered. I thought I could possibly have something with him, possibly have children with him (he said in San Diego that he wanted to begin to try to have a baby with me three months after Oliver was born). I don't know what happened. We never saw each other again.

It was mid-April when we moved back to L.A. Even though I had the same friends, I had new priorities. I knew and felt life was going to be different. It had to be. By the time my son was fifteen months old, I'd return to school to accomplish my goal, getting a college education. Somehow, I knew I'd be the only one who was going to provide for the both of us, and I wasn't going to do it as a high school dropout. I knew we'd live in poverty if I didn't move forward with my education.

During college, I chose to no longer hang out with my friends who were chasing ballplayers or going to the clubs. I easily let go of my relationship with Morgan after one day when I told her I couldn't make it to her barbeque because Oliver and I were sick. She said, "You need to work more on our relationship." I couldn't manage going out to all her events or get-togethers, and I really didn't even want to. I had enough of our so-called friendship. We had some fun times, and she was funny, but we were quite different. Also, she had not treated me great at times. And, like always, I was easy prey because usually I wouldn't lash back or even say anything in response.

One time at Roxburys we were sitting at a booth in the VIP room. She and a friend of hers were talking about me. It was about a week or two after a Clippers player whose attention both of them tried so hard to get ended up hitting on me instead. Maybe they were still mad or jealous. But that night at Roxburys, they tried to make me feel bad about myself because I was in a pretty black cocktail dress, sitting up on the top part of the booth. Everybody back in the day did that. You could look down onto Sunset Boulevard and scope out the scene in the club. It completely backfired on them because Tommy Davidson from *In Living Color* came up to me, grabbed my hand, and told me that he and his friends were talking about how they thought I was beautiful. He said this as he and his friends Martin Lawrence,

David Alan Grier (also from *In Living Color*), and another guy were walking out of the club. It almost brought tears to my eyes because the whole evening "my girl" was making me feel bad about myself, and then someone had just reached out to me to lift up my spirit.

Another night at Bar One, Morgan was talking to me about a ballplayer she liked. She was carrying on about, "What is he thinking by having a girlfriend who is a single mother? Single mothers are held down because of their children. They don't have the freedom like single women do or I do." Morgan made it sound like all single mothers should be on the bottom of the totem pole when it came to good, eligible bachelors looking for a mate. Did she forget who she was talking to across the table?

Like always, I was stunned. I didn't say anything back to her. Our friendship was never truly a friendship but a mutual likeness for the same things—the clubs, the parties, tall, dark men, and going to Lakers games. We were now leading different lifestyles. I couldn't keep up, and I didn't want to. All my life I had never wanted to marry, so I was never looking for someone to "take care of me." She was. I knew I wanted children but had never thought of how hard it would be raising a child on my own. She would've never dared doing it on her own. Somehow, thankfully, I just knew what it would take to make a better life for my son and me, so letting go of being a Hollywood club girl was easy.

I stopped drinking again. I had started a little bit after I moved back, but I was done because it wasn't good for me. I tried to keep focus on the important stuff—working on my personal emotional growth, school, and always and forever Oliver.

I moved back not really thinking of what I was going to do to support us. I had saved some money from before I moved to San Diego, and I knew at some point that I was going to go back to school, but I never thought about work. John helped me out with the initial move, but we depended on welfare. John, the only regular I kept in touch with after I left the business, wanted to completely take care of us, but I didn't want to rely on him. I knew I had to keep in touch with him, though, just in case I needed him later on. The stakes were higher at that time with having to support my son and not living in the environment we were in. I needed a security net, and John always offered that. I wanted to never have to depend on my parents or be without a home. Losing the house in Houston made a big impact on me to this day such that one thing I put before even food is shelter. I will go without food before I skip on rent. I will also not move into a place where the rent is too high in fear of not being able to pay that amount at some given time. I still thought I might need to put myself through sacrificing my body for rent rather than live in the chaos that my parents brought. It was such a dilemma. I knew someday I'd no longer have to even think about that, and that was why school was so important to me. Giving my body for an hour if I needed to wasn't going to take a toll on me psychologically like when I was in "the business" and felt unworthy. I just had to keep in touch with this guy, and it truly annoyed me because I still needed someone other than myself to depend on, and he was just annoying and could be a jerk at times.

People can ask, why have a child if you can't afford barely to take care of yourself? I didn't want to be on welfare, much less be this financially strapped. Going on welfare was the second-lowest point in my life. I had never imagined I'd end up there. No one, I'm sure, ever thought any one of us could end up there. I don't remember ever thinking badly about it, but it was always so far away from being anything we'd have to worry about or think of. It was always other people's problems. I always felt there were so many degrees of separation that I never really knew anybody on welfare until my final year in Oxnard. And finally, when I found myself pregnant and abandoned by the baby's father, I knew I had to sign up for some governmental assistance.

I hadn't been working for a few months, legitimate work, before Oliver was conceived. I did work a real job for a little while in San Diego, but eventually, the savings would run out. I remember when I went into apply in the L.A. office for aid within two weeks of finding out I was pregnant. The office, located on Pico Boulevard on the Westside, had to have been one of their first offices for social services in Los Angeles. It was a run-down building that appeared to be from the early 1960s. When you walked in it, it looked like it hadn't been touched for decades. There were rows of chairs, around fifty in all. People were also standing around, and some were walking around, talking to themselves. I took a number and sat down. I remember sinking into my chair, crying. I was in a large room with not only other people like me and their little children but with people who looked like they had just gotten out of prison and people who appeared to be homeless and seeing or talking to something or someone that wasn't there. I hadn't ever been around that. I was frightened and so sad that I ended up there.

As I attended to my morning sickness and drew some saltines out of my purse, I wondered what my grandparents would have thought. It wasn't supposed to be like this. I wasn't supposed to end up there. My lineage would've been shocked, but all I can now say and realize is that anyone can end up there, broke and with nowhere else to turn. There is no shame to be had; things happen. Fortunately, I was in a country where I could get help for me and my baby. When I later moved back to L.A., I didn't live too far from that office. I'd pass it regularly and remember that day. They eventually tore it down.

When I found out I was pregnant, I didn't think I could get pregnant, so I decided that I was keeping my baby, despite constantly hearing about giving the child up for adoption. I couldn't have ever lived through that because I had always wanted a baby. I thought it was a fluke when I got pregnant with Oliver. I did go through the torment and sadness of how was I going to give this baby what he deserved and needed, but pushed those feelings down. As I look back, I wasn't willing to give up or abort the baby, as it might have been my only shot at having a child. I think, knowing myself, if I hadn't kept my baby, I wouldn't be alive today. I was so lost still at that time, and it seemed like life threw me challenges so often that I felt I couldn't get through them. I still might have lost myself in alcohol or drugs or just given up entirely on living if I didn't have this love in my life who needed me. I know that I made the right choice in having him and keeping him, even though many people close to me suggested adoption. It is sad that finances are such an issue in these cases and judgments are made. It might sound selfish, but he was a blessing that saved me, and I had to use any avenue it took to help us survive.

I spent some of the most serene, beautiful moments of my life all summer long with my son in 1995, right after we moved back. This remarkable little boy brought me certain purpose to care about myself, heal myself, and do the best I could for the two of us. From the start, I saw beauty and *real* love, unconditional love, not just words. By taking care of him, he showed me gratitude and kindness. He showed me true love and his need for me to take care of him and put him first. It was inspiring and the most beautiful gift I have ever been given.

One day, coming back to our apartment from spending a

lovely, warm, sunny Southern Cali day outside was the person I'd spend the next seven and a half years with off and on. His name was Carter. He was in the laundry room, which was right in front of my apartment. His dog ran out of the room, and I leaned down to pet it. His owner called out to him, and I looked up. I had to take a second look, because by first glance he looked very attractive. I gave him a smile and went into my apartment.

Days and days passed, but from then after, I kept on running into him and his dog. I got to know him more and more because he played a lot with Oliver. When he saw us, he'd have a light conversation with me while gushing over my baby. It seemed sometimes there was an interest in one another, and sometimes I thought it was just all in my mind. I also tried to ignore it because my mind was still on Mr. Laker Guy and what could have been.

Carter eventually gave me his number and said to call him if I needed anything. We had our first kiss on October 3, and somehow, I would spend the next seven and a half years with him, even though I knew three weeks in that I'd never want to marry him or have his children. It is amazing the stupid things I get myself into without thinking, but then I'd have these moments of certainty like knowing I wasn't going to end up with Carter (and didn't want to) and knowing I was going to raise my son all by myself.

On October 14, I ran into Keith, a friend of Joshua's, in my apartment complex. He brought Joshua by, and Joshua saw his son twice. The first time he came over was with some random chick, and I do mean "chick", it couldn't be the one he was engaged to a year earlier because this one looked cheap in the way she dressed and how her hair looked, kinda greasy. The two of them were kind of laughing at me and saying how the baby looked nothing like him. I was stunned at how mean they were being; all the while, this chunky, beautiful baby was sitting on the floor looking up at them.

Like always, I didn't lash back. I should've yelled at them and told them to get the fuck out of my apartment.

The next time Joshua saw Oliver was one week after Oliver's first birthday a few weeks later. Joshua came with Keith that time. Joshua came and grabbed Oliver out of my arms and was holding on to him like he was his long-lost son, which I guess he was. He even held his cheek to his son's cheek. He ended up giving me $100 for his "friend's" (me) baby's first birthday. We spoke a few times over the phone after that, and he said that he'd pay me $400 a month for child support, but he couldn't be a part of his son's life; he was still not ready to be a father. Eventually, he stopped calling and disconnected his number. I never saw Keith again, and I wouldn't have contact with Joshua for years.

When I met Carter, I was a single mother on welfare. I came from this alcoholic, abusive family. I had begun heavily drinking at fifteen, lost my virginity to a rape, and was doing drugs at sixteen, and I also dropped out of high school for the last time at seventeen. I hadn't really had a boyfriend, and I recently had this life of selling my body so that I could live independently, not having to live with my parents, and that I could also afford to continue to put myself through school. When he met me, he was still living with his ex-girlfriend; at least that is what he told me at first. He also had two boys for whom he barely paid child support, and he didn't have a job. We were a match made in heaven!

As writer Stephen Chbosky said, "We accept the love we think we deserve." Maybe I was just craving attention. He showered Oliver and me with attention. He was very nice and wanted to cook for us all the time. He wasn't an addict and had never used drugs, and when he drank, he didn't drink to excess. But he was more immature and screwed up than I realized at first. He was all into himself. He was extremely active in sports a little too much because he'd be playing up to three sports every week, rarely taking one day off. He'd do this rather than invest time looking for a job to support himself and keep current with his child support. It even took a toll on his relationships with his sons and then later with me, because he'd rather play his sports than spend time with us. What was really wrong with him besides those things was that he was one of the biggest cheaters and liars I've ever met or known in my life, but I wasn't going to piece that all together right away.

No matter what he said about not being with the ex when we first met, I believed within weeks that he was. I'd be hurt by the fact that he was still living with her, even if he said he was just sleeping on the couch. He'd tell me he had to stay there to recoup the rental deposit they put down on the apartment and that it was just a few months more until their lease was up. We'd spend a lot of time together because she was working and we weren't. It was easy sometimes to convince myself that he was telling the truth; how else could we have been able to go out all the time?

But deep down I knew what was real; call it woman's intuition. This was probably why I knew within a few weeks that I didn't want to spend the rest of my life with him or have his children. I was calling it quits one day, and then we'd find ourselves back together days later. It was typical ACOA behavior; this is a characteristic. It had always seemed that I got involved with guys who were already taken, but as I look back, maybe it was a security measure that I searched for. Maybe by choosing unavailable guys I therefore wouldn't get hurt as much. I can't really understand why I would only end up with guys who were either taken or didn't want something serious. I knew I always wanted something serious, but I remember being a child—my mom would bring this up over the years—and asking my mom, "I don't have to get married if I don't want to?"

She'd always say to me, "No, you don't have to get married if you don't want to." I never wanted to get married. I had always wanted to be in a monogamous relationship, though.

Why did I never want to get married? I think I was always fearful of having something like my parents had. I probably thought all marriages were like what my parents had, and as a child back in Ohio, I knew early on I didn't want that. I'd rather be on my own if it meant otherwise having that kind of love in my life. That wasn't any type of love I wanted. I also grew up thinking that men would cheat. I didn't want that, either. I grew up hearing about my father's affairs, true or not, from my mother when she was drunk. Maybe it was because of this that I believed for so long that men couldn't be faithful.

A close childhood friend of mine from Houston recently told me that my rape probably has something to do with my relationship issues also, which is one thing I had never thought of before she mentioned it. Also, I always say, thankfully, I hadn't gone after guys who wanted a relationship with me, because then maybe I would've gotten beaten like my sisters had by their boyfriends. I believe pretty much, unfortunately, that all but a few of their relationships were physically abusive. We learn what we learn.

Maybe I needed more time to grow so that I wouldn't fall prey to a relationship like that. All along, I'd see that I'd also pick guys more like my father's distant side. And up until a few years ago, I did believe that all men would lie about infidelity all the way to their graves—even Oliver's father, for example. I knew that I wasn't the only one. I even had Oliver's father continuously tell me he wasn't seeing anyone else, even though I knew that he was and later found out the truth on that mid-December night at the club. But Carter would turn out to be the worst of them all.

By the fall of 1995, I returned to school, majoring in a practical major that I knew would get me a good job—business administration—instead of photography, my true love. Throughout the next few months, I put up with the fact that I was becoming too attached to someone who lived with someone else. It tore me apart at times. Even though I didn't want to be married, I could latch on to someone and have serious feelings.

By April, Carter and his ex moved out of their apartment and went their separate ways. He moved back home with his parents. How his ex kept on dealing with him all those months prior, I don't know, but how or why did I? She had caught us one night as we were trying to leave in her car to go to the movies. All along she knew, but I'm sure he continuously denied it to her, lying to her, as well. He later said he lied to her for the sake of her not doing any harm to me. She really lost it the night she caught us in the parking garage trying to leave. For the following couple of hours, you could hear them screaming, and later, I could hear her crying up and down the hallways and that was when I definitely knew 100 percent that they had been together all along.

The next month after they moved out, Oliver and I moved out of the studio apartment. We moved into a one-bedroom apartment down the street. Carter was more available and able to spend the night more often. I remember the first week he spent four consecutive nights with us. I thought it was great at the time.

A month later, I was ending my second semester back at school. I was finally on track for the first time really with the goal of getting a degree. Before that, I think I was just pursuing the act of learning, only a few required classes, as well. Prior to this, I had taken African American history classes, human sexual development classes, and my photography classes. I was a full-time student, a full-time mom (and dad) to a toddler, and I was also now a girlfriend. I thought I was managing my life, but throughout the following year, I came across a side of me that I had never seen before.

The time I spent in therapy I never really got angry. A therapist once mentioned how detached I seemed. She said that I spoke of things just as a matter of fact, almost like they were situations that had nothing to do with me.

I, the sweet, nice, quiet one, was now angry and irritable a lot of the time, and this came out around Carter and Oliver, which was very difficult for me when I noticed it was going on for a while, and I couldn't control it. Once, I hit Oliver on the bottom, and I burst into tears right after. I had never wanted to lay a hand on my children. I couldn't believe myself and my actions.

I was on edge most of the time. I knew I had to get control of myself and my emotions. I didn't want to harm my child like I was harmed. I didn't believe in spanking or any kind of violence toward children. I believed good discipline was intensive explanation and taking away privileges. I knew I had to go back to therapy and somehow fit it into my schedule and figure out how to pay for it. I did, but I didn't stick with it, because I saw a new therapist for a month or so, and it seemed she couldn't keep her eyes open. She'd doze off while I tried to talk about my issues.

I tried looking for the old therapist I had been going to years earlier, Dr. Brian from Oxnard. Once, I tried to schedule my next appointment with the therapist who couldn't stay awake; she was all booked up for the following week. She referred me to a part-time therapist, Dr. Mara. I saw her, and I ended up staying with her for about a year and half.

Within months, I realized my depression had existed pretty much since my preadolescence. It was something I'd really have to work on. She helped me cope with the new stress in my life and some of my past issues. I liked her, but I think I was having a hard time paying, even though I was on a sliding scale, so I had to stop seeing her. This therapy helped me to be who I am now and helped me start thinking with a different perspective.

A few months passed, and Tupac had been shot, who, at the time when I moved back to L.A., wrote me back from jail and gave me the encouragement and confidence I needed for being a single mother. It was rare for me to ever hear words like those he wrote, and that was even while he was going through a series of problems himself, like being behind bars. In his letter, he had turned the focus on me and was selfless. He was so happy that I wrote to him. We had a newfound friendship, and he told me to tell Oliver's father how "Uncle 2Pac" was going to be there for us. He just had a love and appreciation for

Oliver and me that I cherish.

One night, some girlfriends and I were having dinner at Roxburys. Anna, a girlfriend of Morgan's, came to our table when we were finishing dinner. She came to tell us that Tupac was out of jail and that he was up in the VIP, but she said this not knowing I knew him. Morgan turned to me and said, "Go up and see him. All we're doing is waiting for the check."

I went up with Anna and entered the crowded VIP room, passing the bar and stepping down the one step to where the booths were. I finally got a glimpse of the back of him, and he turned around. Immediately, he hollered my name. He lifted me in his arms. And as he was placing me back down to earth, I noticed everyone staring, especially two females who looked at me like, "Who is she?" I was shocked by these two women, because they looked like Faith Evans and Mary J. Blige. I could swear it was them, but didn't make sure because I was too focused on reuniting with my friend. He and I spoke for a bit. I wanted to excuse myself because now way too many people were staring, probably wondering who I was, and I felt uncomfortable. I don't like to be stared at, especially by many people.

The next time I saw him was at a Mother's Day event at the Beverly Wilshire hotel in Beverly Hills, where Uncle 2Pac walked up to me, took Oliver out of my arms, and then greeted me. Even though we exchanged numbers, that would be the last time I'd see him again.

On September 13 (another Friday the thirteenth), Tupac passed away. He had been shot a week prior. It was reported in the news that his mom said he could barely hold on. She was an inspirational single mother he had reflected on in his letter to me while he was in jail. She supposedly took him off life support and let him go. This was exactly five years from the day Lily died. Tupac Amaru Shakur was gone. The rapper, actor, son, and friend to me was dead. This guy that was named after a Peruvian Incan king was never going to be able to make any more changes in this lifetime. Someone who gave me the encouragement that I was going to be a great mother and was Uncle 2Pac to Oliver was never going to have a chance to make a complete change to how the media always pigeonholed him to being this thug. I knew him as this guy with a sense of humor who was in awe of where his life was going.

He was a truly talented guy that I hadn't realized until one day, when I was using his bathroom, I noticed a journal on the floor. I was nosy, so I opened it up. I was amazed to find his poetry, which would later be most of the songs we still hear on the radio today. I knew he was gifted; it looked like it flowed out of him magically. Tupac was someone who reached out to me when I needed someone. His words felt sincere. He had no doubt that I could be a great mother and raise my son on my own. His view of me was something I never felt from myself or my parents. I also wasn't hearing words like that during this time and it was encouraging. Because of this, I have always truly missed him.

After his death, I went into a deep depression not because he meant the world to me but because I have always thought that death cheats people out of their possibilities in this lifetime; the what-ifs are there, but the person is not. Dying at an early age sucks! Now I found myself driving to school one morning, and I was wondering why everyone was rushing to work or somewhere else, killing themselves to make that mighty dollar. Was this what life had become? Why even bother? It could all end in an instant. That was my state of mind after his death.

The thought of Lily's death again and all the other friends who lost their lives too early were getting to me emotionally. Thankfully, I had Dr. Mara to go and see, but it got so bad that she also referred me to a psychiatrist. I didn't like the thought of going on drugs for mental reasons, and that is what psychiatrists recommended. I had no problem seeing Dr. Mara because she had a PhD in psychology. Psychologists don't have a license to prescribe medication.

I had grown up with an addict. Not only was my mother addicted to alcohol and was a chain-smoker but she also had many prescriptions from therapists over my lifetime that I grew up seeing on her nightstand. I saw this as another one of her handicaps—using pills to resolve her issues. But they didn't resolve anything for my mother. For more than thirty years, she had seen so many psychiatrists and was prescribed many pills, but it never helped, or she never allowed it to help her. I was frightened to become like that, but I had to get out of the mental state I was in. I didn't want my child to be around the lethargic, withdrawn-from-life, negative, suicidal, depressed me that I had sometimes been and was now venturing back into becoming. To add to my list of daily-weekly things, I was now including a psychologist and a psychiatrist and was checking in with the city mental health department that helped pay and watch me to make sure I had the correct cocktail. I had my plate full.

Months swept by. I got over my suicidal thoughts. I continued with the treatment that helped me learn to psychoanalyze myself. I questioned my thoughts, my feelings, and my circumstances—and still do at times because it helps me either get out of a bad situation or keeps me away from doing stuff that will just hurt me in the end. Self-analyzing isn't perfect, and I'm human and don't do it all the time, but I do do it.

I eventually got off of the medication. I was still in school at SMC, but Carter and I were having more problems. We had always had problems since day one. That was why I was so off and on with him. I knew he wasn't honest. Sometimes it seemed like I could really count on him, but then most of the time he wouldn't follow through, which was a trait I knew very well. He was never, ever on time, which was one of my pet peeves from childhood. We'd always be rushing late to a movie. I don't think we ever saw a movie from the beginning. I never felt as if I were a priority even though we spent a lot of time together. Carter was the priority. He was just working us into his life, after all the sports he played and after his family; then came Oliver and I, then his sons, then work or making money—and in that order.

We spent a lot of time together, but our relationship was very unpredictable. I continued pushing Carter away and pulling him right back, maybe out of neediness or just that I had become comfortable with having him around. But when I look back now, the patterns are those that mimic my childhood and a childhood from an alcoholic home—the unpredictability, the very good moments along with the very bad, the not feeling good enough or valued enough from the other person, the chaos of never being on time and rushing around. He reminded me of my mother and her unpredictable self. They both are people that think or move through life being late and that just reflects that only their time is important, even if they have a loved one waiting on them. It is a very selfish and self-centered act.

Even with being in therapy, the anger and irritability somewhat remained. It was part of the low-level depression. I was learning to be a mother while being in school full-time and trying to be the girlfriend of a guy who rarely had a job and who I always felt was cheating on me. I wasn't even a whole, mature person, so having someone like him that was so imperfect was a burden in my life.

I cannot explain why I stayed with him for seven and a half

years. I try not to beat myself up about this period of time, especially when I think I wasted *all my pretty* on him. I think it was all a huge, long lesson. I knew he was with a girl when I met him. I had heard of him with other girls at parties, but I just pushed it to the side, never wanting to face the truth. I guess maybe I was just accepting it because I didn't value myself enough. I knew he didn't have a job and rarely had any money. I knew he was in arrears with his two sons' child support payments. I knew—*he did him,* playing sports all the time rather than see his boys or look for a job. I knew the only way we were going to go out of town together was if some sports league was out of town and he was playing. I knew when I offered to help him put a down payment on a car with the $3,000 I had gotten from financial aid for school that it would be a mistake; he still owes me about $1,200, and what he paid was a constant fight and battle to get out of him.

I rationalized that he wasn't abusive in the way I knew abuse. He did very much mistreat me, and in the end, I saw that he was actually more damaged than I had ever been. I knew that I never wanted to end up with him, but I allowed it to continue for too long. I was obviously still damaged and messed up myself, but thankfully, a little piece of me wanted better.

In 1999, I finally earned my associate's degree in business administration at Santa Monica College. SMC was where I finally started to come out of my shell. I think my speech class helped me a lot because I had to stand up in front of the class finally, willingly, for the first time in my life. I gave speeches on things that affected me like being an ACOA or opinions I had on other subjects.

I loved the classes in which I was recognized for my viewpoints and enthusiasm to learn, like an English class at Orange Coast College where I could write about my ideas on abuse and prostitution. I liked my human sexual development classes that actually had a lot to do with psychology and learned behavior. At that time in my life, I was seriously thinking and cultivating my own thoughts. I'd definitely miss this and I would miss SMC especially.

Carter and Oliver were the only ones to see me graduate to get my first degree, even though my family got invited. My mom to this day says she never received the invitation, but I'm sure she did. She was probably just drunk and placed it somewhere that she could not remember or she discarded it and couldn't remember that she had.

A few months later, I was working full-time for the first time in a long time, a real corporate job, working alongside ex–FBI agents and an ex-sheriff. Being in Beverly Hills, it wasn't a very impressive office because the official new office was still under renovations a few floors up. My first day, I had to wait for someone to arrive, because I hadn't received a key to the office yet. As I waited, I paced in the hallway almost in tears because this was my leap and bound to growing up and being an adult, doing adult things, and being completely responsible, but all I wanted was to be a child and to be taken care of. I couldn't turn back. I knew I needed to grow up and take care of my baby, even though part of me felt like I was a baby. I was already twenty-nine years old! Part of me just wanted some of what everyone should have—an innocent, long childhood with minimal worries. I missed mine, or at least it was taken from me way too quickly.

This firm was an interesting place to work. It was a small office with just about six people. I was the receptionist and the assistant to the president of the company. My boss was ex-FBI, and he really wanted to know all the details about me. He also liked to test me by seeing how I would react in different situations. He was a good man, but he was FBI, and it takes a certain type of person, possibly someone who is always analyzing, testing us all the time to see if we would break. He was always profiling everyone.

He helped me out years later to do a background check on Joshua, which helped me start getting the information I needed to go through the court system. I also learned that Joshua had been well off all those years, so he could have paid for child support, and we wouldn't have needed to struggle like we did.

It eventually felt good to be working and taking care of Oliver without financial aid or being on welfare. Life seemed to be turning out pretty nicely. Within a year, though, I remembered my intention was always to get a bachelor's degree. When I wanted to go back to school, I knew that I didn't want to take the business route anymore, because I could barely get through my second accounting class, and I found no real interest in accounting.

Interestingly enough, years later, I found myself doing a lot of accounting at my jobs. It's strange how things work out that way. I had always thought for the most part that I wanted to get my bachelor's degree and that it in itself would be one of the biggest accomplishments of my life—if I could do it. I had wanted it to override the fact that I dropped out of high school in the tenth grade. I would choose what I love—art—as my major. But I had this decent-paying job in the heart of Beverly Hills and I had to figure out a way to go back to school.

I spent a year or two working at the private investigation firm. After I started this job, I decided that now it was finally time to stop seeing or keeping in contact with John for good. I hadn't seen him often since my return to L.A. About a month or so when the paychecks started to come in was when I stopped seeing him. He had already starting declaring he wanted more out of our relationship, but it was always just business to me. He was going through a divorce and had a vision of us, hoping to start a new chapter with me. From the start, in my mind, the only way I could wrap my head around doing what I was doing was that I was providing a service. I didn't even recognize it as cheating when I was with Carter. Though it may sound heartless, it was always just a business transaction to me. I felt as if I were the only one really being taken advantage of and being hurt, because this business continuously reinforced that I was only good enough to have sex with men and that my looks and body were the only things I had to offer. If some of the guys that I had seen may have thought they really had feelings for me, they were under an illusion I created. I acted the whole time and was not myself. They didn't know me. Besides, I felt more like a confidante during a time when John needed someone the most. Most of the time, we would just meet for lunch to talk. About six months after I started at that job, he gave me some money. It'd be the last time he gave me cash. I stored it away for a rainy day.

When I started at the job, Carter and I weren't together; we were on our biggest hiatus. I had broken up with him for days, sometimes weeks or months here and there, but this was the longest—a year and a half! I just would get so upset with him because either I wouldn't stop hearing about other girls or he was never really fully committed. He also never helped me pay rent when he pretty much stayed with us all the time and ate all my food too. To outsiders, we really looked like the perfect couple; Oliver and I were always by his side. Wherever we'd hang out, he'd always have to fit in time to go play at the basketball courts.

I think we were showpieces for him for the most part. He'd even try to claim Oliver as his son because so many people found Oliver so adorable and asked Carter if he was his. He finally stopped saying it because I didn't like it, especially since he wasn't helping me financially support Oliver and wasn't his father. I wasn't going to add another deadbeat to the list, even if he spent time with Oliver.

What is interesting about how Carter loved to have us around was how it was when it came to his family. I think I only met his mother twice when he was picking something up from her place. I also met one of his sisters once or twice, but those times were brief. He really never brought me around his family, because he said that they wouldn't get me; they might think I was stuck up because I was so quiet. I also later heard from him during our fights that they actually didn't like me because I was a single mother on welfare. I found that amusing because his family lived in an area I'd never live in. I believe one of his sisters ended up on welfare, and I don't think at that time any of his immediate family had ever gone to college, and I was striving for better by doing so.

He had no problem bringing around this beautiful offspring I had created and was raising on my own, though. They loved Oliver. Even though I had my first boyfriend, I still wasn't treated like I was acceptable or good enough.

Toward the end of working at the PI firm, I may have just run into Carter one too many times at the park. He'd do that sort of thing, just show up where he thought Oliver and I would possibly be. I sometimes felt like he was circling around our area just to run into me. It felt creepy and flattering all at the same time. This time, he must have caught me at a vulnerable point in my day or at a time when I was just being the really nice girl from my childhood who wouldn't remember how badly I was mistreated before. I allowed him to come back into our lives, but within two months or so, I found out about some other girl that he had hooked up with about a week or so after we got back together. I'm a smart girl, but at this time in my life, I didn't ask better for myself.

After I found out about his hookup and we fought about it, he behaved for a while. He was scared to lose me again. He was very attentive and trying really hard to make us work. I was just existing; I was happy because I was comfortable with him, but I had never changed my mind about the fact that I didn't want to marry him or ever have children with him.

This time that we reunited, we laid everything out on the table, including what I had done for work years prior. He had assumed that was what I did to support myself, but he just needed to hear it from me. I never revealed to him that I had stayed in touch with one man so that I could still lean on him if I needed to. I stayed with Carter for another two years as I battled with him and this girl who ended up not being a one-time hookup but another girlfriend. It seemed like she came back in the picture about six months after he and I got back together. He'd drift back and forth between us. Though I never wanted a future with him, I found it too hard to let him go. I had been with him for so long.

He was the first guy that I brought around my family when they came to visit. My parents were very kind to him but really didn't like him for me. That is one thing to be said about my parents' manners: they are always very courteous to people.

Those last two years with him were the toughest; it was when I lent him cash to make a down payment to buy another used BMW that I never fully got repaid for. This was the time for at least the last year and a half when I definitely knew of someone else—no more suspicions. This was the time when we went to San Francisco for one of his football leagues and his friend's girlfriend and I paid for the hotel we all shared. His friend was another one of those guys that lived off of girls, like Carter did. *YUK! YUK! YUK!*

Thankfully, I had my breaking point one evening and wrote him a long letter that I delivered to his apartment where he lived with a roommate. I made a scene going there at 9:00 a.m., assuming the other chick was there. She was. He finally opened the door and let me in. He was so cool and collected as I cried and threw the letter in his face in the kitchen; all the while the other girl was standing there, leaning up against a kitchen table that I had given to him. All I can say is that I met someone more messed up than I ever was. He may even be a little bit of a psychopath. Who calmly stands there like nothing is wrong, cooking himself breakfast, while he has two females who have been battling each other for the last two years over which one is his girlfriend? It was truly messed up.

I only saw him once after that when I ran into him years later. All I could feel was disgust. Thankfully, I learned what I didn't want out of a guy or relationship. I later found out that there were at least eleven other women during the same time we were together. *So gross!* There were many lessons to learn from all this, but it would take me years to process how I let so many years go to waste on him. I learned two things for sure—that I did deserve better and that I definitely could get better.

After I left the PI firm, I enrolied at California State University in Northridge (CSUN). I had done one semester at another university but didn't like it, so I transferred out to go to CSUN. I began in the fall of 2001, majoring in art. I loved CSUN even though it was a half-hour commute. That money that I had saved for a rainy day helped me afford to go to school full-time, plus the money I was getting from financial aid. Oliver was in elementary school at a magnet school in Brentwood, a prominent city about fifteen minutes from where we lived. I'd drop him off and take classes all day about three times a week. I took many different types of art classes, including photography. I included children and family development courses, as well. My childhood had always interested me in how it truly impacted me and my sisters.

I excelled so much at CSUN that I was now on the dean's list. I was a high school dropout, now on the dean's list at a university. I had no doubt I was smart and that I could learn, but this was just proof.

About a year later and the savings was being spent, I looked for a job for the summer. I found a full-time job at a company in Santa Monica. The owner had two companies; one was an Internet, web hosting, and design company, and the other was an online retail store. He had two small offices near the Santa Monica Airport. I worked in one of his offices that had just two desks, his and mine with just about a foot in between the corners of our desks. I was going to help with the administration and billing. This was going to be my second real job. I had done retail and fast food, but those were entirely service-oriented companies with minimal education requirements.

I liked the people I worked with, except early on I saw signs that there might be an issue with the owner. He constantly fought with the lady in charge of sales and customer service for the online store. Also, he never gave anyone keys to the office, so we all had to wait for him to arrive to let us in. He also had file cabinets that were locked at all times, even though I was doing a lot of billing. He was obviously very paranoid and controlling. And when it came to our paychecks, he did them himself. I'd have to remind him to give me and the rest of his employees our paystubs, which I'd find later constantly needed corrections, and I'd find I was being underpaid. No one, besides the lady that later walked out on him one morning, questioned anything.

By the fall, I needed to work while I continued at school, because the savings were practically gone. Me returning to school didn't go over well, but my boss accepted it, and I accepted staying even with all these little issues I didn't like. I now somehow scheduled being a full-time single mom, a full-time student at CSUN, and working full-time along with participating at Oliver's school, being on the GATE Committee (Oliver was part of the Gifted and Talented Program through LAUSD since second grade), and helping out at the YMCA, which was located on campus. I did this so that I could get a lower tuition that I could afford. I somehow found it doable, but how, I do not know, because I've never been one of those people with a lot of energy. I'd just later feel how tired I was once I sat down, and then the yawning would set in.

I love that CSUN was a great experience for both Oliver and me. He stopped going to the YMCA because he preferred going to school with me. On days when he didn't have school, he completely opted out from hanging out at the Y. He'd prefer spending a full day at CSUN with me and my back-to-back classes with the exception of an hour for lunch. He'd sit on my drawing classes, where we drew from live nudes. I made no big deal of it, and he didn't, either. It was art. He'd take notes on the history of photography and be able to answer questions before any of the other students would because he was probably paying more attention. I'm happy CSUN never frowned upon children being on campus, because I believe this impressed upon Oliver that you should further your education and it is a fun and interesting experience.

The last semester at school was tough financially. Before the summer came to an end, I had to make a heartbreaking decision. Do I screw up my credit that had been outstanding for over a decade or do I continue with my last semester at school to get my degree that I had been pursing for more than twelve years? This was so hard for me, and I cried about it. My good credit covered all the scars that losing everything had caused and taken away from me as a teenager. I had always felt if I built up my credit that I would always be okay and safe, but I couldn't afford to pay my credit card bills and pay for school. I had to let the credit go. I valued my education more and what that could bring. I knew I could always build up my credit. I couldn't let go of my education that I had been trying to conquer for so long. I was too close.

9

Postapocalypse

In December of 2003, I completed my bachelor's degree that technically took me twelve years to get. It was a long journey, but I got there. I'm not embarrassed that it took me that long, either. At least I can say that I did it. I also completed it as a single mother. And I always said afterward if I had to choose between school and work that I would probably choose school. I loved learning, questioning the hows and whys. I'm the youngest of four girls, was uprooted to this country for my education (supposedly), and I did it.

The following June, I walked in my graduation. Everyone was invited. Graduation was on a Friday afternoon on campus, and I made plans to have a lunch at Gladstone's in Malibu the following day. My godmother flew in on Friday for the celebrations and stayed at the Bel-Air Hotel, which was her favorite place to stay. Oliver and I had visited her there once before when she and her husband, Tiyo, came into town. For my graduation weekend, Tiyo was going to join us for the lunch celebration only. He had to work on Friday and couldn't make it to my ceremony.

Guadalupe and her family came. They had been living in Northridge for the last year and we still had a decent sisterly relationship as only we knew how to. Candelaria and her husband came for the graduation but had to leave the following morning. Paoletta didn't come to the graduation, but she showed up to join in on the lunch celebrations. And my parents, this time, drove in from Arizona. My mother, I believe, is scared of flying; she hasn't flown in decades, so they made the long trek through the desert at their age. They stayed in my tiny apartment with us, just as everyone else would do if they were in town.

The weekend was interesting, because my mother and my godmother hadn't seen or spoken to each other since that day my mother called her drunk when I was sixteen, begging my godmother to take me in. All the while, all these years, my godmother was my support system, always encouraging me, saying, "You can do it! You're the star!" She had become my second mom.

Manners can make a very uncomfortable situation more

tolerable. My godmother was very diplomatic the day of my graduation walk. I think she spoke more to my dad than my mom, but who'd blame her? Besides, what would she have to say to my mother, especially when she heard about how my mother was never mentally, physically, or emotionally supportive? She knew my mother hadn't worked in years, so she could definitely not make small talk about work or even volunteering.

I was very emotional that hot summer day. I had the biggest smile, but I was also brought to tears as I sat there waiting to walk up to receive my diploma. The time left me alone to think of what I had done—accomplished. Besides having Oliver, it was my proudest achievement thus far.

The following day in Malibu was really nice. We sat down toward the back of Gladstone's that had full-length glass windows that over looked the Pacific Ocean and sands of Malibu. My family—minus Candelaria and her husband and my nieces and nephews—were there, along with my godparents and two girlfriends of mine, one being Leah from Oxnard and the other my coworker Nancy. I dressed very classily with the new pearl earrings and necklace set that my godmother had given me as a graduation gift. My godparents sat across from my parents with me sitting right next to my mother. It was a very happy moment for me, because I had accomplished so much, and nothing could take away from that, but I was frazzled getting there because—like always—my mother made us run late.

Two things stood out to me, but I didn't address them—Paoletta drank too much, and Guadalupe, knowing my godparents were paying for the lunch, ordered lobster, the most expensive thing on the menu. I found that disgusting and kind of rude. If it was her husband or her parents paying for the meal, yes, by all means, get the most expensive thing on the menu, but she wouldn't have if it were her parents or her husband taking care of the bill.

After lunch, my godparents and two girlfriends excused themselves and said good-bye. The rest of us hung out at the beach, Guadalupe and I playing and taking pictures with all the kids.

Life went on as before. I went back to work Monday morning, and Oliver went back to school. By this time, it had been more than a year that I didn't love my job. I guess I never really loved it. My boss was a micromanager and not very trustworthy even though he was the one who went around not trusting anyone. He was a tall, large man with not only a negative attitude but a bad temperament.

By this time, pretty much every paycheck needed to be corrected. I always had to remind him to print out a paycheck stub, which he hated. But I had every right to see how many hours I was being paid for. In a few weeks, my coworker and friend Nancy was moving back to Wisconsin, where she had family. He decided not to hire anyone right away to replace her but to save the money and have me take on most of her work. It wasn't like I didn't have enough work to do myself. I had taken this job just with the intention of it being a summer job, but then I returned to CSUN, and because I needed the income, I decided to stay. Now I began to realize that this was precisely why I went to college—to have a better life and better circumstances for Oliver and me, besides accomplishing a lifelong goal. Isn't that what a degree or two is supposed to give you—not having to limit yourself to working for fifteen dollars an hour and being confined to not be able to grow within a company?

I started really despising the situation. I saw how he micromanaged everyone and everything. I don't think he was intentionally mean; those were just his quirks. He didn't like me at times because I'd ask for the stubs, but as professional as I am, I bit my lip. Even when I have had people lash out at me verbally, I usually have never said anything back; I just walked away or stand there frozen. I hate confrontation. I'm always scared of what it could lead to, like a quick and unpremeditated assault.

Another year passed, and my boss finally hired someone to work for the retail store. Oliver was doing very well in the fifth grade. He was a well-adjusted, well-liked kid. Since preschool, he had been the boy that most of the kids wanted to be friends with, probably because he was raised in a gentle environment. He wasn't an aggressive, highly energetic boy, and he didn't have a hard time having a handful of girls who were just his friends. He is funny, compassionate, and sensitive to others and what they may be going through.

When Hurricane Katrina hit, he organized his school to do a backpack drive that sent backpacks to the kids in New Orleans and the surrounding areas. At this time, besides working full-time and taking care of Oliver by myself, I spent many hours at his school with the GATE committee, volunteering, or dropping in on the PTA from time to time. We'd spend our weekends at the park or seeing a movie and having lunch together. We'd get away and take vacations or play hooky and go to Disneyland. I had made it a point to get annual passes as often as I could, and he and I went quite a few times a year. These are precious memories I have and I hope that Oliver always remembers.

As a single mother, there were times when I needed that other person to help me with taking care of what needed to be taken care of when it came to my child. I didn't have that, but I made it work most of the time. Some may look at it as being stretched too thin, but thankfully, for the most part, it was easy. Oliver helped a lot by being a very good kid, never getting into trouble, and doing well in school, but toward the end of his fifth-grade year, I needed to run around and check out schools and do their tours. I needed to make a good decision about where to place him for middle school. Not everyone goes to the school that is in their vicinity, at least not in L.A. Because finances were always an issue and living in the area we lived in, I took Oliver out of his area schools from day one, and middle school was no exception.

There was a scheduled tour of one school that I needed to go to. Unfortunately, things like that are only on weekdays. Even though I had three vacation/personal days available to me at work, my request to take that day off to take the tour of the potential school was denied by my boss. He actually said through an e-mail that I needed to figure out like everyone else does to do my personal stuff on the weekends.

I have a world of patience. I've been told I'm too passive, but I'm human, and I do get fed up. There was no more biting my lip. I quit my job. I thought it wasn't right for him to say that to me not because I'm a single mother and should get leniency but because I had the available days to take off. And even though sometimes I find the nerve to put my foot down, I do get scared of the repercussions, like not having a job reference.

After the weekend, I cooled down and apologized, but we left it at that, and I no longer worked there. I'm always scared at first of the unknown but realize almost immediately that I make some right choices for myself. This was one of them.

I took six weeks off looking for a job and being really there with my child, picking him up right after school got out, playing with him, and making him dinner every night.

I take baby steps to do better for me and for my future and to stay on the path that I have tried so desperately to stay on. Things don't happen overnight, especially for me, and they obviously have not been easy, not knowing if I was making the right decisions or sometimes regressing to old patterns of behavior. My financial and work lives are no exception.

In January of 2006 after looking for a new job, I received a phone call regarding my résumé on Craigslist. It sounded like a job I could do, just reception and administrative work, but it really caught my attention because the company was very creative—dealing mainly in the beauty industry. If I wasn't going to do something creative for my line of work, at least I could be around something creative.

I went in and met with the lady who found my résumé, and I came back to have a second interview with the CEO of the company, Jonathan. It was a small start-up but was doing very well. They were a few years in and had another location in New York.

When Jonathan and I met and he offered me the job, he told me how he wasn't hiring me to answer the phones and sign FedEx packages because he knew I could do more than that. He said he and the controller needed an assistant. I accepted, even though everyone thought I wasn't going to return because there was a VP who came in complaining and yelling about how messy the office was. The office wasn't messy. For most of my life, I overlooked people's behavior and how badly they behaved. I never thought that maybe I wouldn't want to be around that. Also at that point, I really had no choice but to take the job because I found myself almost out of savings. Besides, this was a better-paying position. I was aware of the VP's behavior, but it didn't bother me. I had been around worse behaviors, and sometimes you just become immune to things you experience often.

I liked Jonathan and the controller. Jonathan spoke nicely to me and actually didn't require me to do much for him. I spent most of my days being trained on QuickBooks and how their billing worked. I felt left out almost immediately when it came to the girls. There were a group of them who went to lunch together, and I was never asked to go with them. The lady who had found my résumé online may have had her second thoughts after I started, because she and I didn't mesh after my first day. I think she realized I was hired for something other than what she intended me for. The controller's office was the very last office in the back, and she wasn't happy that I was away from my desk for most of the day. Three weeks into working there, she stopped me in the hallway, grabbing me with both hands at the top of my arms right below my shoulders and asked me, "What can I do to make you stay up here in the front?"

I was shocked. She was so abrasive. I'm surprised that I even answered her. She is a type A personality, coming off as very aggressive and overly assertive. I am the complete opposite. I told her, "I'm sorry, but Greg is training me. I'm sorry his office is in the back and I have to be back there."

From that day on, I really tried to not only put up a wall between us but to stay away from even having to speak to her. I was so shocked that someone, especially in a professional setting, would grab someone like that. Even though some behavior doesn't shock me, I dislike situations where there is confrontation or hostility, and this was one of those times.

Within six months, the controller was leaving the company. Thankfully, I was being trained by him all of those months, and instead of assisting him, I had been doing most of the invoicing, billing, and payroll for the company.

A year after I started, we moved to a large office on the Westside. This job was literally seven minutes from my apartment. When the controller left, the VPs hired a financial analyst who became our CFO. He was going to work out of the New York office. He and I met again about a week after the controller left and divvied up the accounting duties each of us were going to do. Since I had been doing the bulk of the accounts receivable, accounts payable, and payroll, I took on the responsibility of doing these tasks with the exception of the international payables, because I knew that it would be too much work for me to handle. I still had to be the office manager and assist the CEO.

The company had multi-million dollars in sales and was growing, adding a few millions in revenue by the year. When we moved to our new office, I got the first inclination that the CEO valued my opinion when he asked me on how to situate everyone in our new digs. There was a sitting area when you first walked in, and you had to walk around the corner after passing the glass conference room to come to your first office on the right and cubicle on the left. The screamer, as I used to later call him (the VP who griped about the messy office) had the first office, and I was situated in the large, three-person cubicle directly across, alongside the project manager who was technically the assistant of the confrontational lady that had laid her hands on me. It was funny that they placed the loudest person, the VP, in the front office, since he yelled at times.

By this time, I had a very conservative-looking, clean-cut image, unlike back in those Klein and Oxnard days when I shaved my head and dressed alternatively, typically all in black. No one knew that I had anything other than a very ordinary, average life. The rebellious-looking chick was gone on the outside, but she still remained inside. The open-minded, antiwar, antigun, antiestablishment, fuck-you-attitude person when she was upset, who wanted to blast some punk or alternative music and wished she could dye her hair fuchsia was still alive in me, just hidden.

This job was a step up. I got a very substantial raise when the controller left, and I had full range of my responsibilities in accounting. Besides the CEO, no one else knew how to do what I did—not even the CFO. I had to train him on QuickBooks and help him understand the process of getting the accounting in the system so it could be later analyzed. He was a person, supposedly, able to see the final picture, but he didn't necessarily know the steps for how to get the numbers in there.

Jonathan was a good teacher in anything that I had to do that I had never done before. Yes, this was a step above the last job, but it wasn't an environment that I'd choose for a daughter, if I had one.

The CFO seemed like a great coworker at first. He was nice and didn't speak to me in a tone I found inappropriate, but there were the hints that he was making every VP think that I was nothing more than an assistant to the finance department. I'd see the organizational charts that the president of the company would send me to reformat, and my title would be *assistant*. Here I was doing all the accounts receivable, accounts payable, and cutting all the checks, along with doing the entire payroll for the employees both in Los Angeles and New York before we moved payroll to an outside resource. I started getting hurt; year after year. I'd recognize that I was nothing to the higher-ups other than someone else who pushed papers. I was getting paid better than I had in prior years, but within this company and what the CFO was making, I was barely getting paid for the work I was really doing. It was a multimillion-dollar company, and I was doing all their bookkeeping, along with being the office manager and executive assistant to the CEO. All along, the CFO was just modifying reports for the partners and being there to answer any questions that they may ask. Also, for more than six months, he told Jonathan and me that he had been reconciling the bank account monthly, but come to find out, he had no clue about how to do bank reconciliations.

After a year, the seed of my frustration and aggravation was planted with this work situation, because I felt like I was being taken advantage of. I did have patience and tolerance on my side; I believe I was born with these traits, but my childhood truly defined them. I could deal with unhappy, unpleasant situations for a long time. I was the quiet, shy, and very soft-spoken girl. If I had to speak, sometimes I would do so in so quiet a voice that teachers would ask me over and over to speak up. There were too many situations and people in my lifetime that made me learn how to better retreat into my shell and not go off on someone. I spent decades not speaking up, because as a child, it never made a difference.

It had only been recently that I learned to vent, probably because of therapy. When I vented, I would sometimes pace while I did it. I never paced before while I talked. I think all those feelings coming to the surface were being filtered out through my emotions, so I needed to move. I'd seek out Jonathan whenever I needed to talk, and he was great, because he didn't see me as crazy (as I thought I was), and he gave me great advice. He'd also talk to me about himself and maybe things that happened in his day or week. He became a great boss and a good friend early on.

For the most part, the first two years I worked at this company were great, even with the agro-girl that I would never understand and the first year with the VP who was a screamer. I learned so much the first six months. I felt I was doing an excellent job as the sales of the company multiplied year after year.

Our company had annual holiday parties, which I reluctantly attended at first because I had been so much out of the loop of being social, outside of Oliver's school activities. I still hadn't had a drink in years. I hadn't even dated for years.

On my second year at this company, I reconnected with Melanie from Oxnard. It was because of Myspace that we found one another. Gotta love social media. We hadn't seen or spoken to each other in years, and we made plans to have a drink after work. She came and met me at work, which was interesting. I came off like a frumpy, plain, bland mom who was just raising her son alone and probably never looked like I had a life or any sense of style for that matter, and here came a girlfriend of mine with stripper heels and a white tank top showing off some of her tattoos. My only tattoo at the time was almost always hidden and went unnoticed. She looked fabulous, pretty, and spirited. I introduced her to some of the designers, and we left to get caught up.

She had a beer, and I had an iced tea. We hadn't seen each other since the night of her first wedding, when Oliver was about ten months old. Carter and Oliver and I had attended that wedding in Riverside. After her ceremony, she cried to me about how she felt so bad for taking off and losing touch like she had done, and yet she had vanished again until now. I never held a grudge. I had learned years earlier that this was what she did, even without meaning to.

She was newly engaged, about to be married in a few weeks. Her first marriage lasted only a few years. I was happy for her, especially for the fact that she had found a profession; she was now a hair stylist. She learned how to use her creativity and take care of herself. It was better than the road she was leading when I lived in Hollywood and she was working as a receptionist. I knew she wouldn't be happy doing that her whole life.

Oliver and I attended her second wedding ceremony. It was in Riverside again, a lovely backyard wedding, but I felt so uncomfortable. I still hadn't been in any non-parent-child activities, and here I had gained one too many pounds for my liking. I was with strangers, Melanie's new friends who had heard stories about us and our wild times, especially about the first evening we met Tupac. I felt like they'd look at me and not believe it or they would just judge me. Oliver and I didn't stay for very long after the ceremony. Besides, our drive back to Los Angeles was more than an hour.

Melanie and I stayed in touch this time, and I invited her to come with me to my company's next holiday party. It had been a challenging two years, both with work and finances, but now I was stabilizing and making a little more money. My credit cards had either been paid off or gone to collections two years prior, during that last stint in college. I got rid of a dud, a car that Carter had sold me when he worked at CarMax and when we were still together. I now had a cute, problem-free Toyota Matrix. Oliver and I had traveled a few times to Cancun and just done a California road trip up north and down the coast, spending some time with my godmother and her husband in Tahoe at their second home. Things were good. I felt like recapturing my single life and not just being Oliver's mom and having just work and parenthood in my life. Melanie coming with me to the holiday party was just the beginning of my road back.

Our holiday party was held at the screamer's condo. He lived in a condo that overlooked the heart of the west side of Los Angeles. Melanie picked me up. She was dressed ultra classy but with a little retro flare. I dressed in a new top and pencil skirt and straightened my bob-length hair. I had just recently cut it a few months prior and was mostly straightening it, rather than having my curls let loose like they used to.

We took the elevator up that opened directly to his place. We mixed and mingled with most of the employees, some VPs, along with others that were in town from New York. Jonathan also showed up with his wife.

This was going to be the first night back to drinking after more than nine years. I wanted to "just taste," to sample new drinks I had never had—like a pomegranate margarita. It had been so long that I had a sip of alcohol. Even with just sampling about three drinks, I did feel a little buzz happening.

The night felt like old times. No longer was I feeling too uncomfortable being social. I was back to taking pictures like I had always done. I had always been that girl with the camera in her hand or purse. Here was no different, and there were enough people, including the president of the company, who loved striking a pose.

After that night, I started drinking, going to do happy hour or out with girlfriends, but just about three times that first year and maybe five times the next year. I was keeping my drinking completely under control and not allowing myself any more than two drinks at a time. I now mentally thought about not getting drunk every time I drank. It had to be analyzed. It wasn't like I said to myself, *Okay, well, if you start drinking, you must overthink it.* It just happened that way. This was how my thinking had evolved. I needed to make an effort to think about everything I did that could lead to a detrimental state or even get me into trouble. Even though I hadn't had a drink all those years, I knew that I had picked up another addiction, shopping, to replace the drinking. I thought about that for years, and I knew I had a tendency to do things that weren't always good for me. I did sometimes things that helped me escape or made me feel better.

Everything needed to be evaluated sooner or later.

Around the time when Oliver was six, I had gotten into a car accident. Because it wasn't my fault, I received a settlement that allowed me to take my son for the first time on a real vacation. I took him to the place that brought me peace. It was the same place where I got my thoughts and emotions centered right before I conceived him—Cancun. We went almost annually after that for a few years, even though every year the question of my legally having custody of him would come up. At first, it wasn't a problem, because Carter would go with us to the ticket counter. It became an issue later where we were returned in Houston, Texas, not being able to go on our connecting flight because I didn't have legal documentation that I had custody of Oliver. In 2007, I'd find out that I couldn't get legal custody without serving his father court papers and that at any time because I didn't have legal custody of my son, his father could also take him away from me. Nothing could be done until he could be located, though. And the San Diego Department of Child Support Services and soon Los Angeles County Child Support Services Department were going to give up trying to locate his father; they had been trying for years. I completely understand the laws to protect children from being kidnapped from the other parent, but with circumstances like mine, when the other parent hides or disappears for years, was it fair to deny my child from his birthday vacation out of the country or even to possibly see the world in the future?

At the end of 2007, again with the lovely thanks to Myspace, I had reconnected with an old acquaintance, Julian. I had known him from my old Hollywood club days. He used to be a club promoter. I reached out to Julian to see if he knew how to contact Joshua because they use to be friends. Because of what happened recently, when Oliver and I were turned back in Houston on our way to Cancun, I needed to someday deal with this situation. I needed to ensure that I'd be able to show I wasn't kidnapping my child if we were traveling outside of the United States. I was relieved to hear that Julian and Joshua had stayed in touch all these years. Julian couldn't believe Joshua had left us high and dry like he had. He apologized to me, even though it wasn't his fault. It is funny when I think of how we all say "I'm sorry" like it was something we did.

I was elated and nervous once I had Joshua's number. After thirteen years of the San Diego Department of Child Support Services and Los Angeles County Child Support Services Department and me all looking for him, I had his telephone number in front of me on my computer screen.

The following days, I held on to the fact that I had a way of contacting him. I had always been thankful that he knew at that time that he couldn't be a parent, that he was too young to be a father. I was pleased that he knew that then instead of drifting in and out of Oliver's life, like so many men do because then Oliver could've taken it personally, asking, "Why doesn't my daddy like me anymore?" How I have always seen it and raised Oliver was that Joshua doesn't know Oliver because he knew at the age of twenty-four that he was too immature to be a father. This, though, doesn't take away from Joshua's legal and financial responsibility to take care of the child he helped create. The only money I had ever received from Joshua was the $100 he gave me a week after Oliver turned one. There were promises to pay $400 a month, but within a month or so, that never happened, and he disappeared.

After a few days passed, I started Googling Joshua's number. Gotta love Google! Immediately, a résumé of Joshua's he had posted somewhere came up.

Let me mention a very key component to not having been able to find Joshua all those years: I wasn't sure of his last name. Judge me if you'd like, but this was just another stupid, immature thing that I didn't do, and when you mix immaturity with a person who doesn't speak up and with a little bit of no self-worth or a lot of no self-worth, this is what you get. It really is just sad when you think about it. I also didn't think that a one-night stand would lead into more than seven months of seeing each other. Eventually, there came a time when I was at his apartment in Hollywood off of La Brea that I had asked to see his driver's license. I wanted to see his picture on it, but he wouldn't let me see it. His words to me were "No, my full name and address are on it, and maybe one day you might want to find me for child support or something." That has stuck with me all these years. It was the oddest thing I heard out of a guy's mouth at the time, but I guess it was very smart of him. I never made a fuss about it.

I'm sure it sounds so strange, but this is coming from a girl who really had no backbone back then to stand up for herself and know any better or care to. All those years I had assumed his last name could possibly be Solomon because there was a time he was at my apartment calling a bank in New York, and he told the receptionist to say it was "Solomon" to whomever it was he was calling. On every document I had written down for child support services, I wrote "Solomon" in parentheses and wrote "not sure." On Oliver's birth certificate, with the best of my knowledge, I listed Joshua's first name (though I didn't spell it like he spells it) and that he was born in Haiti and wrote down his birthdate (but, I didn't know he was born in 1969, which I'd later find out). Now on his résumé I saw his last name. I'd have never been able to guess that name. It isn't even a French name, like DuBois or something. He had always claimed to be more French than anything, so I had surely been expecting a French sounding name.

I Googled his full name, and a lot came up, including things that I will not reveal or judge but that I had always had my suspicions of. I didn't know what to do with this newly acquired information. I was too afraid to call him. I'm still a coward when it comes to situations like this, because my first instinct is that it will turn into a confrontation that therefore will lead to a physical altercation. I had been hardwired to feel like this, and I'm truly aware where it comes from and that I still need to work on this among other things.

I went to Jonathan and told him what I had and asked his opinion about what I should do next.

Jonathan took Joshua's printed résumé that I had downloaded from the Internet and started plugging away on Google, even though I let him know I had already done that. I paced, just out of nerves, around in his corner office that overlooked Westwood as he searched. He Googled the address that was on the résumé and found a business associated with it and a different telephone number. Jonathan wanted to call the number to see if it was working and to see if Joshua would answer. I felt like we were schoolgirls calling a boy we liked, but I was so fearful of what could happen next.

Jonathan called, and the number was still working. He gave me the courage to stand up for myself and especially for Oliver.

A few days later, I called Joshua. He was very surprised to hear from me. He did ask a few times how I had gotten his number. I think he wanted to know whom he could trust or not trust moving forward. *Sorry, Julian, but you did the right thing!* I didn't tell him who had given me his number.

Joshua and I caught up. He told me how hard things were between him and his ex-wife toward the last few years of their marriage. I believe they had broken up for a bit, and Joshua had started seeing another woman by the name of Natalie. Then he began going back to see and sleep with the ex-wife (but at that time they hadn't been married yet). This is the female that Michelle had told me about all those years ago that had inherited money after her mom passed— the one who had him going to Washington, DC, while we were seeing each other. Maybe she came into more money, and that was why he started trying to reconcile with her. Who knows! All I know is that he told me he ended up seeing both of these girls at the same time, up until the ex-wife got pregnant for the second time. They already had a daughter who was about a year and a half younger than Oliver. Joshua told me over the phone that their second pregnancy was the point that he decided that they should get married. He stopped seeing the other girl, Natalie, but a few months after he and the soon-to-be wife were engaged, the other girl told him that she was three months pregnant. He said he wanted to kill himself at that time. He told me that he had never wanted to be one of those guys who had different baby mommas.

On the day of his wedding, Natalie supposedly tried to crash the wedding but was escorted away by some of his friends. Natalie has a boy whom Joshua sees and has supported off and on for years. Her child was born just a few months apart from his now ex-wife's second daughter and he has always been in the picture and supported his two girls. He told me that they divorced years later, about a year or so prior to my finding him.

While we spoke, there was no mention about whether or not I had a child. He later told me that he didn't remember seeing Oliver when Oliver turned one, but then how did he know I had a child?

He continuously questioned me about how I knew Oliver was his. I knew because if there was any doubt in my mind, I would have pursued the other options where I would have gotten a substantial amount of child support, and they were public figures, so I'd always know where to locate them. I wouldn't have gone after the guy that I knew wasn't capable or willing to be there.

I also knew because of the timing. During the couple of weeks that Joshua and I spoke before Christmas in 2007, I learned from him how Oliver's double-jointedness (I never knew that is what that was) came from Joshua. Besides that, I like to smile and say to myself that Oliver is my twin, my child. He has a calm demeanor, especially for being a boy. He is never aggressive, competitive, or all over the place. He is very giving, patient, and inquisitive—not by testing things out but by learning from what he was told and looking further into it. I possess all these traits, though Oliver was able to eventually stand up for himself, like when a child would take something out of his hand that he was playing with; he learned to hold on to it. As a child, I would have just let someone take it.

The day after Christmas, Joshua called me to check in to see how we were doing and asked how our Christmas was. He told me how this was the first Christmas without his girls and how hard it was. His eldest daughter (with the ex-wife) had had a hard time when Natalie's son came into the picture. By that time, the boy was about four years old. Joshua wasn't there in the beginning with that son, either, but he came around years later. He introduced his son to his daughters one day at the beach. The eldest daughter must have been around nine and even at that age took notice of her dad stopping to talk to this boy. His daughter mentioned, "Look, dad, he has a necklace just like you."

Joshua told me it was hard to blend these siblings together, especially for the eldest daughter. Moving forward to 2007 and the day after Christmas, Joshua told his eldest daughter that he had a dream that she had an older brother. He told me, "I wanted to see her reaction." He said that she was silent for a bit, looked at him, and then said, "That's not funny."

He knew from that point on that he couldn't introduce Oliver into his life, because he thought she wouldn't take it well. I couldn't believe it. I think that was the last time he called willingly.

We spoke one more time in January, and I got very upset. He again offered to pay me child support like when he had offered all those years earlier, but now he had raised it to $450 a month. At the time, that wasn't the most important thing, I wanted Oliver to actually have a dad. He said he couldn't be in Oliver's life because he and his children had a different lifestyle than Oliver and how unfair that would be for Oliver to see what they all had and then come home to his mom's one-bedroom apartment after spending some time with the rest of them. He said he'd contact his lawyer to see what could be done about me getting legal custody drawn up and that I'd hear back from one of them. I never heard back.

On January 31, 2008, with the information I had, I filed to

establish paternity and custody for my son. I was holding off on the child support because I had met with a few professionals who told me to wait and first file paternity and custody. Based on what I'd told them, it appeared that Joshua may not contest paternity and custody, but with child support, he more than likely would show up to court. If he didn't show up for paternity and custody, the courts would see what his true character was when it came down to the situation.

He was served personally by an Orange County sheriff. He never showed up to court, and because of this, he was established as Oliver's legal dad. The courts saw this as he wasn't contesting it. I also got sole legal custody of my son. About two months after I received this action by the court, I filed for child support.

I was going back and forth for the next year or so to the courts, learning what and how to file and to follow up with my court proceedings. Oliver was in middle school and still doing very well. He had picked up drama and was in a few plays. I was no longer participating in any parent committees; once he began attending middle school, that all came to an end because he wanted his independence.

At my next couple of court hearings, first the courts had agreed to award me child support going back to a court case I had found from 1996 from the Los Angeles County Child Support Services Department. Unfortunately, it was just a "complaint," and there was no money established. When I went back to court, they wouldn't establish child support going back to 1996. So then the final award was established. Joshua would only have to start paying child support starting February 1, 2008, the day after I filed the court papers for paternity and custody, even though my son was born in 1994. The law in California states that you can only establish child support once a court case has been filed and served. Because he couldn't be located all those years to be served child support court papers, a case couldn't begin.

There was a family code that I had found and I tried to bring it up many times that states that if you can prove a parent has evaded child support, you can go back retroactively. I couldn't prove it on my word, and every time I tried to bring it up to a lawyer or a paralegal in the facilitator's office down in the courthouse, they had never heard of it and were surprised when I had a copy of the code. No one ever wanted to assist me with fighting to go back to when Oliver was born or even to when the 1996 complaint was filed. I'm sure if I had found money to hire a lawyer that maybe I would have been able to go back all those years. Joshua didn't have to pay for the first thirteen years of Oliver's life! That is all I could establish on my own.

This news tore me up inside. The private investigation firm that I had worked for had run a full background check on Joshua, and with this and my brilliance of searching online of public records on Orange County's website, I was able to find out how Oliver's dad had lived all these years. He was a smart, self-employed man; there were no wages to garnish. Did he do this intentionally from the start? Before the economy took a downturn around 2007, his house was valued at $6 million. He had owned several different homes with his ex-wife and had cosigned with Natalie, the other baby momma, on a condo for her and her son. This was not a deadbeat dad by circumstance. When I think of a deadbeat dad, I think of a man who can pay but isn't willing to do so. It was unfair that we as a country let him off the hook for not paying for all those years I was taking care of the child we created. It wasn't fair that Oliver, who had asthma, had to share such cramped quarters with his mother next to one of the busiest freeways in America. It was not fair that he had to hear me say one too many times that we couldn't do that or this because I didn't have the money. It wasn't fair that I couldn't have him continue in after-school activities because I couldn't afford it while I attended my last years in college— and by the time I could, he had no interest in rejoining the competitive field of sports. It isn't fair because we didn't have to struggle like this when the guy that fathered him had plenty of money.

Throughout my court hearings, I turned to the Internet and searched for information I could gather in case I needed it. I found Natalie, the other mother, and contacted her via Facebook. She called me the following day. She told me later after she had spoken to her father about it that she had known about me for some time; Joshua had told her way before I reached out to him.

We had our sons meet. Her son was more excited because he had always wanted an older brother. At this time, she was going to court regularly with Joshua over custody. She asked me to attend a few hearings with her. The first time was actually when I first met her. She seemed nice. It was then when she showed me a December 2007 bank statement she had recovered that showed the extent of Joshua's money—it had a balance of around $172,000. She believed it was from the recent sale of his house. I used it a couple of years later when he took me to court in 2011 to try to vacate our child support order.

I no longer speak to Natalie, because she was pissed that I used the bank statement, and she was sticking up for Joshua.

At the time, I still wasn't dating. Work was becoming very hectic, because business was doing very well, and I was still managing the majority of the accounting while still managing the office and assisting Jonathan.

Since moving back to Los Angeles when Oliver was five months old, I'd see the family almost once a year. My parents had moved to Arizona for my dad's work, a year or two after we had returned to the City of Angels. Candelaria and Paoletta were still living in San Diego. Candelaria seemed to be doing much better than the homeless crystal meth addict that she was when Oliver was born. Candelaria and her new husband had lived in Chicago for a bit after we moved and were now living back in San Diego. Paoletta was divorced and was raising her son. His father was in the picture, also living in San Diego, and they shared custody of my nephew. Guadalupe was living in Northern California with her husband and three children.

The times that we'd get together for family reunions were miserable for me. I'd get so anxious worrying about what verbal fight or confrontation would happen. I never really wanted to see my mother; I always saw her as the center of the issues. She didn't drink on these occasions when we got together, but she was still who she was, self-absorbed, and she had become critical toward me. When we'd all get together, I still saw addiction; my two older sisters smoked like my mom did, and all of my sisters drank, one or two of them drinking more than I would have liked. It just took me back to my childhood every time, because the behaviors were still there, and nothing had changed. I wouldn't behave like who I had become; I'd behave like the adolescent me, and even though I now started drinking on occasion again, I didn't drink when I saw them. I didn't want to fight with my mom again, trying to prove to her that I didn't drink those nine years I had said I wasn't drinking. She never believed me. I guess she could never believe I could do it. I didn't want to argue with her anymore about the fact that I wasn't going to be like her, because I'm sure if she saw me with a glass of wine now, she would not hesitate to say, "You see? You are just like me."

I will be the first to admit that she was still a thorn in my side at that time. I despised who she had become. I was ashamed of who she was. This woman that had beauty, brains, and potential had amounted to this—a woman with no dignity or self-worth who did nothing for others and carried herself like she had no care in the world about what she looked like or how she dressed. Worst of all, she got drunk and mean and made no apologies about it. I never saw it at the time as sad, and I had no compassion toward her. Unfortunately, I was still disgusted by what she had amounted to and of her weakness to not try to fight for a better self or a better life.

Right before I turned thirty-nine, things at work had become a little too much to handle for one person. It had been more than a year that my boss, the CFO in New York, knew I needed an additional person to help me out with the accounting, managing the office and whatever Jonathan needed. The company had been sold off. The company was now around $40 million in sales, and I was still doing all the receivables and payables. I was also setting up new employees, managing the office, and helping Jonathan, who had gotten rid of his executive assistant. I also was the liaison between the bankers and the factoring company and assisting with the transition from one company to the other. Let's just say that I was overwhelmed. I had rarely seen a real lunch break in over six months. I didn't want to be like some of my coworkers who worked ten-hour days. I still wanted to work only my eight hours, plus the lunch break I no longer had time for. The workload being compressed into eight and a half hours was stressing me out! If I found time to bite into something very quickly to eat, I'd almost throw up because I was trying to rush everything. I was still doing a great job—no typos or errors in my work. But as soon as I knew it, something else was added on to what I'd have to deal with.

I had always mostly dealt internally with stress or things that upset me. Throughout my lifetime, I had insomnia off and on. I had also been grinding my teeth since about the age of ten. When Oliver was about five years old, I had chronic knots in my upper back and neck. I internalized everything and moved on. But I was now having spontaneous coughing that was the result of heart palpitations. It had become so frequent that I knew I had to go see my doctor.

At this same time, I was looking for another assistant; about a month or two earlier, they had allowed me to find help. The one I had for about a month and a half didn't work out. I was working at night, looking through résumés, and I somehow had to fit in a doctor's appointment. I went to see my doctor, and she referred me to a cardiologist to find out why I was having extra heartbeats.

On the very first day that my new assistant, Emma, started at the company, I had a monitor strapped to my waist counting how many extra times my heartbeat in a day. We laughed months later reminiscing on that first day together. How she wasn't alarmed, I don't know. I had more than two thousand extra heart beats per day, the doctors said.

After all the tests, the cardiologist at Cedars couldn't pinpoint the culprit; she said it was more than likely stress, but she also said it could have been brought on by the fact that I just started drinking again. Funny how here were two things in my life that had always haunted me and even though I thought for a while I had control over them, I surely still didn't. She said she could give me a prescription, but she recommended that I lower the amount of whatever was stressing me out. It subsided a month or two later, but never completely went away.

This heart issue was a small wake-up call. I was going to be forty soon. I was moving forward, evolving. They may have been baby steps, and I may have taken two steps forward, one step back, but I was evolving. I was no longer an uneducated woman. I was no longer a rape victim; I was a survivor. I was no longer a troubled person that lost herself in alcohol or drugs. I was no longer stuck in the negative. I was no longer a single mother on welfare. I was not perfect, my life was not perfect, and I still had some emotional and family issues that were still healing, but things were better. I was optimistic, and I was growing.

The one area that I hadn't really worked on was that of relationships.

Approaching the age forty was really a stepping-stone to a higher belief system of knowing what I had to do to make the changes for the life I wanted to live all these years and with whom I wanted to spend my life with. At this time, it had been more than six years since I had dated anyone, much less even kissed a guy. What did I want for myself as far as friends and a love?

I was now asking myself what kind of people I wanted in my life. I had fended off the agro-girl in the office; I knew I didn't like these types of people in my personal life. I had become friends with a girl named Nicole whom I had met through Katy (from Oxnard). Melanie and I had reunited with Katy one night, and she had brought along Nicole.

Nicole was cool. She is Puerto Rican and had what I think was a tough childhood, being raised by her grandmother, never seeing her father, and rarely seeing her mother because her mother had a lot of issues. She was brought up in downtown L.A., in the Pico-Union district, a pretty rough part of town. I thought she was an amazing girl because of her background and because she also was raising a daughter on her own (though she did get child support), and despite all this, she wasn't a mean girl or angry about her situations.

Melanie and I also hung out from time to time.

I wanted positive, supportive people around me, because I'd be that to them as a friend or as a love. I'd rather be alone than have any more negative people around me, so I knew I had to choose wisely from now on.

When I was about to turn forty was when I also realized I wanted someone to love me and someone to love. Why couldn't I have that person who wanted to spend the rest of his life with me? I knew I was beautiful, supportive, and strong; I saw how much I had to offer. I knew now that not all marriages were like the one I grew up seeing; I didn't need to be afraid of getting married anymore. I wanted to possibly have another child, because it would soon be too late for me to have any more children. I had always said I wanted five children and could settle for three, but if that didn't happen, I was so grateful for the one I had. How fortunate I was to have him with all he is!

I was ready to start dating again after six and a half long years, but how? The only guys who did say anything to me all these years were toothless guys with their beer bellies sticking out, saying something indecent to me, even in front of my son. I was never a magnet for men, at least to the men that I'd consider. Even back in the day at the clubs and parties, it was rare that anyone approached me. Now I had to try something different. Though it wasn't easy for me, I reluctantly tried online dating; I knew I wasn't getting very far with just letting things happen.

10

A New Road

The first few dates I had were interesting. I had placed my profile at the beginning of January, two months before I turned forty. I did receive a lot of e-mails or winks from guys who viewed my online profile. I was, for the first time in my life, being approached by many different types of men. I was never one of those girls who had grown up thinking of who I wanted to marry or fantasized about my wedding day, so I tried to find someone with many common interests and someone I could relate to and who could relate to me or understand me. I also wanted someone who wouldn't judge me because of where and how I lived.

I always felt misunderstood because of my views on religion and God or my relationship with some of my family members, so it was important to me that he understood and accepted me. He needed to be a nice, ambitious man who could communicate, wanted some of the same things out of life as I did, had a similar upbringing—ideally minus the abuse—and was someone I could trust and be happy with. It didn't seem too much to ask for.

I had a few dates. I didn't want to rush into meeting up with anyone until I really had an interest. I did e-mail back and forth with a few, but this online thing was an instant gratification for most that were on there, so a lot of them were rushing to get my number or were trying to see me right away, and I wasn't having any of that, because I needed a spark to happen. Yes, I wanted to find "the one," but I wasn't desperate. I could have settled a long time ago. It was important to find someone to be happy and compatible with. But most importantly I wanted someone who wouldn't hurt me, either emotionally or physically, so I had to be careful.

There was one guy in late February whom I dated three times. The only thing we had in common though was that we both had gone to CSUN. I went on more than one date with him, trying to convince myself that I liked that he had good values, but really we had nothing more between us. My search continued as my fortieth birthday crept up.

Melanie and I celebrated our birthdays together that year in

West Hollywood. It reminded me of the time we had celebrated our birthdays the night we met Tupac; we invited numerous people, but only a few showed up. I went earlier to dinner at Le Petit with my old friend Yolanda from Oxnard along with my friend that worked in the same building I worked in. Melanie had to work that day at the salon, and since she lived an hour away, she couldn't meet up with us until later.

Dinner was nice, but the rest of our evening at the club, Coco de Ville was fun. Part of me felt like I was back in my club days. Melanie looked hot. I looked elegant, but even back in the club days— for the most part—I dressed classy like that.

I had a few cosmos that evening and loved that Emma from work showed up and brought some friends of hers. Melanie's other close friend Micky and Micky's boyfriend came, and even my boss, Jonathan, came to celebrate with us. I'm sure he had fun, sitting between Melanie and me, hearing stories about us back in the day, even about meeting Tupac. He knew a lot about me, but now he was hearing so much more! I didn't mind it, because Jonathan isn't judgmental in the least. He loved hearing stuff like that—the juicer, the better.

We ended the night at last call. It had been more than a decade that I had heard that. And I ended the evening by receiving a rose from a guy ten years younger than I, which was the best compliment. I just giggled, was amused, and left it at that.

My actual birthday had been spent about a week earlier in Las Vegas with my son and my dad. My dad had actually traveled, without my mom, to Las Vegas to come and join us to see the Beatles' Cirque du Soleil. Oliver and I had gone about five months earlier, and I was so moved by it that I knew I wanted to return for my fortieth and bring my dad to experience it with us. In more than twenty years, he hadn't done much more than go to the movies or grab a bite with my mother. To me, my mother is antisocial and really never had the spirit to try new things, so I wanted my dad outside of that box to join us to see this magnificent show that I knew he'd enjoy. When I told him about it in January, even though I made it clear I was only inviting him, he later invited her to come. I wanted to share this moment with him and my son only. I knew if I had even wanted my mom to go, that she would have somehow ruined it with her negativity. By this time, he knew I no longer wanted to speak to her, so it really bothered me that he invited her.

A year earlier, when 2009 was wrapping up and I was thirty-nine, I knew I no longer wanted a relationship with my mother. Unfortunately, I had to separate myself away from her. I really needed her to remain out of my life. I saw her as being the center of the toxicity in our family. She wasn't the source of all the problems—we all played our own part in this family—but I just believed her alcoholism and behavior had such an impact on our family and the fact that nothing has changed or been acknowledged by her was a big problem. I didn't want to speak to her. I didn't want to see her. Why would I?

For years, I had been letting her know that how she lived was not okay with me. I had to put my foot down and say enough is enough and let her know that I just didn't like her as a person when it relates to me. I don't accept that nothing about her and her alcoholism has changed or that there hasn't ever even been a care to change and that also she has never shown an ounce of remorse or guilt, taking any responsibility. Her addiction and her accusations that her problems for the past forty years were because of us or my father—that everything is everyone else's fault or problem and not hers was just something I could not accept anymore.

Finally, I had had enough and tried to break ties with her. I was done. I thought that there was no point to having her in my life. She had nothing positive or encouraging to say to me. She had criticized my weight, even though she is overweight. She didn't contribute anything positive, but the fact that she gave birth to me. She wasn't fully there for me when I was growing up. She wasn't there to take care of me after we lost the house and everyone moved away and I was still a teenager. I couldn't turn to her after being raped, because I did not trust her. She didn't help me with continuing my education, even though they always told us growing up that they moved to the United States for our education. She wasn't there to help their only child—physically, emotionally, or financially—who had a child and was on her own. She never asked if there was anything we needed or if she could help. She did not encourage me, she did not inspire me, she did not instill that I was good or that I could be great. She even told me once that I couldn't even be a good maid because I could not clean well (she may have said this while being a little drunk, but it has stayed with me all these years). For the nine years I didn't drink, she never said, "Great job!"

She once said to me, "You will be exactly like me and look like me." When I countered that I exercised, did not drink, did not smoke, and did not eat like she did and therefore would not look exactly like her—and certainly wouldn't behave like her or end up like her—she dismissed me with, "You'll see."

Yes, I shamed her, but wouldn't most parents encourage their children to be better than they had been rather than try to keep them down because they are so low?

So by the age of forty, I was completely done with the family reunions where I would always somehow be left in tears, usually because of a comment by my mother. She'd either criticize me about the way I looked—*my hair color being dark, even though it was actually closest to my original color or she'd also comment about my weight.* She'd also tell me once in a while how another sister needed something, never thinking that all my sisters had help and I didn't. Every time I'd get together with most of my family, I'd retreat to behaving not like myself but my old self and react to anything that she said. I hated getting together, because my insides would go through so much stress and anger. I was done with how the world had to revolve around her. She somehow would change the occasion to be about her when it originally wasn't. She also could never call me just to hear about how my life was going and maybe see how she could help or say something positive to encourage me to keep my head up. So I was turning forty, and I was done with her completely, and my dad was made aware, even though he sometimes ignored my choice and put her on the phone. "But she's your mother," he would say to me.

When we were setting a plan to go to Vegas, I tried to let the anxiety of her coming go, because it was so important for me to have him do something like this before he died. He already had been diagnosed with leukemia, and I couldn't wrap my mind around how sad the state of his life had become over all these years.

She did me a favor though, days before we were going to meet up in Vegas; she went on a binge. This was huge to actually see if he'd be allowed to go without her or if he'd even leave her for twenty-four hours to go to Vegas and join us. He knew if he went without her that he would just come home to her drunkenness and her rage, which was probably why he invited her in the first place. The anxiety of a ruined fortieth birthday vanished when I saw him at the baggage carousel at the airport in Vegas. I couldn't believe he did it! Up until that point, I wasn't sure he was going to come without her. Maybe because of the diagnosis of his cancer, he had realized his life was being half lived because of her.

We stayed at the Mirage where the show was playing. It was so great being with the two people that I loved most in this world. We had dinner at the hotel and went to the show. He loved it! We kindly laughed later when we mentioned how mother would have hated it. She hated circuses and anything that was on the borderline of dangerous, like the Rollerbladers flying through the air in the show. I'm so glad she didn't come, and surprisingly, two years later, she mentioned how sorry she was that she didn't make it. I wasn't rude to tell her the truth—that she had done me a favor by not coming and that I didn't even invite her—I just kept my mouth shut. Manners are what she taught me, and I was utilizing them at that moment. Besides, I wasn't going to be mean just because of how I felt about her.

Less than two weeks later, I was online looking at my profile, going through all the pages of guys who had viewed my page. I had recently found this feature and would either delete or keep profiles there to view or reach out to later. There were so many guys who had viewed me and didn't reach out to me. I guess some things don't change. Throughout looking pretty in my lifetime, I've seen men look, but they rarely approached me. This was no different. This whole time that I wanted to get back on the dating scene, I thought of who would be more up my alley, so I thought to really just look at the white guys because I thought of my childhood. I wanted a connection to the same views of life and some of the same experiences and interests I had, and unfortunately (ignorant or not), I only envisioned a white guy because that was mainly what I grew up with.

On the dating website, all you could view was a tiny picture on a person's profile before you opened it up, so when I viewed who had viewed me, I kept seeing a profile that I had seen for a week or so, but for some reason, I never clicked on it and just left it there. His little, tiny picture kind of haunted me, so I put it on the back burner for when I was ready to focus and view the entire profile.

On March 27, a Saturday, I finally clicked on this profile, and his picture said so much to me. Pictures sometimes just speak to me, like a piece of art. He didn't say much about himself on his profile, but he did touch briefly on what his likes were and what he was looking for. I could tell instantly that I dug him. I couldn't believe that I waited so long to check out his profile. He was handsome, tall, and liked cars and racing (I had always thought I would have loved to be a race car driver). He was successful, therefore ambitious—which is the opposite of someone like Carter—he had a few tattoos, he liked some of the same music (the '80s, the Smiths), and he wasn't strong in his religious beliefs; simply put, he said he "believed in God, and that was it." That sounded like someone who wouldn't crucify me for my beliefs or for not really knowing what I believed in, and that was so important to me.

I sent him a wink to let him notice I was interested in him because even though he had viewed my profile, he hadn't reached out to me. I think there are a lot of guys out there that have noticed me but have thought they weren't my type, so I wanted to see if he responded. He did almost immediately, and we sent e-mails back and forth. He thought he was too immature for me but was flattered and immediately reconsidered his maturity level when I told him maybe he just thought he was too immature for me. We continued e-mails the following day, which was his birthday. By that evening, I gave him my number. This was the first guy I believed could possibly be something.

We texted for the next few days and planned to get together later that week, but he had to cancel at the last minute because he said he was having problems at work, and he told me he needed to go on the road. He was a VP for an apparel line for a rock band that was on tour at the time. It was partially run by some of the band's family members, and he thought they were up to no good. We planned on meeting as soon as he got back.

About a week and a half had passed, and I hadn't heard from him. He had said he'd be gone for a few weeks, but I didn't want him to forget about me, so I texted him. I was out with my girlfriend Nicole at the SLS Hotel lounge, and we were talking about him. He immediately called me after receiving my text. This was actually the first time we spoke over the phone, and I was excited that he called, but I was actually taken aback because I wasn't putting the face with the voice. He sounded so nice and thrilled that I reached out to him. He said he'd be back in town soon and that we'd get together. I was so relieved that he was still interested, because I was definitely so interested in him. It was like a spark had gone off since I had first opened up his profile, and I didn't want that feeling to go away.

He called me as soon as he got back into L.A., and we planned to meet up that Friday, a few days later. He wanted to meet in Beverly Hills at the Urth Caffé, not too far from where he was staying at his brother's place. I wanted to have a drink and not necessarily grab a sandwich or salad and be in such close quarters of everyone else being able to listen in on our first date. I switched our plans to instead go to a cantina up on Sunset Plaza. I didn't know until he told me when we were there that he didn't drink. I felt bad.

When he had gotten back into town a few days earlier, we spoke several times for hours over the phone. I really got to know more about him. He laid out all his cards. It was intriguing and refreshing to hear someone tell me all about himself, even the little white lie on his profile that said he was thirty-eight when actually he had just turned forty-two. He told me how he had two boys—by two different mothers—whom he truly adored and that he wished that he could be a full-time father to them. He said he did pay child support and he did see them, but to him, nothing would've been better than being a full-time, hands-on father. He told me a lot about himself, and maybe some matchmakers may say not to reveal everything or too much before or on the first date, but it just made me think that I liked him even more. He was also so polite, and this was a first for me.

Emma was so excited for me that Friday at work. She knew I had been single for so long, and she, like quite a few of my friends close to me, had heard about him for weeks. She couldn't wait until Monday to hear all about our first date.

The night of my first date with Matt was hectic. I was hoping to look my best and began prepping early once I got home from work. Melanie had cut and colored my hair the weekend before, which was perfect timing. But that night, right before I was going to get into the shower, Oliver called me. He was on his way to Venice Beach and needed me to pick him up. I couldn't believe he was doing this to me at the last minute. He knew I had plans, and then he just told me, "Never mind; I will find a way home."

Excuse me? I love him too much to just let that fly. He had never taken the bus home from Venice or been in Venice Beach without me. He had gone to a friend's house, and he told me not to worry and that he would figure it out. Oh, no! I was worried. Nothing mattered to me more than making sure my baby got home safely. Venice is right next to Santa Monica, and even though he knew how to get home from Santa Monica, I wasn't comfortable with him walking around Venice; it was getting dark. He was only fifteen at the time, and although Venice isn't Compton, it can still be dangerous. What made matters worse is when I went to go and get him, he gave me a street name that I couldn't find, and his phone went dead! He had already left his friend's house by that time, and I was frantically driving around looking for him and also calling Matt, pushing back the time for us to meet up. This was Matt's first impression of Oliver. Lovely!

Oliver is the best kid anyone can ask for; he doesn't get into trouble, gets good grades, and does what I say most of the time, but there are those few times when he does things that remind me that he is still a child.

Finally, after close to two hours of senselessly driving around, I reached Oliver. He had found a bus and had just gotten home. If I didn't have the patience not to blow up, I don't know what I would have done. I am sure though that my stress levels were through the roof!

I came home quickly and showered and did my hair and makeup. I looked pretty, but I was flustered because of the time crunch. By the time I drove up to the parking lot that was across from Red Rock on Sunset Plaza, Matt was already there waiting for me. For some reason, he didn't want to walk up half a block to the cantina. I guess it is always awkward walking into a place looking for someone you have never met before. He walked up to me as I was paying for my parking validation. He was this tall, very skinny, dark haired guy with a Pendleton on.

I wasn't nervous seeing him for the first time. I felt like I was meeting up with someone I had known for years. He gave me a hug. I could tell he was nervous, but hopefully I made him feel comfortable by the way I spoke to him, like we saw each other all the time.

We had dinner over two hours, and we talked a lot. He found it cool that I had taken Oliver to see the Pet Shop Boys and Depeche Mode in concert the previous year; he also loved those two bands. He had manners like I had never known, opening up the door for me and pulling out my seat even when I had to use the restroom. Even though he had tattoos, including a big one on his neck, I could see myself bringing him home to my family with a sense of pride. He was polite, spoke well, had manners, did not act tough, and had been a successful entrepreneur. What family members wouldn't love that?

After dinner, we walked to the liquor store to get him some cigarettes. He offered me his Pendleton and took my hand around his arm. We found such commonalties, such as music and punk shows back in Oxnard (around the same time I went), the beach, cars, and driving. We had all these things in common.

After getting his cigarettes, we sat in the car for a bit while we talked about Hot Wheels. We both had had them as children. He was asking me if the ones I had were these certain types, the ones with the white stripe on the wheels. I just smiled and was fascinated as he was giving me the history on Hot Wheels cars. I didn't know which type they were; I just loved the fact that this guy was finding it so interesting that here was this girl loving something he had as a child too and that we could reminisce about it. No one else had ever taken interest in it before. We decided to go for a drive up in the hills and not call it a night so early. We wanted to see how this Cadillac could drive. This first night that I met him, he was driving this rental car. He excused the fact that his car was in the shop. I didn't really care what type of car he had.

We never made it to drive in the hills because we instead drove around looking for a place that was open so I could use the ladies' room. It was hilarious driving and driving, not being able to find a place that was open. We finally found a gas station at the corner of Beverly Glen and Santa Monica Boulevard. It was priceless, little me with his big Pendleton on. It reminded me so much of my days in Oxnard. All my guy friends used to wear them.

As we drove back to my car, he told me how nice it was to be able to talk to someone who knew what he was talking about. He had only been dating younger girls and found it such an eye-opening experience to be with someone close to his age. We parked next to my car and just kept talking. There was so much to talk about and so many things we had in common. We talked about our kids, he told me how he wanted just one more, a girl, and so did I. He said he just wanted "his" own family and just to be happy. I did too. Could it be that simple, us wanting the same things and having such a common background and interests?

Just then, he kissed me. We made out for a bit. In order to let him know that I was going to take it slowly, I had to tell him right there that it had been a while since I had been in a relationship or even made out with anyone—over six and a half years! The only reason I told him this was for the intention of letting him know that I was going to take it slow. At least that was my initial intent. He seemed first shocked and then excited to hear that I hadn't been with someone for over six years. We continued to make out, and let's just say that what he did next was pushing the limits. It's a funny, personal memory between us. Matt was sometimes a risk taker. Months later he'd tell me how he liked to push the envelope as much as he could to see how far people would allow him to go or see people's reactions. We kept kissing for a while. What is it with men? Did my remark that I hadn't been with someone for a long time turn the night into a sort of conquest ... as if I was a virgin all over again? Guys are amusing.

He stopped kissing me and looked over his shoulder to the backseat. We laughed, and I said, "I'm not about to do you in the backseat of this car, especially on the first night." We made out for a little bit more before I stopped it; I knew if I kissed him for one more second, I may have not wanted to stop. We took a deep breath, exhaled, and composed ourselves. We spoke of getting together again later the following week. He walked me to my car, opening up the door for me. I got into my car, he leaned in and kissed me good night and said he'd call me.

He texted me about ten minutes after I got home to see if I had made it home safely and to let me know that he had a great time. He told me how his brother that he was staying with in Beverly Hills was going to Hawaii the following week and that maybe we could go see a movie and then hang out later at his brother's crib. I liked that idea, but I was not completely sure how I felt about him. I liked him, don't get me wrong, we had a lot in common, and he was good looking, but I was not sure if he was my type for something serious—and wasn't this what this was all about? It seemed like he was skinnier than the picture he had texted me about a week and a half earlier (it must have been an old one or a weird angle, and I was still used to liking more muscular guys) and he smoked, which was my number-one pet peeve.

I had been disgusted by smokers my whole life, even though I smoked for a few years during my teens; my mom has always been a chain-smoker. Her smoking always bothered me so much as a child that one Christmas I bought her that electric ashtray that sucked up the smoke—and then of course there is that memory of reaching for that glass, thinking it was water, just to be disappointed with a gross combination of the taste of beer and cigarette butts. That taste was awful and sometimes over the years I'd remember that taste. And, I'm also allergic to cigarette smoke; my nose will close up.

After some thought, I thought maybe he could be interesting for a little while. He was good company, and he liked to talk, but I wasn't sure how he would fit into the life I had pictured for myself. I didn't know what "he" would look like. I was looking for something deeper than what was on the surface and had never pictured who. So for the meantime, I thought that I'd just go with the flow and see what came of it.

He texted me the following day; he had to go down to Orange County with his assistant to check out a band that he was possibly going to manage. He sweetly told me that he'd rather hang out with me.

We texted a lot later that day and throughout the night when he went to get "L.A." tattooed on his arm. Over a year later, he told me he got that tat to remind him of how he wanted to conquer L.A. and to always remind him of his intention to return there (he lived in Santa Barbara when he told me this). He had made it big in Santa Barbara County and Orange County. He had been quite successful in apparel and as a producer of videos. He had started with an apparel line that became a huge company in just a few years, he told me. He had named it after his band at the time. He had launched it either right before he was getting sober or had gotten sober in rehab. This is why he said he didn't drink; he was a recovering addict. He later sold this company and then started a line of car-racing videos that were sold in places like Best Buy.

It is funny how we find things or people we are familiar with. Yes, we had a lot in common; I also liked how he was a surfer and skater. I had always been into skateboarders since my early days in Cincinnati when Candelaria's and Paoletta's friends used to skate at our house. I felt very comfortable around him—almost *too* comfortable—but why didn't I flinch at the fact that he was a recovering addict when I also had a history of addiction? I should have run the other way, but there were no alarms going off like he had a problem anymore. It was me at the cantina who had that one drink. Would I want someone to judge me and think that I could possibly relapse and start having a problem with alcohol or drugs again?

After getting his tattoo, he went to a club. He planned out the next week of when he'd like to see me—Sunday, Wednesday, and Friday, he said. *So specific*, I thought, *but funny and cute!* I still wasn't sure if I wanted to see him. I liked the attention I was getting, but I started thinking a lot, analyzing like I do, to see if I wanted it to go any further. Maybe I was making too many excuses. I tend to do that and overanalyze. Sometimes this is beneficial, and sometimes it isn't.

He didn't help the situation by texting me a lot. He seemed more excited about seeing me again. We texted about a lot of things, but then it began leading to a sexual nature. I can't remember exactly how, but I was just starting to think that he was only interested in me because of that.

But the real question was, was I? It had been over six and a half years. I loved sex. I had some good times in my lifetime, really never having issues with it and not being satisfied. I had just been busy with other things like raising my boy, getting my degree, and getting my life straight. Was Matt someone I could see as long term—or, as some of my friends saw it, someone to just finally have sex with; *it had been too long*. I leaned more toward wanting someone to be into me, liking me, and eventually loving me. Did I really want someone to use me again? I'd had too much of men not caring about me in my lifetime. Where did I want to take this with Matt? Should I just stop conversing with him completely?

That is where my overthinking was taking me. I also thought of how I was a grown, smart woman. I knew how to make my own decisions, so if I decided to go hang out with him at his brother's and if I didn't want to have sex with him, I could just say no and leave. I knew it was possible that if I did have sex with him so soon, he'd more than likely lose all respect for me and not really want to see me anymore. What was I going to do, and what did I really want from him?

It was not until later in the afternoon on Sunday that I decided to go through with it and see what happened once I hung out with him and what I decided to do if it was leading to the bedroom or not.

He was outside walking his brother's dog as I drove up. He came to the car and gave me a hug as I handed him the Betty Crocker sugar cookies I had baked. (Did I also mention how he had a sweet tooth, like me?) He was so thankful that I thought of him.

We went inside, and he gave me a tour of his brother's place. I had brought over some movies for us to watch, and we sat down and watched *The Stepfather*. The beginning is gruesome, as the father murders his family. Matt covered my eyes because, as he said, I didn't have to picture that, much less see it. The movie kind of ends on an intense note; Matt had to smoke a cigarette because of it, and I remember him clutching his heart as we were talking about it.

He came back down and sat next to me. For the first time in my life, here was a guy who had so much to talk to me about. We just talked and talked and talked. I kept thinking, *Do I just do him and get over this dry spell, or do I stand my ground, not have sex with him, and see what we could be?*

In just one moment, for a second, there was silence, and he looked at me, and he leaned in and started kissing me. Oh, oh! Here was that moment I was kind of scared of—the moment that I had been overanalyzing for the last twenty-four hours. What would I do? What *should* I do?

We kissed for a while, and then he stood up and took my hand, and I paused for a second or two before I stood up and walked up the stairs with him. I thought, *I like him. I really, really like him. This is the point of no return.* I knew at that point I wanted more than just getting over the dry spell and that I was possibly ruining anything for a future with us, but I really wanted to be with him, because I felt something with him, even way before we actually first met.

Having someone touch me again after all those years was sweet. I lay on the bed after we were done having sex, and he sat on a chair to smoke, all the while talking and talking. He told me so much about the last decade of his life and of how he had lost everything the last couple of years. It was more than ten years earlier that he and his brother had built a highly successful apparel company almost overnight. He had bought a place in Orange County where he moved in with a girlfriend, and after he sold off the company, he had bought a second place in Santa Barbara.

After selling the apparel company and paying off a lot of investors, he started a new video-production business with the leftover money, but that tanked after a few years when video pirating became rampant. He tried starting other ventures, but nothing seemed to work out.

Around the same time, the video company had stopped doing well, the economy started to tank. His longtime girlfriend, fiancée, a makeup artist, went on the road with some kitschy band, and after six months, she decided she wanted to stay longer on the road, but he told her to come back home. She didn't. She instead ended up marrying some guy that she had met, but that marriage didn't last.

Right before the economy really sunk millions of people, he had two homes, had a business that was doing well, had a fiancée, and had been sober for twelve years. And then the economy happened. Life happened. His video company was over. Mortgages went through the roof. He lost his two homes. His fiancée walked out because, as he saw it, once the money was gone, she was done. He couldn't get any kind of business started, so he had a hard time supporting himself. He also told me that along with the fiancée walking out, his friends were no longer around because he could not give them work, and they could no longer use him for something.

I was silent, taking it all in. I was honored that he was being so vulnerable with me. It was sad and tragic to hear because also then he told me that was when he relapsed. Everything had gone. He felt so alone. I was silent, taking it all in. I was honored that he was being so trusting with me. All I wanted to do as I lay on the bed hearing him bare his soul to me was to reach out and give him a hug, letting him know that I felt sorry for his loss. I had known that loss of losing everything.

What he said next, though, was the first moment when I thought, *I really do like him.* He told me that he was somewhat happy that his years of struggling—losing the businesses, the houses, the friends and the fiancée had happened, because he had learned a great deal. He knew now what and who was important and what he'd do differently in the future. He said that he wouldn't spend so much time working and just enjoy life, his family, and his sons. This is what he valued and was most important in his life. That got to me. Some people don't get to that realization. Most people just want to have the success again and will work and work and work at any cost. Right then, I felt like we were at the same point in our lives, knowing what was important and appreciating who and what we had. We could relate.

His plans on seeing me Sunday, Wednesday, and Friday turned into seeing me more than what he had originally thought. I went over the next night, Monday. We both were working that day, so I went over after work and after I'd made Oliver dinner. I was still working at the cosmetic packaging company, and he was now working at an apparel company that specialized in organic shirts. When I went over, he gave me some T-shirts for Oliver and me and a Ralph Lauren polo, all organic, for Oliver. I wasn't sure if it was an instinctive nature of his or if he was reciprocating because I had baked him some cookies the night before. Either way, it was nice of him to do; off the bat, he was showing me how thoughtful and appreciative he could be.

The next few times we saw one another, we talked a lot, watched TV, and were together. Woman usually find men that roll over and go to sleep, but he only did that one night we were together. Instead of rolling over, he'd lie there hugging me, talking, and rubbing my back. We both spoke more about our pasts, our likes, and what we wanted out of life. I was taken aback by what he was sharing. I heard more about him than he did about me, which might have been better, because all I was hearing was how similar our lives had been. He was sweet when I opened up to him, telling him how I always thought a black cloud was following me, and he then said, "We need to change that."

He shared with me how much music meant to him. I didn't tell him that I used to get lost in hearing music for hours or even days and that music had even saved me sometimes from trying to kill myself. When he went on for a few minutes talking about how great the '80s music was and how most people didn't realize how much of a new sound was being created, I nearly fell off the bed. We both had taken on the New Wave / punk scene. I told him how I had even shaved my head as a teenager, later only keeping my bangs. When we were teenagers, we lived just about thirty minutes away from each other. We had both been to the punk shows in Oxnard. We knew some of the same people. We were both high school dropouts, dropping out around the same time. He was a drummer most of his life and when he was in high school, he had walked off campus during lunch one day to go on the road with his band—and the other band orchestrating the tour actually consisted of some guys that I knew from Oxnard at the time. They grabbed him from his lunch period. They told him to leave with them, that his bandmates were all getting ready to leave to go on tour. He never returned to school, he said.

We both had gotten very involved in partying a little too much that later resulted in both of us having problems. We both were very close to drug dealing and had immersed ourselves in that lifestyle, later contributing to our substance use. I had gotten myself together a little earlier than he had, but we both did get our acts together—I becoming a mother and seriously pursuing my degrees and he getting sober, becoming a father and becoming a successful entrepreneur.

I saw both of us in our own way becoming very successful and having moved forward. And now we both recently had to readjust our lives because everything that was going on with us: I had already been notified in this bad economy that my position was being relocated to New York, and since I was not willing to move I'd be out of a job soon; and he had just lost everything. When I thought back to what I was looking for—someone who could relate to me and to whom I could relate to, someone with similar common interests and someone who had a background like I had—I couldn't help but see how parallel our lives had been for decades.

Somehow, instead of meeting twenty-four years earlier, living thirty minutes apart—knowing some of the same people, doing the same things, then both of us also living later in Orange County, we'd somehow meet in Los Angeles. All our experiences—wild, extreme, rich, poor, and then just trying to find our way, making sense of what we wanted in our lives—had us both now at the same point, where we realized what was important and what we truly wanted. Was it a mere coincidence that we met?

All I knew was that I was stunned because I had never met someone like him, and in a weird way, I felt we somewhat shared some of the same history. In so many ways, when I looked at him, I saw myself. It was easy to relate and feel for him.

We hung out two more days after Monday, on Wednesday and Thursday. On Friday, he wanted to take me out for a "real date," as he saw it—a dinner *and* a movie—and to pick me up at my place. I made sure to look extra nice on our date night.

He made reservations, and I went ahead and bought us tickets online to go see a movie that had just opened with JLo. He picked me up around 7:00 p.m. Because it was too soon to meet Oliver, I had him call me when he was on his way so I could go out and meet him. We were running late to dinner because he said he had lain down to take a nap and overslept. I can still remember him driving and doing a U-turn in front of my place, and, like the gentleman that his grandfather taught him to be, he got out of his car to open my door.

We jumped onto Interstate 10, and it seemed like every moment we spent together was more perfect than before because here he was listening to New Order, which was one of my favorite bands, and it was rare to meet someone who would be playing them in the car. When "True Faith" came on, a song that reminded me so much of my first days in Chicago and the freedom I felt from my life in Houston, I reached for Matt's hand because I thought he was going to change the song. He told me he was just turning it up.

I never had felt so in tune with someone like that before. He didn't know that New Order, Duran Duran, and the Pet Shop Boys were my most favorite bands and got me through my toughest times. The next time he'd pick me up to go somewhere, he was playing the Pet Shop Boys. That was mind blowing and just made me wonder how it could get better than that.

When we got to the Grove, it was crazy as I had hoped it wouldn't be. The Grove is a small outdoor mall in West Hollywood, a tourist attraction and a mecca for overcrowding on weekends, holidays, and the summertime. It's really nice, and I'm sure that was why he wanted to go there—and the fact that he wasn't a local meant that he didn't know of many places to go, but it wouldn't have been my first choice. It was noisy.

The Farm restaurant had outdoor seating, and he wanted to sit next to the large fountain because he said he liked the sound of water, that it was calming. I could barely hear him as we talked. There were kids with their families running around screaming. It was hardly romantic, and you could barely hear the water from the fountain.

We went in and watched one of JLo's worst movies. The premise was good, but the acting was bad. He didn't want the night to end, so we walked for a bit and talked. Somehow we got on the subject of immigration again.

During our week together, there were two things that we disagreed on—immigration and guns. These are two things very close to me and important to me. I came to this country as an immigrant and stayed illegally for a while. If it hadn't been for my parents making this choice, I wouldn't have been sitting right there with him. My views are that the majority of people that are coming to this country to escape a bad situation are coming here for the possibility of a better life. He viewed immigration as something that needed to be handled because, as he saw it, it was that the people coming over here were terrorists, and he also feared the rising drug wars in Mexico that he said were now crossing over to Texas.

My issue with guns should be apparent by now. Before Lily died, I never really had a view on them, knew where I stood when it came to gun possession, and the use of them. I never really cared. I liked that England barely had any guns though. When I was a teenager living in Oxnard, I was surrounded by guns because some of my guy friends had them, and they'd sometimes be strapped. When I was young and ignorant, there were pictures taken of me and of guys holding guns near me, even one in which I'm laughing and sitting on a friend's lap while he has a gun to my head. I did not think anything of it. It wasn't until Lily's service after she was shot that I thought about it and hated it. I decided that no one should have guns—that they just kill mostly innocent people.

Matt and I had our own views and agreed after speaking for a bit, trying to understand the other's view, that we'd never speak of these two things again. But for some reason—I think it was when immigration was all over the news—the issue somehow came up in our conversation on our date night. It ruined the evening.

I ended our conversation and acted really tired, ready to go. He knew it had turned sour, but he still asked me if I wanted to come over. I said no, that it had been a long day. He apologized about talking about immigration, and I said it was okay but that we really should never speak about it again.

He drove me home and opened the car door for me, and we gave each other a hug and called it a night. I thought about it all night and next morning. This situation couldn't be perfect, but how could I ever bring home someone with these views on immigration? I would never do that!

By the next morning, I found some middle ground and understanding on the fact that he had this fear and really didn't know all the facts when it came to immigrating to the United States—why people do it, what they sacrifice to have a better life, and how this anti-immigration thing is actually more, as a lot of us see it, against Hispanics than anything else.

He called me the next morning to again apologize for bringing up immigration on our date. He said he understood somewhat where I was coming from and that he was happy we had come over to the States because, yes, if it hadn't been for that, he wouldn't have met me and never would have had these last few days with me. He was relieved to hear that I didn't want to end us from seeing one another.

We made plans later that evening to hang out at his brother's because his brother was getting back into town the following day.

I went over with a new batch of warm cookies and another movie to watch. He didn't waste any time to start kissing me. We made out for a while on the couch and then had sex. We were back to chatting up a storm afterward. He talked and talked. I liked how sometimes out of the blue when he was smoking a cigarette, walking the dog, or getting us something to drink, he'd just come over and kiss me—just one sweet kiss, out of the blue, in the middle of our conversation. I sat there lying on the couch listening to him as he talked in the doorway of his brother's place, smoking.

At some point—I don't even think I was listening to what he was saying—I just remember looking at this really tall, skinny guy with black hair, smoking a cigarette and feeling like I was shaking my head left to right, saying no to myself because of what I was now thinking. I was thinking that he could be it. He was it. He was everything I never knew I was looking for. I thought if we got married, it would be a marriage that would last; it would be a good marriage with trust, communication, respect, and laughter.

How was I even thinking this? He was doing my pet peeve, smoking. He was too skinny for my taste. Even though he would eventually make a business work, he barely had any money right now and not a place of his own. The thought of him being the one, I wanted to easily ignore, but it was too strong to ignore because it was more of a feeling than a thought. It was crazy. It was not similar to anything I had ever felt before though. I had been infatuated a few times in my life, been really into guys, but this wasn't like that. I had never seen or thought of anyone in that light before, being my husband. *This is right where you are supposed to be and who you are supposed to be with— at least for now*, something told me.

I left after 2:00 a.m., and Matt called me the next morning to let me know that he was going up north for a few days to see his family and his boys and that he'd call me when he got back. The day when he was supposed to get back passed, and then more days passed. We texted each other for the next two weeks, but he didn't ask me out again. He said he was still interested, and it showed in his texting, but I wanted to see him again. Little by little, my heart was breaking. How could it have been going so well and then almost nothing?

He called me a few times while I was at work. I'd go and talk to him in the conference room because our calls were never that quick. There were some calls that he was just checking in to see how things were. There were other calls when he needed a friend to talk to because he was very sad and feeling lonely. There was one call when he was on his way to Orange County to go to a movie premiere about a skater or skateboarding, and he wished that I was sitting next to him going down there with him. I'd put him at ease, he said. I'd make whatever drama he was going through in his life go away.

Another time he called me was right after his ex-fiancée called. The trophy fiancée was calling him to see what he wanted to do with the cat that they had rescued during Hurricane Katrina; she was moving and couldn't take the cat. Matt told me that he was upset because he was worried about what would happen to the cat; he thought she might just abandon it. I'm not sure what he was upset about, the cat or the ex-fiancée, but I did something I began doing with him, making him feel better, at least that is what he would later tell me. He had called me upset, and I changed his mood. He recognized it and thanked me for it now and constantly.

He said the reason why he couldn't see me was because he was dealing with a lot of stuff. The organic apparel company was now only offering him only a retainer of $750 a month to keep him on because they wanted him to come on board as a sales manager but really couldn't offer him that position until they officially took off in the States; their headquarters were in the UK. I knew he spent a lot of time going to AA meetings, so that also hindered our time. He also was having a hard time bouncing around from his brother's place—which was actually also his brother's girlfriend's place—and staying at his assistant's place. He said his assistant always had a bunch of people and "dudes" over until the wee hours and that it would keep him up.

I tried to express my patience, but I felt a little bit emotional inside as the weeks progressed and we didn't see each other. I was sad. Didn't he see the possibility of us? I had never met anyone that I saw myself with like I had seen myself with him. Something inside me was telling me that this was not over and that I was supposed to have him in my life.

I cried thinking about why I had these feelings, what they meant, and why I couldn't just let it go. I'd go to my friend's office. She worked in the same building, just a few floors below. Every day I'd talk to her and vent. I wasn't only going through this turmoil of him and me; I was going through months of not knowing when my last day of working at the cosmetic company would be. I had been living with that fear for over nine months. I knew I was going to be handed my pink slip, but when—and then what?

My life began to feel uncontrollable. When I was talking to my friend in her office one day in July, I started crying for the first time to her about Matt. All my feelings were at the surface when I had an immediate awakening that the sadness I was feeling was not entirely about him; it was a culmination of years and experiences of not feeling good enough for someone else and that I wasn't loved or could be loved.

This all stemmed back to the first people who should have truly loved me—my parents. I don't know what made me have this revelation, but I'm glad I did, because I felt dumb at first that it could possibly be about a guy. Maybe it is because I have spent many years analyzing a lot of things that my brain is so programmed to go on like a light bulb sometimes. I was like, "WOW." My heart wasn't fully breaking because of Matt; he was making little cracks in it, but my heart was already broken by the two most important people in my life. I had been contemplating a tattoo for weeks, and I knew exactly at that point on what I wanted it to be: a beautiful broken heart.

I couldn't wait to get my new tattoo. I had only one from all those years back when I was twenty-two. I thought I'd never get another one because I was happy with just one. I went to Art & Soul Tattoo shop, which was very close to my apartment. I asked my girlfriend Nicole if she wanted to join me after work. She met up with me just as the tattoo artist was finishing up.

We decided to go have happy hour in Culver City at Rush Street. I felt like I'd just had an aha moment. I was energized and happy because I had my tattoo, and I had my awareness to the true status of my heart, even though it was still broken. I had a broken heart, but don't most of us?

I knew I was spending years repairing it and learning to love myself and heal myself. Over the years, I knew I'd be okay, because I knew what was best for me.

Nicole and I sat down upstairs at the outside patio and ordered ourselves some drinks—a cosmo for me and a chocolate martini for Nikki. When the drinks came out and we took a sip, whew, were they strong! I said, "Well, we will only need one, and we will drink it slow." I ordered a few appetizers; I hadn't eaten all day.

That night ended up being a foggy one. I don't remember finishing my drink. I remember taking the first bite or two of our food. I remember going to the restroom, being drunk, and texting Matt. It wasn't until Nicole mentioned it the following day that I remembered falling as I was walking back to our table. That I will chalk up to the layout of the outside patio, being half-wood and half-sand!

The next morning, I woke up with that too-familiar feeling of being hungover. I was in bed the whole next day. What sucked more than the hangover and constant throwing up was that I had gone that far. How could I do that to myself after all these years? Wasn't I better than that? Hadn't I learned? Two steps forward, one step back.

Around noon, I received a text from Matt. He had already been living in Santa Barbara for a week or two. He could no longer couch surf at people's places, and the $750 a month wasn't even paying his car payment or what he needed to pay each month for child support. We texted back and forth as he apologized in his text; he said how I was a great girl and that he was sure I would find someone but that he had too hard of a time trying to make L.A. work and that he had found someone else.

I felt sicker than how I was now feeling. *Really!?!* Why did he even keep in touch with me? I was pissed, and I expressed it. I didn't curse him out or call him names or anything; I just told him to never reach out to me again.

As per usual with my hangovers, I hurt all through the night. The next morning, I was moving slowly, cleaning myself off and getting rid of that feeling of what I had just done to myself. Just then, I received a few texts from Matt. He wrote, "I'm pretty over this new chick, anyway." He wrote that he was sorry he even told me about her. He said, "I need a few weeks to get my head straight, and then after that I'll reach out to you."

I didn't know what to say, but to just go along with it, I texted back, "Okay." I still felt like shit from drinking too much, so I didn't care too much of this roller-coaster ride he was putting me on.

Almost exactly two weeks passed when I told myself that enough was enough. I was ready, I thought, to move on and let go. I thought I was never going to hear from him, and I never wanted to be capable of reaching out to him again. I deleted all his texts, photos, and information off my phone on a Friday night.

He e-mailed me Saturday morning. *Oh my gosh, really!!!* I was so ready to ignore the connection I felt to him, but something kept "us", it, going.

He said that Sunday when he had last text me, thirteen days earlier, he entered rehab in Malibu. His life had spiraled out of control so much since I last saw him back in April, he said. It was now the third week of July. We e-mailed back and forth. I was trying to let go or at least put a distance between us because I couldn't take the emotional bind I was being dragged into. I wanted whatever it was that was pulling me in to staying with him to go away. I e-mailed him that I was proud that he went to seek treatment. I told him how I knew he could battle his addiction—that he was better than it and had so much going for him and that he was smart and creative. He asked me in his first e-mail for my number because he no longer had his phone and anyone's numbers. I ignored that question and the request for me to call him.

A few more e-mails went back and forth. He said he knew his addiction stemmed from the loss and abandonment of his father when he was very young; he had spoken about it in rehab and that his first vivid memory was of his father walking out on him, his brother, and his mother. At the time, when he was a child, he couldn't make sense of what was happening. All that he remembered was his father walking out and how he was sitting on the couch and turned to see his brother crying.

I already knew that his father had walked out on him and his twin brother and mother, leaving his mother to go on welfare. He had told me that story back in April, right after I had told him how I had to go on welfare for a few years when I first had Oliver. It was a way he related us together, his mom and me. But to have his father walking out as his first memory tells a thousand words. Loss and abandonment, especially by a parent, can be a crippling thing that will just reappear intensely if you don't seek help. It all made sense to us right then why he relapsed; loss and abandonment were issues he could not cope with. He relapsed when all was gone—the money, being a successful entrepreneur, the company, the homes, and the fiancée. The loss was too intense.

The next day and a few more e-mails later, he wrote me as he sat on a hillside overlooking Santa Barbara. I finally decided to call him. The gravitational pull was too strong, and he was a friend needing me. I felt like I had to give him my hand once again. We spoke, and it just felt like I had felt always with him, just so right. When we spoke or saw each other, everything—life, him, me—made sense, and there was this balance and calmness in my life. It is hard to express and to have anyone else understand, but all I can say further is that it is like when you know you are supposed to be there at that very precise moment because everything makes sense in the world. This was that feeling. When we didn't speak or see each other, I felt confused because it—us—made so much sense ... but then again at that time, it made no sense to me.

I had always said I never had a type, but now when I think of him and my type, he was my type. I had dated mostly black guys who were either jocks or worked out. They were nothing like who I truly was or into. And after many years, here came along someone who was truly up my alley: edgy, sweet, thoughtful, and kind of looked like Speed Racer; I loved Speed Racer as a kid. It took a while to recognize all this, and I thought I was a new, more mature, conservative woman now at least that is what I had been portraying all these years. I had just let life and whoever came along make me lose sight of who I was deep down inside, and now I was shocked and confused when he came along.

I tried to fight every emotion and thought I was feeling. I had this constant conflict going on. My rational side always wanted to prevail and not let this thing that I felt win. I knew he was a good-looking, nice, thoughtful, and ambitious guy and so forth, but my thought was that I wasn't crazy goo-goo gaga over him, so why was this feeling taking precedence over my rational side? It was weird. I lusted over guys a lot before, but this wasn't that. I spent months being so confused about all this when he was out of the picture. It drove me nuts at times when I was alone, but all I now knew was that I had to keep my heart open to him in any kind of way. It didn't feel right if I closed the door.

About a week later on a Friday, after months of dying to get out of town, I texted Matt and Melanie (from Oxnard) and asked the two of them, "Who wants me?" I needed to get out of dodge. Matt texted me back immediately. He said I could come up there and that he'd be happy to see me, but he did have a few things he needed to do. I packed up my stuff, beachwear and all. I chose the Motel 6 at East Beach, which borders Santa Barbara and Montecito. I was so excited not only to see him but to get out of town; I needed it so badly. It was the first time I left Oliver home alone. He was sixteen already and was looking forward to being home alone.

I felt like a teenager driving up north on the 101 freeway, blasting my music. I took the Cabrillo exit that led to my motel. I started the slight curve to the right on Cabrillo toward the ocean, and just then, something happened to me; it was like the heavens opened up and sang to me. I don't know if it was all the months of uncertainty with my work and future or what had been going on with Matt and me, but I had been climbing the walls emotionally for a while and just then all those feelings went away. It almost made me cry. I love this spot and remember this every time I take that drive.

I checked in and changed into my bikini to go to the beach. Matt had to do a few things around his parents' house and couldn't come over until about 5:00 p.m. I lay out, listening to music and taking in my views. I was honored to be able to witness a wedding from beginning to end right there in front of me about fifteen yards away. I cried. I wanted to one day be loved like that. When it is real, it is beautiful. I think when a man asks a woman to spend the rest of her life with him, it is truly magical, because you are saying to the other person, "I don't want to go on in life without you, because I love you that much." I wanted someone to feel that for me and vice versa. After all these years of not wanting to get married, I now wanted it more than ever with someone I wanted to spend the rest of my life with.

When Matt came over around 6:00 p.m. to pick me up, I was still getting ready and talking to Melanie over the phone. She had finally called me back after me texting her the day before. I was so glad I didn't wait for her to get back to me! She was so excited to hear that I was in SB and going to see Matt again.

There was a knock on the door, and I got off the phone with her and answered it. He gave me one of his big, tight, long hugs. Off the bat, he started to talk, and I finished my last five minutes of getting ready. We began to walk outside to go to the car, but we stopped to talk. He sat on the outer part of the air-conditioning unit that went inside my motel room, telling me how bad things had gotten emotionally, financially, and with his addiction. He looked good, and he had gained some weight. I just stared very closely into his face while he spoke. I gave him a hug afterward.

We went to State Street for dinner and continued talking, now leaving all the bad stuff to the side. We had a nice meal, and in between, he took pictures of us. He told me that if we hadn't known each other and he just saw me walking down the street that he would have had to meet me somehow.

I asked him, "So would you come up to me?"

He said, "No. What would I say?"

I said, "So that is why maybe sometimes I do not get approached. Would you actually let that chance go by? What if you could be missing out on someone great?"

He said, "It would just make me feel weird going up to someone I didn't know. I'm not that type of guy."

I said, "Well, thankfully, we already know each other."

I left to use the ladies' room after we finished dinner, and when I came back, there was a cosmo sitting there waiting for me. I would've ordered a drink if I had felt like drinking. Why had he done that? He said he wanted me to have fun despite the fact that he couldn't. I didn't feel like drinking. I liked that he didn't drink. All these months, I took in more of what I saw than what he recently had told me about his addiction. I guess because I didn't see it, I didn't see how bad of a problem it was. It kind of went in one ear and out the other. I took a few sips. I didn't like the way it tasted; it was too strong.

I said, "Let's go," and he then took a few sips from my glass prior to getting up and walking out. I felt uneasy about it, but he was a grown man, and it was already done.

We ventured out around State Street, and it was kind of romantic. We spoke, walking slowly, me holding on to his left forearm like I had done before.

It was late, and we decided to head back to the motel, but before we went back to my room, he wanted to go to the liquor store. I paused. Not only did I not want to go, but wasn't this a problem for him?

He said his real problem was with drugs, not alcohol, and he had this kind of teenage spirit energy going on that made me take in the moment, and I just went along with it. I allowed him to drive us to the liquor store in Montecito. We got back to the motel, and he made himself a small cup of vodka and cranberry juice and a cup of vodka with mango juice for me. I had to add more mango juice because it was too strong for me. One thing to know about me and my drinking is that I really don't like the taste of liquor. I spent years getting wasted, but toward the end, I rarely had very strong drinks unless I was too drunk to realize it. The only time I really tasted a lot of liquor was when I used to take shots or when I was really young in Chicago or in Oxnard—and then and only then was when I'd drink straight Schnapps or Jack Daniels.

I only had one cup. He had three cups. I made him stop there, even though they were really small cups. I noticed how he drank, and it was not a pretty sight. I had never seen someone drink a cup so fast; it was like he was dehydrated. I knew right then he did have an issue with alcohol, and that is why I made him stop when I did.

We went down to the beach to try to hear the waves, but we only stayed for about ten minutes because it was so freaking cold. We went back to our room and had sex. I barely could sleep afterwards. I was perched halfway on top of him while he held me sleeping. When I was awake, I just stared at him, thinking too much. My rational side was saying no. He was yummy in every kind of way I felt about him, but I was really trying to get to the heart of what I fancied. The few times I fell asleep, I had really quick, vivid dreams. I have an unbelievable photographic memory sometimes. My brain is wired for visuals like that, so sometimes in my dreams also, I have very precise visuals, like a camera. That night I had two, but they were magnified in deep, rich color, and they were like flashes taken out of a movie clip lasting a few seconds. The first one was of me in a burgundy dress, slight lined with black beading, in a backyard walking down an aisle toward Matt. He had a black dress shirt on with a tie that matched the color of my dress, and the last second I had was of looking at him, smiling, and he was smiling back at me with the biggest grin I ever saw him make, and then when I was right about to reach for his hand, I woke up with a slight jerk.

The second vivid dream I had was of what appeared to be in a hospital room, and it was just of Matt in full medical scrubs holding a baby and smiling, looking at me … and then I woke up with another small jerk. I slightly woke Matt, but he immediately fell back asleep. I still to this day cannot shake those dreams. I see them still as I saw them just as I woke up that night. How fascinating and how sometimes hurtful our brains can be.

The next morning, he felt bad that he had even suggested drinking at all. Not only did he see it as bad, bringing his addiction issue to a wonderful visit from me, but he couldn't believe he slipped like that on his recovery. It was stupid, he said, and he would not do that again.

Lying on the bed, I agreed with him. He was sitting on the booth next to the motel's tiny table. He told me what he needed to do from that point forward, and one thing he spoke of was how he needed to not be with girls just because they had money. He was speaking about that flame he had that he originally told me about right before he entered rehab. He was still trying to shake her and get her out of his life. He said it wasn't worth it to just date someone because she had something like money to offer. I agreed.

I told him how I liked how his hair wasn't done. He styled his hair most of the time with gel, and it was spiky in the front. I had never seen him without all that style. I told him that all the styling of the hair and the clothes took away from really seeing him. I liked how I could focus just on his face and not his look. He finally really looked extremely handsome to me. He made that smirk that I loved and thanked me. He kissed me a little bit and then said good-bye for now. I spent the next few hours lying out on the beautiful sands of Santa Barbara before I headed back down to L.A.

We spoke for the next few days, and he made plans to come and stay with me the following weekend. He came over Friday night after visiting his old assistant, Hannah, because she was leaving L.A. to move back home to New Mexico. They had a falling out back when he was staying in L.A., and he said he wanted to make amends with her before she left.

While over at her place for not too long, he was waiting on me, desperate to come right over. I think he didn't want to be around Hannah and her friends because they were about to start drinking, and he probably feared relapsing. I was waiting on Oliver to get out of the shower and get dressed. He was going to be out of the apartment for the weekend; I was sending him to stay with one friend Friday night and another one on Saturday night because even though all those months when I had offered for Matt to couch surf at our place, he didn't want to take me up on it because he was concerned about what Oliver would think.

Matt came over right after Oliver left our place. We hung out, catching up and watching TV. The following day was a beautiful, warm summer day, so Matt and I decided to go view the shops out at

Third Street Promenade in Santa Monica.

We walked through the crowds of the promenade and made a beeline toward Ocean Avenue about a block away where we could overlook the beach and the pier. Matt had only been out of rehab for just a couple of weeks, and he was talking about his issues. I took some pictures as he chatted away. He spoke of how he wanted us to visit his uncle who lived east of Los Cabos, Mexico, whom he was partially named after and whom he felt more like than anybody else. I smiled. It was sweet, but I told him how I was still waiting for the real Matt to show himself. I knew and told him he still had a long road to recovery, and until he got there, we couldn't proceed with such plans. Matt had just done a stint in rehab, but as he told me, he was taken out too early. He had only been able to stay for those two weeks because that was all his parents could afford to pay for. He wished he could have stayed longer, because he knew he needed more time.

He had gotten off of Xanax—which he said was the worst thing ever to detox from—and whatever else he had started using in L.A., but he was still on his Suboxone, which was given to him about two years earlier before we met. Suboxone is a drug that is used to wean someone off of opioids, but it is addicting too. At the time when he was first prescribed it, he wasn't aware, nor did it seem like the doctor knew that it could be addictive. When we saw each other, he was on a very low dosage of it, and I really couldn't tell if he was on anything. It was the times when I didn't see him that he took more than he should, and then he'd drink or use other drugs. Early on, I didn't take his addiction seriously, but now I was being cautious.

We had a good time there talking in the sun, offering to take pictures for tourists so they could all be included in their picture. Matt seemed energized, happy, and focused on us and life in general. With a slight laugh, he told me that this was the real him, but I knew I was only seeing glimpses of him this whole time we knew each other. I knew addiction too well. When an addict is barely using or has recently stopped, that person is still under the influence because the brain takes longer to adjust to being completely clean. They fight to stay sober, so they aren't completely their full sober selves yet. I told him that maybe in a few months we'd go to Mexico and visit his uncle.

We went back to the promenade and had a bite to eat before we headed back to my place. He took a memorable picture of us. We look like such a happy, good-looking couple.

Oliver was home when we returned. He had come home earlier and was ready to be driven to his other friend's house. Matt and Oliver met for the first time. Oliver had heard so much about Matt and liked him from what I'd told him. He'd say to me often, "You two should get married." In Oliver's sixteen years of life, he had only met one other guy who was in my life; there weren't any others.

Oliver and Matt meshed so well together. Matt's oldest son is about a year and half younger than Oliver, and at the time, Matt was still young at heart, so he knew how to make the situation comfortable.

Matt and I drove Oliver to his friend's house in Venice. Oliver loved this because Matt had a Mercedes AMG, all decked out and fast. We drove to Venice, and Matt showed Oliver what his Mercedes could do. Oliver loved it! It wasn't the same as my fast driving, because I never had a cool car.

Matt and I came back to my place, and I ordered Chinese food for dinner. We had such a good time together. From the very first night we met, it always felt right and comfortable to be with this man, and I felt like I had known him all my life. It was a connection that I had never felt with anyone. When we spent time together, we talked about our very serious issues, emotionally supporting the other by giving insight, encouragement, and understanding. There were a lot of moments when we laughed, Matt cracking more jokes than I. There were also moments of us talking about our past, present, and future, and in between our conversations, he'd walk over to just give me one of those sweet kisses out of the blue.

Both nights, he told me how happy I made him. This night I was lying on the couch, and when he was done smoking, he bounced over to lie with me and put his arms around me. "You make me so happy. I feel good to be around you." I heard that a few times from him.

By this time, I saw glimpses of how good things could be—*the possibility of us.* I had fallen for Matt and wasn't only attracted to him but loved the essence of him—how he thought, felt, and treated me when we were together. He was one of the most thankful, appreciative human beings I had ever met. He was kind, considerate, compassionate, and thoughtful, and like he once put it, he was sensitive, despite what others thought when they saw him. He told me how he strived for the underdog or kids who were less like the rest of us in school. I thought if and when he was to get his life straight and have me in his life, that I'd be the luckiest girl in the world.

Matt left late Sunday morning. He told me he didn't want to go. I remember walking him out to his car, and he told me, "You are like the best friend I never had. Well, no, like the best friend I haven't had in a long time." I wipe tears as I recall this moment, because he was that to me also, and I never said it back to him. I just kissed his hand I was holding. We kissed good-bye, and I couldn't feel any better of how things were now that they were back on track, because I always knew if we tried, we could be something special.

I couldn't wait to see him again. He called me on his way home and thanked me for the great weekend and for having him over.

The following weekend, I was sending Oliver off to Stanford University. He was part of a leadership ambassador organization, People to People, and was going to be staying in Palo Alto, California, on the campus for a week of learning to develop his leadership skills. I couldn't go and see Matt in Santa Barbara. We spoke a couple of times a day. It sucked that he lived there, despite it being only a little over an hour away. I was still working, and I didn't have many vacation days to use. Oliver was flying up to San Francisco, and the People to People organization had a pickup service from the airport because kids flew in from all over the country to do this weeklong event. I planned on driving up to Palo Alto, about five hours north from where we lived to get him when the program was done. Because it felt like Oliver and I hadn't spent much time together recently, I wanted to use some of my unused vacation time and take three days off so that we could drive back down the coast together, making a few pit stops and seeing Guadalupe and her family. They lived about forty-five minutes north of San Francisco.

The apartment was very dark and quiet without my son there with me for that long week. My days were filled with work and talking to Matt in the evenings. I was trying to plan out how I was going to pick up Oliver that following Saturday morning. I was going to drive up there, but I didn't want to go up on Friday. I could have gone after work, but then I would have arrived around midnight, and I didn't want to waste more money than I needed to on a motel room. Matt suggested that I come up to SB and then leave around 2:00 a.m.

I said he was crazy. I said, "I won't get any sleep, especially if I'm going to come up around 8:00 p.m."

He said in a jokingly Matt kind of way, "You'd better come up here and see me."

I told him, "I'll see."

That was on a Tuesday. By Thursday, he didn't seem so eager to see me and told me to do what I thought was best, and I heard how his mood had changed about the whole thing. I decided to go and see him and hang out with him in the shack that he created on his parents' property toward the back of the house.

I drove up that night and got there in an hour. It was a beautiful summer night's drive. Once I drove out of L.A., the stars came out. I parked on the private road that led to his parents' driveway. Matt came out and took me by the hand. I walked with my head facing upward toward the sky. It had been too long since I had seen stars like that.

We were very quiet, trying not to wake up his parents. I hadn't met his mom and dad yet. At that point, I wasn't even sure they knew anything about me. When we talked and the subject of his mom knowing me or not came up, he'd tell me that he had mentioned me to his mom, but I never knew if he did. He told me that after some point, his mom didn't wanted to meet any more girls that were in his life because she became too close to some of them, and she was left in an awkward position once the relationship didn't work out.

I was only sure that his friend Ryan knew about me because of the night we went out to dinner on State Street a few weeks earlier. They had been texting back and forth about me. I'd heard so much about Matt's family, though, that I already felt like I knew them, and part of me already cared for them, especially his mother. Matt and his twin brother had not made life easy for her and her husband, their stepdad—which Matt referred to as Dad. Matt was truly aware of how much he had put his parents through, because he told me so, but I don't think he really got it until about a year later, in mid- to late 2011. I felt a true connection to his mom because of all that he told me and because we both are moms. I could never imagine dealing with the lack of sleep, worrying, and stress, wondering if your child will be all right and just the constant hope that your child will find his way to his ultimate happiness and be content in life. And unfortunately over the previous few years, he seemed to have lost his way.

The shack was a two-room structure, a small entryway with a kitchenette and a small bedroom with a small, open sitting area. It was not really a shack; he just called it that. We watched a movie, and just as I thought, around 11:00 p.m., Matt got this ounce of energy and was talking my ear off. I was able to hush him up around 1:00 a.m., but he was still wide awake, chomping on popcorn sitting next to me as I tried to get some sleep before I had to drive up north. The moment, as crazy as it was, didn't make me regret going there as I thought it might have. Matt is one of those people that you just love to be around.

I left closer to 3:00 a.m. from his place, and that was the scariest drive I've ever made. For close to two hours, I drove in complete darkness and rain and fog. I didn't know if there was a cliff right beside me to the left of my car or not. It kind of felt like there was. This part of Central California is mostly agricultural, and there wasn't a light in the distance at all.

At daybreak, it was cold and still lightly raining, and I saw farm laborers out working in the dewy, vast farmland. I appreciated my life at that moment. I thought of how hard that life is. Not many of us are aware or would want to go out in those conditions and have to be bent over picking fruits or vegetables in the wee hours of the morning and in the cold and rain. So many people in this country say how the farm laborers are taking away our jobs. I heard this a lot, especially when the economy went for a nosedive. I'm sorry, but I don't picture one American doing that kind of work in those conditions for that pay.

By the time I reached Palo Alto, the rain had passed. I stopped at a gas station and used the restroom to freshen up my makeup before picking up Oliver. I was so happy to see my baby and so proud of him.

We headed into the town of Palo Alto to get some Starbucks. He told me about what he had done at the program and was glad that I had signed him up. He initially was supposed to go to Japan, but I could not afford to pay for that trip. I'm happy that he enjoyed it, because it was the last of the big spending efforts I was able to do for him before I was laid off a month later.

A few hours later, we went into San Francisco and met up with Guadalupe and her family for lunch. That was nice because it had been some time since we all had seen each other. After lunch, we walked around Chinatown. We said our good-byes, and Oliver and I headed south into Redwood City, where we stayed for the night.

The following day, Oliver and I went to the Santa Cruz Mountains. We walked through the redwoods and stopped at a small ravine where there were a few people sunbathing and swimming. This is why I took a few extra days off from work. I love moments like that. Vacations don't have to be these big, lavish expenses; they can just be your cheap road trip, stopping off at places along the way. I love moments like this with my son. Nothing is better than spending that one-on-one time with him and talking with him, either about important stuff like what is going on really in his life or just his views on things or just talking about nothing. I've always said that I love my son because he is my child and there is much love for him, but I truly like my son. He has so many likable qualities, so I enjoy spending precious time with him.

After taking our hike through the Santa Cruz Mountains, we went to Carmel-by-the-Sea for dinner. We had been there before, years earlier. It is such a beautiful spot along the central coast. We walked down their small main street that had little boutiques, restaurants, and art galleries. We checked out the menus before heading to the shore to view the turquoise water and take some pictures. It was cold and windy at the shore as families, like ourselves, were there admiring the beauty of Carmel-by-the-Sea. We had dinner and then jumped back into the car again for another lengthy drive, heading south into Buellton.

The next day, we went into the Danish-influenced town of Solvang, which I had wanted to check out for years. I thought we'd be there for hours, but it was so small, and not everything about this center part of town was Danish. We did find some amusement seeing an ostrich farm along the way, and we got out of the car and took some pictures. We decided to head over to Santa Barbara a little earlier than expected. It was Monday now. We had plans to meet up with Matt on Tuesday because that was when our road trip plans had us in town.

Oliver and I checked into the Motel 6 at East Beach that I was so in love with. I took Oliver to State Street and the wharf. We had only been to Santa Barbara together once before, a few years earlier at the end of another road trip. This time around, I was able to show Oliver a little more of Santa Barbara. We jumped onto the trolley and had dinner in town.

The following day, we walked straight out of our motel and had a day at the beach and ate at the East Beach Grill. I love this area so much. Everything is so clean and convenient, and it has a spectacular view.

At this stage of my relationship with Matt, even being crazy about him, I was still wavering if I wanted to continue seeing him. The problem was that I was always holding on to what I had learned about him that first week I had met him, and I wasn't able to shake the thought that had run through me on that sixth day after meeting him—that he could be the one. I saw the possibilities. I felt that he had been everything I never knew I was looking for. I felt like I had known him all my life. I felt like he was home to me, but now I also saw that it wasn't a perfect situation.

I wavered back and forth; since that first week we met, so many things had happened—and not for the best. He had spiraled out of control, and his life was so out of sorts. He had so many good qualities, but there was also still a part of him that would go and be the old Matt—destructive, one who valued material wealth, one who thought he was nothing if he wasn't a successful business guy, and one who also had a fear of getting old. He couldn't see what I saw.

I heard from him that he had remorse and regret about how he allowed the unimportant things and people affect him so deeply. He also felt really bad about what he had done to his family and his sons by not being there and not being sober. I saw the positivity he had shown me when I'd sometimes get lost in my angst of not realizing everything good I had done for my son and me. I saw the generous man that was giving, even to strangers, especially when he really had nothing left to give. I saw the appreciative man that even if you gave him the smallest of gifts that he acted as if no one had ever given him something and that the gift was the best thing ever. And, I experienced the thoughtful man that was present in whatever you were sharing with him.

But with everything I was holding on to that was good, I was letting my rational side think more. I realized I loved an addict. I did see him as entirely different from my mom, though, because I heard over and over how desperately he wanted to get sober and how remorseful he was because he knew how this affected everybody that loved him. He took responsibility for it. In my heart I believed that he'd get sober, but part of my mind thought—what if he didn't. I had also known that there were other girls in and out of the picture. These two things—being a using addict and seeing other girls—I couldn't deal with sometimes. When it came to the girls, it was not like he ever promised me anything or that I was his girlfriend, but it still hurt. I wanted so much more. And unfortunately, I knew from the previous weekend that something had happened. I just felt it.

The previous weekend, when I sent Oliver off to the program in Palo Alto and I was at home by myself talking to Matt all week long, things were great. We stayed in touch, and his connection with me was there as it had been since he had gotten out of rehab. But the weekend that I didn't go was the end of Old Spanish Days Fiesta in Santa Barbara, which is a weeklong annual event celebrating everything Spanish. It has a lot of cultural events, but down on lower State Street, a lot of locals and people come into town and get drunk. I think it was Friday night that I was talking to Matt on the phone. He had just gotten out of an AA meeting and had gotten pulled over. He called me back after getting warned about the tint on his windows of his car. He told me how he was just trying to stay away from all that partying going on and away from getting into any trouble because he didn't want to get caught up in all that again.

The next day, Saturday, was the end of Fiesta, with a big parade down State Street and more drinking at most of the local eateries and bars. A lot of the restaurants and bars on State Street have outside sitting areas, so much overcrowding and drunkenness happens annually. Back in L.A., I was in for the evening watching TV. I took a long, hot bath, and once I got out, there was a phone message from Matt. At first, it was hilarious, and then later it made me worry. The first part of the message didn't even sound like him. He was trying to speak Spanish all loving to me, and it wasn't until he couldn't figure out any more Spanish words and started speaking English that I realized that it was Matt. After I first heard it in its entirety, I thought, *He really has fallen hard for me.*

I called him back and just got his voice mail, so I texted him to call me. A few minutes passed, and I thought, *Uh-oh, come to think about it, he sounded like he may have been tipsy.* The worry set in.

I called a few more times and didn't hear back from him until about 12:30 a.m. He said he couldn't talk because it would wake up his parents. *That hadn't been a problem before,* I thought.

He kind of sounded rude in his text, telling me to not worry, that his phone had died, and that he'd speak to me tomorrow. Though I'd felt like we had gone to right where I wanted us to feel about each other, in less than three hours, I suddenly felt like someone he barely wanted to speak to, much less had any feelings toward. I hated that evening.

The next day, he apologized and said he hadn't drunk and that his phone had just died and that was it. I was old enough and experienced enough to know better, but I let it go.

Push forward to a week after the phone call. Oliver and I were in Santa Barbara, and I was back to pondering where I was going with this Matt situation. Would I just say enough at some point? My tolerance threshold was very thin when I was getting ready for meeting up with him for dinner, because the night before when we were in town, I had wanted to see him, and he said he couldn't. I just thought of the weekend before when he didn't call me back and that his phone died. I knew better, and I thought he had met someone— probably right after he left me the loving, hilarious phone message.

Despite this, I bit my lip and went to go for dinner but was almost about to cancel when we were just about ready and Matt said he'd meet us there. He had shown me such a gentlemanly side to him, so I was very surprised to hear that he wasn't picking us up. I tend to want to fly off the handle, like so many of my family members do, but somewhere inside of me, I tend to breathe and push down that tendency and find some patience and tolerance. He said he couldn't pick me up because some of State Street was still closed off because of the farmers' market and that he was already down there wrapping up an AA meeting. That—and the fact that he said he was bringing his close friend Ryan to meet me—saved me from canceling the dinner date.

I got stares as I walked through the farmers' market. There is something to be said about looking your absolute best! Matt and Ryan were outside smoking a cigarette as we walked up. Matt gave me a big hug, and I shook Ryan's hand. They already had the front booth in Joe's that Matt loved so much. I had Oliver enter the booth and I sat next to him, not realizing that Matt had already ordered me an iced tea and that I was supposed to sit next to him. I sat directly in front of Ryan.

It was a good dinner. Matt and Oliver spoke a lot, and I got to know Ryan and learn about their friendship as well as a little more about Matt.

We walked out to a warm summer night. Ryan gave me a hug as I told him to watch over Matt when I couldn't. I hugged Matt, and we made plans for me to go over to hang out at the shack after dropping off Oliver at the motel. It is amazing how I can lean toward wanting to end it one minute and then in a matter of hours lean back over to be open to the possibilities of us. I can push bad feelings down very quickly at times.

I went over, and once again, he walked me to where the shack was. I walked in the highest of heels with my head toward the sky, admiring the stars. I sat on the side of the bed listening to Matt talk about how his week had gone. It was interesting that we had spoken so much during the last week, but he hadn't filled me in on everything that was truly going on. He told me it was time to really do something about his addiction. He needed to stop because now it was bringing up the possibility of taking away his freedom and that was about all he had left. He told me that the week had been bad because he had bought drugs off the street. I'm not sure if he was speaking of painkillers or his Suboxone, but they sounded like prescription drugs. He said he felt strong enough mentally this time to detox because he thought if he didn't that he'd more than likely end up in jail, and that was the last thing he wanted to happen.

I told him that I was there for listening or helping him find a place but that only he could do it. I told him that I knew he could do it; he had done it before. I told him he had to remember that.

We hung out for a few more hours, and all those feelings from earlier were gone but not forgotten, because as he walked me out, he grabbed a lighter and said, "Is this yours?"

I quickly said, "No, it's the other girl's."

He was silent.

I knew right then that I was right and whomever he had met the previous week was over the night before. I was crushed.

I was hurt by the others that had entered Matt's life, but I never felt cheated on. He never said he wasn't dating other girls. He even later told me how he didn't want to talk about them before because he knew how I felt and how it would hurt me.

For the next three weeks, we stayed in touch, but there were not those daily calls from him; it was more like every other day. He was slipping away from me again. Whether it was his addiction or a girl or both, I'm not certain, but I knew I was losing the opportunity to see what could happen between us.

We spoke about it one day, and he apologized. He said that he was struggling again with his dosages of his Suboxone; they had increased, and even his mother had said to him just the day before how she had noticed him avoiding her, as well. He told me how he handed all his medication to her and that she was going to give him his proper dosages and therefore lowering his dosage with the intent to wean him off.

The next day, a Thursday, he posted a picture of us in his Mercedes on his Myspace page. By Saturday, I was in disbelief when I saw a few other pictures of another girl. He wasn't in the picture with her; they were just of her. He tried to tell me it was his brother's girlfriend and that she had been bugging him to put up pictures of her. His Myspace page was for his new apparel company, not a personal page, even though he would use it as if it was a personal page. He said she wanted to be a model for his company. This was the first time I knew he lied to me. All the time I knew him, I thought he'd never judge me or lie to me. After that first week and months later, I told myself because we spoke about *everything*, even the other girls, that Matt would never lie to me, no matter how much it hurt—and here he was lying to me, and I let him know that I knew it. He took down the pictures.

Two days later, I texted him, "I'm done."

He begged me, "Don't do this! You are the only good, positive person in my life."

I told him that he needed to focus on what he needed to do to get sober, and then we'd see.

He said, "Great! Okay, thanks!"

By early October, we barely spoke.

Since the days that I took off for our road trip, I had a hard time for weeks going back to work. I'd go in later and later each week. I was supposed to start work each morning at 8:00 a.m., but every week, I'd find myself sitting in the car, anxiety stricken and then crying, not wanting to work for a company that was getting rid of me after all the hard work I had done and everything I had dealt with. I was taken advantage of by my boss, and he took credit for my work. He barely paid me, giving bonuses that were just a little higher than the receptionist in New York and then taking my job from me by recommending that accounting be in New York instead of in Los Angeles.

My feelings about Matt didn't help my state of emotions too at this time. My own life was in chaos and not perfect.

I called up the new controller in New York, Andrea, and cried to her, begging her to force them to just lay me off and do it already. I was panicked for more than a year of what would become of Oliver and me if I couldn't find work and pay my bills and feed us, but at that point, I was in a serious depression, and I knew something had to give. I needed the uncertainty to end, and I needed to stop feeling used and mistreated. The whole office could hear me crying and speaking loudly while I spoke to her over the phone. I wasn't calm until I got off the phone with her. But, then the calls started coming.

The first one was from the CFO who had taken credit for my work over the years and a few months prior had stolen from the company. He had to give me BS over the fact that I should have come to him, and he wanted to know why he had gotten a call from the girl in my office regarding an outburst I was having over the phone. He was speaking of the agro-lady that I'd never gotten along with. She lived in a swanky and expensive part of town and had a man mainly supporting her lavish lifestyle and their children, while I struggled with no one to count on. She wasn't in my shoes, because if she were, she would have lost it too! So when I heard that she called to complain about me, I just remained quiet, as there was no point arguing with him or saying anything. He also told me that my last day would be September 30.

Then the other CFO, who took my boss's job about nine months later, called to inform me that Andrea came to him and that my last day was September 30 and to try to keep everything levelheaded there because he also got a complaint about my phone call to Andrea.

I even got a phone call from Jonathan, and he let me know it was the woman in our office calling everyone in New York and complaining about me. Damn, only if she and I could trade lives for a year. She was already a very unhappy person, but as I saw it, she didn't have the stresses I dealt with, at least not at that time.

As soon as I knew my end date, most of my stress and anxiety subsided. I was just happy to cut off that dead limb I had known was coming off for over fourteen months. I was ready to conquer whatever life would bring.

Later, I also tried to date, and at first, it was okay. I was trying to keep an open mind, but soon I'd be crying while getting ready to go on a date because I was upset that it wasn't Matt. If I wasn't crying before, I was crying after. Since I'd met Matt, there were these periods of time I consider us being off. I tried to date throughout that time, but no one could get a second date with me. I didn't feel like I met anybody I could relate to or that could understand me and my not-so-perfect life. I look all clean-cut and like I've had a really good life, but there is half of me that most guys wouldn't understand—that I don't get along with some of my family or see them regularly or about my situation with Oliver and how I have been left to my own devices to raise him. Matt got me, and I got him; he was just lagging a little behind me.

In mid-October, I texted Matt to check in and to see how he was doing. We did this when there were those times that we were "off." I always wanted to just hear that he was okay and to let him know that I was still thinking of him. It wasn't like Matt to not immediately call me back or text me back, so when he didn't this time, I freaked out.

He texted me back about two hours later. He had overdosed the day before and was just about to enter rehab in the next two hours. He let me know how he wouldn't have his phone for two weeks and that he'd call me as soon as he got phone privileges. Right then was when I realized he was really an addict and it was really bad. I don't think I got it before then. I couldn't believe I almost lost him.

He got back on his feet and cleaned up his act, but he was still on the Suboxone, though it was back down to a low dosage. When he was on his low, even medium-to-low, dosage of Suboxone, it was like he wasn't on anything. This is something that my friends didn't understand. And when he was on these low dosages, that was when we were "on" and talking and seeing each other, and he seemed okay and normal. If anyone had ever met him under these circumstances, they would have never known he was on anything. I never saw him when he used other drugs or drank heavily, so until he overdosed—even though he told me things would get bad—I always thought things weren't as bad as he made them out to be.

He entered rehab and called me when he could. He was happy and grateful that I was there once again for him as a friend. We weren't back "on," per se, but we were back to being tight as friends there to support one another.

After this incident, his mom had had enough. She already had Matt's fourteen-year-old son practically living with them because things weren't all that great in his life. She was trying to be some type of role model to him and help guide him in the right direction. She couldn't have Matt influence this child or have to deal with Matt's addiction in her house anymore, so she made Matt move out, and this was his first stint since I'd known him that he lived in a sober house.

I kept in touch and was surprised that around Christmas he was texting me a lot. He wanted to come and see me. He sounded well and more grounded. We made plans for him to come for New Year's Eve. I offered things to do, but we just agreed to have dinner at home rather than be out there with all that craziness. I wanted us to do something at first but was so relieved when he didn't want to do anything, because I started to worry that I would have a problem on my hands with his sobriety.

I sent Oliver over to a friend of his who lived on Sunset Boulevard in Brentwood. Matt had a twenty-four-hour pass from his sober house. He said he'd get to my place around 8:00 p.m., so I was surprised when he was already on his way at 6:00 p.m. and I had not even showered; I still needed to take Oliver to his friend's place, which was about twenty minutes away.

I was just leaving Brentwood when Matt was just about to reach Interstate 405 from Route 101, not too far from where I was at that moment. I took about the fastest shower and did my makeup in record time. I was pretty satisfied with myself when I opened the door and Matt did a double take and said how beautiful I looked.

I made us lobster tails, Peruvian-style scallops (Conchitas a la Parmesana), and some veggies with potatoes. The man couldn't stop devouring all the food I had made. I just sat back like I did most of the time, taking in his energy that was filled with happiness and enthusiasm. When he was around me, there was this energy. It was part energy, part of his personality, and part of just him… *being*. It was like I could get glimpses of him at the age of six on his birthday or other times when I could get a glimpse of him how he would have been at fifteen years old with the exuberance and enthusiasm of life. I'd see this happiness and playfulness in him that just made me love being around him, but also with a balance of deepness and maturity on how he summed up his life at times. I saw so much in him and in his eyes, which I never told him.

When he spent the weekend with me back in July and we were in Santa Monica talking, he interrupted me, telling me how beautiful my eyes were, but I find it hard to take a compliment, so I just smiled and kept talking. I also didn't tell him how his eyes said so much to me. I saw all of him through his eyes.

He filled me in on his overdose and the stupid things he had done. I was in disbelief, but I had to be a friend and listen and let him talk to me. I couldn't react. I knew this was why he depended on me so much; he could tell me anything, and I wouldn't turn around and either run or react like a girl usually would, flipping out that he was seeing other girls while we weren't together or judge him by his mistakes. But it was so hard at times. I knew, though, by what he told me and how he told me things that he knew right from wrong, and he tried so hard to do what was right, but sometimes his addiction got the best of his judgment. He'd beat himself up about doing bad things that he knew hurt people who loved him. I just tried to convince him over and over that he could get better, get sober, and have the life he longed for.

We rang in 2011 together. I lay on the couch flicking between all the shows that were on while Matt bounced around, jumping on the couch, lying next to me and kissing me, and sitting on my three-step front porch smoking a cigarette.

When all the cheering of the new year came on the TV, he came in and kissed me as we said to one another that this year we were going to have a better one than these last few years we both had had. I thought of how true that could be and how we had to have a better year, for both of our sakes. We deserved it!

We went to bed, and the next morning he was off again, back home to SB. It hurt so much every time he left or I left him. I missed him even right before we had to part, and with all the times he texted me that he missed me, I'm sure I missed him more. He thanked me again for having him over and told me that he'd had the best time ever. I'd smile, hearing that. Him saying that he had the best time ever was especially sweet because we were just doing little things like grabbing a bite or watching a movie. He was truly a man who was appreciative of good moments and good people in his life and never held back from telling me so. He also always had a response to whatever I was trying to tell him that was going on in my life, good or bad. It was always "I'm sorry" or "That sucks" or "Great job" or "You can do that!" He always did that. He took in what I told him and expressed back to me that he cared about me. *Always.* I had never met someone who was so in tune with what I was saying and cared so much on how that possibly affected you.

I was happy that I rang in the new year with Matt. I was being optimistic and positive that this had to be it, the year when things were going to give us an upswing toward the things we wanted, and he was going to overcome this challenge on his sobriety. He seemed too together and smart to not get completely sober again. Optimistic and hopeful was the only way I could be.

By mid-to-late January, Southern California was having an influx of warm, beach-like weather. I had spoken so much to my girlfriends about Santa Barbara that Melanie and I made plans to go on a road trip up there. We were just going to wing it and see if we'd stay up there for the day or if I would fork over money for a room so we could have one full day there.

I let Matt know that we were coming up, and he said he would try to meet up with us, but he wasn't sure if he could because his namesake uncle was also going to be in town, and he had meetings to attend and things he had to do at the sober house.

Melanie came over the night before. We got into Santa Barbara around noon and ventured immediately to State Street. We went to a sports bar to just have a place to sit down, talk, and catch up. It had been years since Melanie had been to SB. She used to go up there during Fiesta, like I had, when we used to live in Oxnard, but never with the intention of checking out Santa Barbara—just the intent to party.

We decided to stay and checked into the Motel 6 that I loved so much. Matt canceled his dinner plans with us. It sounded like he had some anxiety in meeting up with us, but what could I do? I just tried to sound understanding, but I was crushed to not be able to see him.

Melanie and I had dinner and a drink at Joe's. We met some guys who seemed very cool, and they joined us next door for drinks. It wasn't the type of situation where we were interested, but I did find one of the guys to be cute. I can find someone cute or attractive, but that is it; it isn't like I want something to happen.

We hung out and talked, and I ordered water because I didn't need or want to have another drink. When it was time to wrap up the evening, we went to hang out with them at one of their places, and it ended like most of those memorable, funny nights Melanie and I always found ourselves getting into. The owner of the house, the cute guy's friend, had a house like one you see on those hoarding shows. We had never seen anything like it. It was amusing and gross, but when I reflect and think about it, I think, how sad. And how did they think of bringing back two beautiful girls back to a house like that? I would have been embarrassed. Christ, I am embarrassed by my apartment on a clean day. So we excused ourselves and got a cab back to our motel.

The next morning, I called Matt and talked to him for a while. Melanie was so over him, like my other friend Nicole was. The night before when we were talking to those guys and I dared mention him, Melanie called him "just some druggie" to one of the guys who asked who I was speaking of. I lightly hit her on her arm when she said that and told her to be nice, but now when I was talking to Matt on the phone, she was like, "Fuck him, Fuck that … fuck, fuck, fuck." It is all I heard out of her mouth while she headed out to get us coffee.

The degree of her insensitivity for someone I cared for and Nicole calling him a "junkie" once or twice made me feel like I couldn't go on talking to them about him anymore, good or bad, and I wondered at times how true our friendships really were. I thought they knew me enough to know that I was a smart girl and that if I didn't think that he could get better then I wouldn't have kept in touch with him all this time. I continued "us" because I knew in my heart that he could get sober once again, like he had so many years earlier, and he was an amazingly good person and made me happy when we were "on." Who were these friends of mine to judge him? It wasn't like they didn't overindulge in alcohol, drink more than I thought they should, or even use substances other than alcohol. And the guys that they were with or were seeing weren't the greatest of situations either. It wasn't cool of them to be so mean and judgmental when he just had a weaker side and he couldn't fight his addiction at that time.

I could have said really insensitive stuff back to anybody who judged him, but I didn't. I know that my girlfriends love me and that they were just acting out in this way, but it is sad that I couldn't continue to lean on them for support. They didn't need to like him, but they did need to be a friend to me. He was a good guy, and all they could do was judge him.

He apologized that morning for not being able to see me because he did want to see me; he just had some things to do. He told me to go have some fun with my girlfriend, and that is just what I did. We packed our things, left the car in front of the motel, and walked straight out to East Beach for the day. It was just what the doctor ordered too. We laid out my blankets and towels and vegged out, halfway in between the ocean and the East Beach Grill. I loved days like this because usually I could spend hours in the sun.

Melanie went off for long walks and playful times on the swings. We drove home later that afternoon.

The next time I saw Melanie was in May, a few months later, when I went with her to Vegas. Even though we stayed in contact, I wouldn't see Melanie for almost another year after that. That is just how our friendship worked.

I wanted to see Matt when we were there, but I did notice a change in my expectations of him. The feelings of us were not diminished on my part at all; I just sensed that it was still not the right time to see where this thing we called "us" really could go. He had his sobriety to work on, and I continued to look for a job and continued to take care of myself by going to the gym a lot and riding my bike to clear my head and center myself.

When I look back and think of what state I was in, I was still kind of a mess. The years at the packaging company where I was overworked and taken advantage of, the health problems with my heart from all the stress at work, losing my job and my financial security, and then meeting this guy who had such an impact on my beliefs regarding fate and destiny took a toll on me. I was getting better emotionally, and the depression that I had encountered before being laid off was gone, but I was still in a fog and confused mentally. Sometimes when one is having a growth spurt to change and evolve, it does not come with many pleasant days but with countless hurdles to cross over. We do not know at the time that is what is occurring, because it just feels like we are being tested all the time, but if we hold on and get through it, we learn and evolve. It was very surprising to me that in this time of my life, I was still so kind, gentle, and understanding and could laugh.

Valentine's Day came around, and it had been about two weeks since I'd spoken to Matt. I remember him having mentioned how he hated Valentine's Day because they always had been awful. I think I sent him an e-mail, and after a few days of not hearing from him, I panicked again. He had overdosed in October, and now here was the second time when I wasn't hearing back from him almost immediately. I never like to force an issue on guys, but I went ahead and sent a letter to his mom. I had to introduce myself and have some kind of contact, just in case. I let her know how I felt for her and her situation with all of what Matt had put her through and that to please keep my information just in case something happened to him. Because of what had happened in October, I had found myself looking at the obituaries now, but I never thought that it would actually happen. I guess maybe a part of my brain and intellect knew better. I now imagined him probably in a coma somewhere from an overdose. I needed to be kept in the loop.

It was about two o'clock in the afternoon a few days later that she called me. He had overdosed again and had barely made it. We spoke for about twenty minutes, and she urged me to stay away from him for my own sake. I told her I had to be his friend, if anything. I knew he relied on me for this.

A couple of hours later, he texted me and let me know he had overdosed and was in a bad state and would get ahold of me when he was out. Matt later said that it was really bad. Supposedly, he was locked down in a mental facility because they didn't know what he was on or if he was just "mental." When he got out of there, he didn't have the sober house to go back to, and his mom said enough and told him he couldn't stay with them. The ex-girlfriend in Santa Barbara with all the money moved him into her house, where he supposedly lived on one side of the house. He said he had no other choice.

We continued speaking, but around April, he told me he was with her. I told him, "That's it. Don't call me, don't text me, don't see how I am doing."

There was no point in having contact if he had a girlfriend—at least not for now because I still wanted us to see what could develop when he got sober.

He ignored my requests a few weeks later, and thankfully, I had been on my bike when he called, because then I had a moment to gather my thoughts, which I typically cannot do instantaneously. I texted him back to please not reach out to me, and his response was, "I'm sorry. Okay."

The last couple of months after I had spent New Year's with him were quite different from the earlier times when I used to freak out over why he meant so much to me and it never making sense. I didn't understand in the beginning how messed up he was, but I knew now, and I knew that this girl or others would come and go. I also had gotten back to remembering what was important to me, which is my son, my life, and my sense of balance or calmness. I was working on it, and Matt's problems were working against where I was trying to be. I knew I'd always be there for him if he really needed me, but I only help those who are trying to help themselves, and he wasn't trying or reaching out to me for that purpose anymore.

I was shaken up by his phone call for a few hours, but I let it go and moved on with what I needed to focus on, which was finding a job and the upcoming court hearing I had with Oliver's father.

Oliver's father was now taking me to court to try to vacate or modify the child support order that I had begun in 2008. I was stunned. *Really?!!* He wanted to get in front of a judge and tell the judge that he didn't know about any of this. At first, his paperwork was issued by his lawyer, but now his lawyer had dismissed himself from the case, and the case was pushed back a few months. I don't think my son's father ever realized how smart I was. My response to the order was long and detailed, and I submitted copies of proof for my response. I also asked for proof of his fiancée's income, because he claimed that his fiancée somehow was paying for their expenses, which totaled over $4,000 a month. I wondered if the response that I filed with the courts was the reason why his lawyer backed out. Without his lawyer representing him, I knew that I'd now be on the same level playing field once we went to court. It was good that I didn't have the distraction of Matt, because this was my time to get prepared for my day in court.

Short lived moments in my life because on June 7, I heard from Matt. He was desperate. He e-mailed me that he needed to get out of there (the rich girl's house) and that he was willing to do anything, even wash cars. He needed help finding some work in L.A. Some may think he was callous or was using me, but I was a friend he could always count on, no matter what. Not many of us have that.

I called him and told him that he didn't need to wash cars—that we just needed to finally get his résumé together and start looking. He said, "Great" and thanked me and said that he would come down to L.A. in a couple of weeks to stay with his brother and come and see me. I said okay.

A couple of weeks passed, and Father's Day was getting closer. I assumed he had just gotten settled again with his situation and decided not to try to get his life back on track down here in L.A., but I didn't want to pass up wishing him a good Father's Day. Even when we were "off," we always sent one another well wishes on the holidays.

For about two days, I questioned whether I should reach out to him. I felt kind of childish thinking, *Well, he didn't reach out to me on this past Mother's Day.* Even though sometimes I think like that, I try to do what I feel is right and what I want to do, so I sent him an e-mail.

This was the third time in our relationship that he didn't respond to me immediately or at all. I knew the first time it wasn't like him to not respond, and that was the first experience I had with him having overdosed. The second time was when he overdosed again, and his mom reached out to me hours before he did. Now this was the second round of looking for his obituary. Not good!

What kind of mess had I gotten myself into? Was I really wrapped up in this kind of situation? But at that point, he was already like family. I wouldn't stop caring for him. He wasn't just some random guy I met. Six days after we met, every fiber of my being screamed at me that there was a reason for us. Yes, it drove me to tears and made me in constant conflict against all my beliefs, but there was a purpose, a reason, and I couldn't just walk away now.

I didn't want to reach out to his mom again. I could just imagine her telling me to go help others, not him. I thought to reach out to his younger brother, but how? I remembered seeing that his brother who also lived here in L.A. was a friend of Matt's Myspace page, which then led me to his brother's Twitter account. I reached out to him there.

His brother didn't know who I was. We e-mailed each other, and I gave him my information. By the time his brother had gotten my first e-mail, I came across an arrest record online. On June 10, three days after Matt had reached out to me, he had been arrested.

Matt would later tell me was that he was awakened in the morning by the rich ex-girlfriend. She was yelling at him and pulling on his arm trying to wake him, wanting to know who this girl was that he was e-mailing and calling. She had gone through his phone and saw us e-mailing and calling one another. They got into a fight about it, and she threw him out and called the cops on him. The cops were waiting for him at the end of her street.

Matt's brother said he'd pass on my information, but the next morning, I had an epiphany. I didn't need to wait for him to get my information to Matt. Back in my Oxnard days, a few guy friends of mine had gone to jail, and I knew if I called Santa Barbara County Jail that I more than likely could get his information to write to him.

I wrote him and encouraged him, tried to tell him to stay positive, and said that I was there if he needed someone to talk to. I told him that this was probably for the best and that finally they would have him detox from everything!

We wrote and talked on the phone all the time. His first letter to me said how he was thinking about having his mom track me down. Thankfully, I had found him first. He told me some of what had happened, and he started to talk about us, like if "us" was still an option or if there was still a chance. After a few letters back to him, I told him that I was there for him as a friend but for him to not go there about "us." Eventually, as Matt would do, he lassoed me back in, and "us" became more than it had ever been before.

He sounded like he had never sounded before, more grounded and with a stronger well-being, even though he was in jail. I wasn't all over the place emotionally at this time and it helped that I knew he was safe and clean, at least from narcotics.

At the end of July, I went to court with Oliver's father—the first and only court hearing he had ever shown up to. Nicole had come to support me. Oliver's father represented himself, which was probably the first time without his lawyer's help. I barely had to speak when our case was being heard by the judge. An attorney from the Los Angeles County Child Support Services Department had joined me because they were working for me by enforcing the child support order made by the courts. This attorney kept on trying to tell me to stop trying to speak up. Most of the conversation, questioning, was happening between the judge and Oliver's father. Oliver's father tried to claim that he didn't know about this child or the court order and that he didn't have any money. The judge did not believe him.

In the end, Oliver's father had to pay $56 more a month, and his request for the order to be vacated or modified was denied. He further agreed with the judge that he did make somewhat around $5,500 a month. It was one of those glorious days, and I walked out of the courtroom crying into Nicole's arms.

It is and was the principle of the matter. For so long, maybe even longer than thirteen years, I didn't get justice, mortally and lawfully, for my son. It was bad enough he was given a life without one parent, but my son has missed opportunities also, and that didn't have to be the case. It wasn't because his father couldn't afford to; greed and selfishness poisons lots of people, including Oliver's father. I understand that what has happened wasn't personal toward Oliver. Joshua didn't know him or get to know him; the disconnection happened way before Oliver took his first breath, but there should have been more justice for the child who didn't have to go without.

On that court day, I felt once again vindicated. I might never get more than the $13.33 he has paid in child support so far, but at least some justice was served. It was if the judge had said, "Oliver deserves this and you have to stop bullshitting the court system because we are not buying it anymore."

After this court hearing, I filed a contempt case for not paying child support. He again didn't show up. He has only paid me the $100—a gift for my son's first birthday—and $13.33 for child support. Again, the Los Angeles County Child Support Services Department and I are not entirely sure where to locate him because he ignores all the paperwork the agency sends him. All they say they can do now is suspend his driver's license and passport and run his social security number, but that has been going on for years and doesn't help in any way. He knows the system and knows how to play it. The agency is keeping track of the child support amount plus interest, and even though it stopped once Oliver finished high school, it never goes away. We'll continue to try to retrieve what Joshua should pay if we can ever find some of his money.

Matt appeared in court a few times while he was in jail. He had a long list of offenses against him; he later told me that most of them were dropped. Toward the end of August, he told me there was a possibility of him getting out soon. Our relationship was on such another level, but inherently, I wanted to still keep an arm's distance between us, because he and I had so many things to work out. I was riding the ride, but I was far from completely taking the leap all the way.

He told me how his mom had told him that this was his last chance with her; I was giving him one last chance to get it right too. He thanked me for showing him how supportive and loving his parents truly are; I reminded him of how other moms could be and they could put themselves first before their children. He wrote his mom a long letter in the last week or so that he was in jail, and he told me it was because of me. He also said that he'd never forget what I had taught him. He had always loved his parents and appreciated them, but he really never understood that not all parents were like his, loving and supportive. He wrote me that the letter he wrote her moved her so much that she read it to his stepfather. He just couldn't wait to get out and see me and for us to just go to the beach together. I couldn't wait, either.

11
End of a Dream

At the start of Labor Day weekend, Matt got out of jail. He almost gave me a heart attack because we spoke the day before, on Thursday, and he was supposed to be released at midnight that evening. He was being ambivalent on whether he'd actually get out or not, and then I didn't hear from him until after 11:00 a.m. the next day. I was worried he hadn't gotten out, but it was just that he didn't get out until after 3:00 a.m. He told me how he was the last one released after all the "poor Mexicans were getting deported." He felt sorry for them that they were being deported. He told me that he saw for the first time how sad their situation was.

Matt's father picked him up. He came home and crashed and called me as soon as he got up. I was so relieved, and I couldn't wait to go up and see him on Sunday.

Excited, I drove up to Santa Barbara. I felt like we had made the strides we needed to see whether we could be really good for one another. This was the first time I was going up to the mountaintop house on the winding road during the day. I had been up there just a couple of times but never even got a good look at the main house, because it was always dark, and I was always with my eyes facing the sky, looking at the stars. Matt didn't have his cell phone turned back on, so he and I had been talking through his mother's cell phone or the house's landline.

I called when I thought I arrived, but I was confused if I was at the right place. From the times before and the glimpses of the house, I thought I had seen a two-story house, but here was a single-story home, so I thought I wasn't at the right place.

His mom, who so many months before told me to stay away from him for my sake, answered the phone and seemed happy to hear from me. I had partially driven into the circular driveway and began pulling away when she answered. She told Matt to go out and find me.

As I was pulling away, I saw him out of my rearview mirror and stopped to get out. He just stood there looking at me with his grin. I backed up and turned around and parked. I was so nervous. I had never been nervous to see him, even when we first met, but here I was feeling like I was seeing him for the first time. He gave me one of his big, hold-on-tight hugs, and I finally pulled away because I was starting to get emotional, and I told him, "I don't want to start crying." I pushed back the tears that welled up in my eyes.

We went in, and his mom greeted me with open arms. She and I immediately sat down and talked around the kitchen table. Matt was still getting his stuff together for us to leave to go down to State Street and later to our motel that I had gotten in Carpinteria, a town ten minutes south of Santa Barbara. She and I talked about the last few months and how we were just happy it was all behind us.

She handed me something to read. It was something she had written for a couple that she was going to marry. It talked about being there for one another and being strong for the other one when the other one couldn't be strong and vice versa—basically being each other's rock. I handed it back to her after reading it halfway through because I got emotional. I had tried since the beginning to be there for him, and most of the time I was successful, but only when he turned to me and needed me to be that comfort and enlightenment. There were so many other times that he had just escaped through drugs or drinking too much, so I knew there was only so much I could do. I knew and wanted to be his rock, and he had been so supportive of me when I needed someone, but I knew I couldn't force it with him, and there was a part of him that didn't want to deal with the fact that he needed help sometimes.

It was another hot summer day in Cali and it felt as bright as it was. *The possibilities.* The happiness of the possibilities was running through us, and it was evident on our faces. We left and went to grab a bite near lower State Street and then later cruised around for a bit around State Street and the coast. Later, Matt drove us to Carpinteria to spend some time together and get ready before he took me out to dinner. I felt home again. The universe was hugging me and reassuring me that this was where I was supposed to be at that very moment. I had always told Matt how I had felt so comfortable to be around him. It was a familiar feeling, like I had known him for decades, but by now, I had felt like I had known him my whole life. When I was either in Santa Barbara or with Matt, I felt like I was home again.

Jonathan had noticed back in 2010 that it was like a spark in me went on. It felt like I came back to life. Jonathan had even wanted to meet the guy who changed me. Matt didn't change me; he just made me feel alive again, the true essence of me reappeared. I felt like I had been lost for so long and just found my old real self. The little girl who was sweet, not trying to conform for others and edgy at times, and was free to be her real self without any judgment was back again.

Being around Matt always just felt right. It felt like the universe was whispering in my ear, "Everything is well now," and all those times before when we were not together were torture, because the core inside of me felt out of balance. At those times, I'd cry out in frustration because I didn't understand my feelings or what was going on. My feelings were so conflicted with my thoughts. Yes, he was a good-looking guy, and yes, he was thoughtful and sweet and so on and so on, but he had his problems. I didn't care. All I know is I didn't feel right inside when we weren't together.

I never believed in fate or destiny or that some people really are supposed to come into your life for a purpose or a reason or that maybe you are supposed to come into their lives. My whys did not matter now, because we were once again together, and I was once again feeling like everything in the universe was right, even though on the surface it wasn't such a pretty picture. He had just gotten out of jail and was still weaning off the antipsychotic medication that the jail had put him on while detoxing from the Suboxone and whatever other narcotics he had started using before he got arrested.

I, meanwhile, was still unemployed, fighting my battle to get child support, and trying to keep an arm's distance from my mother, who started e-mailing me about her decisions about what to do after the selling of her parents' house. Despite all this, we were happy and couldn't stop smiling all the time, because he was out, and we came through it together without any bitterness of the past.

For the moment, we basked in the present and the future. Matt treated me to a beautiful dinner at Blush down on State Street. We sat on the patio and listened to a man playing the Spanish guitar. We couldn't help just staring at each other and our surroundings in amazement. Were we dreaming?

After dinner, we walked around a bit and then headed back to the motel. I loved sleeping in his arms again.

The next morning, we headed to Butterfly Beach in Montecito, the wealthy neighboring town of SB. It was Matt's favorite local beach. When we began driving around the Biltmore looking for a parking space, Matt pointed at the hotel and said, "If we get married, that is where we'll stay for our honeymoon." Then he pointed at Butterfly Beach and said, "And there is where my mom will marry us."

I smiled and added, "After we are done honeymooning there, then we will take a long honeymoon in Cancun at my timeshare."

It wasn't the first time we had talked about wanting to get married, how intimate we wanted it to be, and what kind of ring I *didn't* want—a diamond—but it was the first time it felt to me like such a possibility. I had never thought or spoken to any guy in my life before about it.

We found a spot, and I lay out while Matt and I talked and talked. He asked me if I wanted to take that long walk on the beach that he wrote me about so many times while he was in jail. At about the same time, we laughed and said, "Nah, it's too hot."

I watched him as he went close to the water and just stood and looked out into the vast ocean. I wondered what he was thinking of. He jumped in to cool off, and I saw a person who loved the ocean like I did.

He came back and sat next to me. He mentioned how he had dreamt of this day. All I could tell him was that I had also. I don't know if he would have ever imagined how much that moment meant to me.

We left the beach and stopped by the sober house where he needed to live for a while. He introduced me as his girlfriend, checked in, and gave them all the information about where he just was (jail), what had happened (it seemed like everyone knew everyone), and what they needed to allow him to stay there. We then headed up to his mom's house, thinking we'd cool off up there. It was one of those late summer days in Cali where you felt like you are on vacation and time is not a factor.

We pulled up, and his parents were sitting by the pool with his soon-to-be ex-sister-in-law and his niece and nephew. He was excited to see his niece and nephew. I had heard about them and their mother since day one—how she stayed with his brother through thick and thin, and he admired that, but he still didn't care for her ... and by the looks she gave us when we walked up, it seemed mutual.

He introduced me to her as his girlfriend as I cringed inside. Part of me was touched by his feelings toward me—*finally!*—but he had just gotten out of jail by being thrown into jail by another girl. I didn't want to come off as a stupid chick. No one knew of our backstory or what we talked about and how we saw things between us, so I could have just imagined what his ex-sister-in-law was thinking of me right then.

I was very courteous and quiet. Everyone besides Matt was feeling the tension and awkwardness of the moment, but it was also quite obvious that we had interrupted a conversation. Matt jumped in the pool with his nephew and tried to get his niece to open up. He came and sat next to me after his nephew got out of the pool.

Almost immediately, his dad called him over to talk outside of the pool area, and then Matt called me over. I said, "Good-bye; it was nice to meet you," to his sister-in-law and her children and walked out to the driveway where Matt was. He said that his dad had told him that we had just walked into a private conversation and that he had asked us to please go to the main house. I was scared they were asking us to leave, but they weren't.

Matt and I sat on the patio in the back of the house. He called his brother to tell him that his soon-to-be ex-wife was over talking to their mom. I sat back taking in the situation. We were real now—no more dating or hanging out. I was just staring at him. He was finally raw to me. He had always worried so much about his appearance, and here he was with a little weight gain from jail and some gray showing and this random, inch-long hair that was located on his left shoulder that I plucked out. I loved it! It was real.

His mom came out to us and said that they all were headed to the country club so that they could finish talking. She said good-bye to me because I would be headed back to L.A. soon.

Matt was on the phone, and as I saw his mom get her things, I went in to say good-bye once again and give her a hug just in case I was never to see her again. I told her that I may not be back, and she gave me her business card for me to call her because I couldn't get into it right then. I hung out with Matt a little while more before I headed back to L.A. I hated leaving him, and I knew later that night when he called that he hated me leaving him too—or he just hated being alone—because his first words were "I'm lonely." Right then, my inner self said, "Uh-oh!"

The next morning when he called me, he apologized for the weekend. It was a great weekend, but it wasn't perfect. There was an apology and an issue to address—he drank beer all weekend. This is why I was on the fence of returning when I told his mom that I may not be back. He knew I wasn't going to let it slide, and we had to discuss it. We had come so far and started off on the right path this time around, but the fact was that he was an addict; even though it was only beer, I knew it could lead him to other things. He made every excuse over the weekend for why he was doing it, but he knew by Tuesday morning when he was calling me to apologize that it wasn't the smartest thing to do around me and that I wouldn't just let him continue down that path. *There were other girls for that!*

Once again, he told me how he needed me, and because of this, he promised me it was hopefully not going to happen again, but he reminded me that he was an addict and that it would be an uphill battle—for him and me. I had thought for the following days that this was what I had signed up for and it still wasn't time to let us go; we had unfinished business, whatever that may be.

Six days after Matt and I met, I had thought, *If I marry this guy, it could be a really good, solid marriage.* A year and a half later, even after talking about marriage over the weekend, I didn't know if he was just meant to be my very good friend (or as he had mentioned a couple of times, my best friend), my lover, the father of my next child, or my future one and only husband. It didn't matter; I was still riding the Matt wave, because I thought I'd know when it was time to get off. And he knew it wasn't time for us to be over, because the next weekend at his mom's house, he'd say to me very jokingly, "You are not going anywhere. We are not done yet." One would have to know his sense of humor to know he was joking and wouldn't force anything. I just half grinned because I knew we were not done yet either.

It was great that it was a short week, and I headed back up there early on Friday morning. I went to his mom's where he was still living; it would be another week or so before he'd move into the sober living house. His parents weren't there, and I sat down in my comfort spot around the kitchen table. I was so comfortable with him and so comfortable with his mom and their house, like I had known her for years and had visited many times, and that was atypical of me; I don't even feel that comfortable at any of my sisters' homes. It may have just been that he had shared so much about himself and his family that I felt like I had known them for what seemed forever.

We walked and sat down outside at a different part of the patio overlooking the hills of Santa Barbara with a direct view down to the ocean. He sat on the sofa that faced the mountain, and I sat on one of the chairs facing the Santa Barbara coast. He talked to me about how rough the last few days had been but that he was getting through them. He was thinking a lot about not only the last few months but what had gotten him to this point. I'd go back and forth looking at him and then looking at this spectacular view, all the while telling him how all this wouldn't be easy, and it was okay to feel sad about what had happened, but that he was okay and free and had every chance to not fall down the trap of making things worse again.

He asked me, "Why are you even with me?"

I began to tell him how he was a good man. "You are smart, positive, and thoughtful, and we have things in common." I stood up and walked toward the edge of the patio balcony, looking out to the ocean.

He smiled and said, "Yes, but I have so many issues."

I jokingly said, "Well, maybe I have unresolved mommy issues."

I wished I hadn't said that to him, because yes, some part of that might have been true, but he was truly almost perfectly made for me.

He came over and joined me where I stood and I said, "No, really. I like you because of your qualities, and I believe in you that you can turn this around again. You've done it before."

He kissed me and then said, "Let's go."

We went driving around Santa Barbara getting some things he needed. He took me all over, even to what he said was a sketchy part of town, but I was coming from Los Angeles that had really sketchy parts, not like what I was seeing. I didn't even see this part of Santa Barbara as unkept and unsafe as L.A.'s sketchiest parts.

The rest of my visit went smoothly, and he didn't use. We talked about some serious stuff, and we laughed and kidded around with each other. I came back up the following weekend and then the weekend after, sometimes just staying for one night or two. Even though I was still unemployed, I still had a lot of my savings that I had saved for fourteen months before finally being laid off in 2010, and my mom had recently sent me some money directly into my bank account, which helped me be okay with spending a little bit to go up and get the cheapest motel there.

My mother and I really didn't speak at all in 2011 until September when she e-mailed me about the sale of her parents' house, and this was when the lines of communication opened up again. They didn't open up because I wanted anything from her, especially "her" money, as she had always said to us growing up—*her* money, *her* things. Actually, she offered me some cash, and I shut the door to that by not acknowledging it twice. I just commented to her e-mail that finally all the fighting within her family over the money and inheritance would be over and that was a good thing. But even though I kept it brief in my e-mail, she knew she had an opportunity with getting back in my life, because the door of communication was slightly ajar.

As I've mentioned, my mom ended up with only 12.5 percent of the proceeds from the sale of my grandparents' house in Lima. For months, my father talked to me about whether or not they were going to get lawyers involved—not only to find out what had happened to the other 12.5 percent but what had happened to the last thirty or forty years of her rent portions she was supposed to get all these years from other properties my grandparents owned in Peru, as well. Atlantic City was gone, Philadelphia was gone, but from my understanding there was still some property in Peru and she had been complaining about how she had never received any of the rental income from these properties. In the end, my mom decided to not do anything. Over the phone one day, I told her that it was okay, and I asked her why she would put herself through another battle with her family. I also told her that in her heart of hearts, she needed to be okay with it, or it would be just another thing she'd be drinking about.

I hope she is okay with the decision she made. I believe it was the right one. Life is too short to continuously fight evil and greed.

Over the last twenty-one years, I never asked her or my father for money, but here they were including me on this income that she was about to receive. They wanted the three of us to do something with it so that it would continue to grow. I was at a standstill financially, and they were in their retirement years. I couldn't go into business with them, though. Well maybe, I could with my father, but; I knew my mother was not a worker bee, and I didn't believe that she could get out of bed before 10:00 a.m. So that would not work!

I told them that I thought they should hire a ghostwriter to help her write the book she had always wanted to write and to also find a manufacturer to create a condiment that she had concocted that was similar to something that we grew up having but couldn't find here in the States. When my mother directly deposited money into my account in late September, I was actually very upset that she had sent it; I didn't ask for it or want it. I did not trust her. I was weary of her turning the tables on me and feeling like I owed her something, which would be just like her to do. All I thought was as soon as I'd make some money, I would repay her, not owe her anything! My parents had had my account number because they had sent Oliver birthday and Christmas money in the past. It would have been smart of me to just return or reject the funds, but I didn't even think of it, possibly because I really did need it.

Matt didn't completely understand this. He knew I had issues with her, and he sometimes giggled about it because he never fully understood how she could be. He just said, "Take it and don't talk to her because you need it."

I did need it, but all I could think of were the strings attached— that I'd owe her or at least be obligated to talk to her and have her in my life. I was still trying to keep her at a distance. By the time I turned forty and transitioned into mapping out what I saw for my life and who I wanted in it, she wasn't part of the picture. To me, she was a cancer. There were those moments that weren't so bad, but they weren't great, either. It was kind of a gray area, like remission. When she was fully engaged, being herself, we butted heads; how she lived was unacceptable to me. She was still drinking and now hoarding while my dad—whom she criticized for "not doing anything" even though he had worked a full-time job with leukemia—didn't need that. She came with the attitude and told me a few times, I don't care, this is my life and I will do want I want, besides your father doesn't do anything *(he had Leukemia and was still working a full-time job when she would tell me this!)* and she would jab at me every once in a while about how I needed to lose weight and I was only like 120 pounds! She was toxic. Her negativity needed to remain out of my life.

She never gave me encouragement concerning the job I was doing with my son or myself. The money and the opportunity of creating a business was her way back into my life—not because she loved me but because she knew I was intelligent enough to do it and to work hard. She wasn't going to use me, I thought. Matt had such a good mother who wouldn't do things like my mother had done to me, so it was very hard for him to feel my dilemma or truly understand.

After this, I had a conversation with my father about how I felt after all these years that they were never there for me, especially her, even if it was just to be emotionally there for me. I was now forty-one, and she and my father knew what I really felt over the last twenty-one years when they helped out their other daughters. I felt I needed the most help, even non-financially, but I'm hardly the type to ask for help, even from my parents. Still, I believed they should have seen it and known. My son and I lived on a lower scale than everyone else. They knew I didn't receive child support. No one was around to pay some of the rent or watch my son when he was sick when I had to go to work. I was the only one that went to college and had student loans that I'm still paying. I believe I didn't have to ask for their help. I did it all on my own, at a price sometimes, and without the help of them or a boyfriend or husband, like some of my sisters had.

That was when my mother kept offering me more money in September and I finally acknowledged the fact that she was offering. I kept turning her down because it was a little too late. They could have helped me all those years. Even Candelaria bought my books one semester when I was first attending college because even though I worked full-time, I couldn't manage the costs of tuition and books. My parents had rough financial times over the years, but not always.

Thankfully, she only deposited cash into my account one more time, and I knew I'd try to do everything in my power to pay her back. I needed to prove the point that money cannot buy love. I didn't need her money; I needed way more. I needed her.

The third weekend I went to go see Matt was a real test. I refer to it as panic attack weekend.

I stayed for two nights. I went up early Friday just in time for us to have lunch on State Street at Chipotle; his dear, longtime friend Ryan was going to meet us. It was going to be nice to see Ryan again. Matt and Ryan had been friends back in the days when Matt had his apparel line; Ryan had been his graphic designer.

It was another beautiful, warm, sunny day in Santa Barbara. It was so nice to have it feel like it was still a summer vacation. The reality was that Matt and I didn't have jobs, so every day could feel like a vacation; Oliver was older now and extremely responsible, so I didn't have too many worries about leaving him for a night or two. I knew he wouldn't have a party or friends over in our crammed, tiny one-bedroom apartment, and we had made the agreement that he wouldn't go anywhere, so all was good.

Ryan, Matt, and I sat on the outside patio eating our Mexican food and talking. After a while, I leaned back in my chair looking at the Spanish architecture that lined State Street, feeling how wonderful this Friday was. We then walked across the street, and Ryan and I started to talk about our concerns regarding Matt. It seemed like Ryan was about to tell me something about Matt and a liquor store just as Matt walked back toward us. That was all I needed to hear to put a little thought in my mind that Matt was still struggling to stay clean.

Matt and I said our good-byes to Ryan, and we headed over to Cabrillo Boulevard to catch the 101 freeway southbound to go back to our motel. We loved taking this route, because we could drive alongside the beaches and ocean and see their beauty.

When we got to the motel, Matt mentioned how he started feeling uneasy, so we just stayed in, watching some television. I could feel him tossing and turning all night. Both of us were very poorly rested the next morning when we woke. He mentioned how he'd had a hard time sleeping; he said he felt anxious and stressed.

He called his sober coach and talked with him for a while. His sober coach had told him to do jailhouse push-ups to alleviate some of his stress. It made him feel a little better, but only for a bit. He was in and out of the room talking to his sober coach most of the morning and smoking cigarettes. He couldn't sit still. His sober coach told him to come to an AA meeting with him later at 6:00 p.m. Matt felt so bad for me, but I told him to do whatever it took to get him through it and that I was okay with it because I knew it would be part of our lives together. It wasn't going to be a big deal for me to go walking around State Street by myself for an hour. I loved doing that any way.

Before going to the meeting, we went to his mom's house for a while. He thought maybe sitting in the Jacuzzi would help him relax. His mom greeted us with open arms. Matt told her how he thought he may be having an anxiety attack and how bad he felt for me having come all this way. He wasn't feeling well enough to do anything. I told her how it did not matter, that I knew there would be times like this.

He went into the Jacuzzi while his mother and I talked. Then Matt came in after about twenty minutes. He still wasn't feeling well. His mom had mentioned to us how there was this new type of meditation she wanted him to try. Matt's mom had a yurt in their backyard. She told him to get dressed and to meet us in the yurt. He had shown me the yurt the first time I came to see him at her house, and I thought it was so cool.

While sitting in the yurt and talking with her, I could get a clear view to part of the backyard where there was a swing bench. We had seen him approaching the yurt and saw that he went to sit down on the bench and began to cry. And then I began to cry, but I let his mom go to him first. She sat next to him as he broke down. She asked me to come outside, and she grabbed a few chairs for her and her husband, who had just arrived. I sat next to Matt rubbing his back. He so desperately wanted to go to the emergency room. We worried that he just wanted to be prescribed something. We tried to talk to him, coaching him on what he was feeling, and I told him how I knew he could do this. He snapped at me, "I'm not as strong as you."

I was shocked. I told him that I wouldn't be there if I didn't think he could fight the disease. It was true. I didn't know after six days of knowing him how bad his addiction was, but over time, I had no doubt in my heart now that he could get sober again like he had so many years earlier. He just needed to find that willpower once again and the fight to want to be clean.

We tried so hard encouraging him, but he still wanted to go to the emergency room. It would have been very easy for him to go if he'd had insurance, but he didn't, and he already owed so much money for the last overdose he'd had. If any one of us had thought that maybe he needed to go and wouldn't be prescribed something then, we would have been all for it.

He began texting whomever and then got a call back. His dad had gone inside to get something while his mother and I tried to listen to the phone call. Matt obviously didn't want us to hear because he walked away.

His mom asked me, "Did you hear that?"

I couldn't hear anything. I look back now and wish I would have handled that weekend so differently. I would have definitely taken him to an emergency room to see what was really going on with him. Was it just anxiety, or was he still detoxing, or could it have been something much worse?

We left his mom's place so he could meet up with his sober coach and go to his meeting. Their meeting was on one of the side streets in lower State Street, and I dropped him off, being introduced to this older man who was his sober coach. Supposedly, his sober coach had known him and his brother for years and had really felt a need to help Matt through his recovery.

I walked around State Street window-shopping for the hour while Matt attended his Alcoholics Anonymous meeting. He seemed a little better when I picked him up.

I decided to treat us to a nice seafood dinner at Enterprise Fish Company on State Street. We needed something good to eat; it had been such a long day for the both of us. While we ate, I felt like an old married couple who had spent many years together. Truly, it didn't feel like we had only known each other for a year and a half. *Where did the honeymoon stage go?*

When Matt and I were done with dinner, he had to take a cigarette break. I took a moment to call my son to check in, and Matt just stood at the edge of the parking lot looking out to State Street toward the ocean. This was just another time that I'd find him looking out and thinking, observing, or contemplating life or the view he was looking at. I wish I would have known what he was thinking about.

I drove us down to the end of State Street and made a left at Cabrillo, taking in the scenic route we liked so much, heading back to our motel in Carpinteria. We got back to the motel, and it was a relatively quiet, almost somber end to our day. I immediately got into my pajamas even though it was just 7:00 p.m. We were both exhausted. The emotional stress and not having gotten much sleep the night before made my body want to shut down.

We spoke for a bit, and Matt apologized for the hundredth time, saying he had ruined my visit. He crawled into bed with me trying to sleep, and I fell fast asleep by 7:45 p.m.

The next morning, he didn't complain about having a panic attack, but he was just drained. He looked weak and tired. My weekend visit was coming to a close.

After we checked out of the motel, we stopped in Montecito to get a slice of pizza at Giovanni's. After we ordered, I joked with him about being able to beat him at a game of Galaga—a video game from our generation. Giovanni's had a Galaga arcade machine there, and about a year prior in Santa Monica, I had told him that I always played as a child and that I was sure I could beat him. He had told me no way, that he was the king. No matter how bad he was feeling, he still had his way about him, the joy and the playful side.

He immediately took me up on my challenge and put two quarters in, but I couldn't muster any concentration while playing, so I had him play both players. He ended up getting the highest score. Yes, he was the Galaga king!

The mood was still as it had gone all weekend—slow paced and gentle. He was sick. Whatever it was that was ailing him was still there, and he definitely was going through it.

We drove to his mom's listening to some old Go-Go's songs from their first album. His mom hugged us as we came in. I'm sure we looked beat. Matt went gently to lie on the couch and watch some football while I sat and spoke to his mom. After a while, it was time for me to leave, and I sat with Matt for a bit. I rubbed his third eye, telling him to just get some rest and not to think about anything. I told him how I used to rub Oliver's third eye when he was an infant, and Oliver would go right to sleep. Matt gave me his smirk that I love so much. He found some strength to walk me out, because no matter what, he always found it important to do that special thing for me. I hugged him and kissed him good-bye and cried all the way home, because all I wanted to do was be there for him.

All week long, I worried about him. One thing that was good was that he checked into the sober living house. He had to because his mom was going out of town, and she refused to allow him to stay at the house by himself. I worried just a little less because I was sure the sober house would constantly keep an eye on him. Supposedly, they tested them all the time, but only for narcotics, which was better than nothing. I had my suspicions that he hadn't totally gotten off the psychotic meds from jail, but I wasn't really sure and didn't ask. He had written to me that he had ended up on Thorazine, but toward the end of his stint in jail, he was weaning himself off. I believed that the panic attack weekend was the main result of detoxing now and possibly being clean for the first time in years. I thought his body was just reacting to not having any substances in its system, including alcohol, so he was just going through withdraws.

I couldn't wait to go up the following weekend, but I wasn't looking forward to staying by myself at the motel. Matt couldn't stay out for the night because he didn't get those privileges off the bat from his sober living situation. I continued all week long, twelve or so hours a day, looking for a job and sending out countless résumés on employment websites. Spending all these hours looking for a job was taking a toll on me, especially because I wasn't hearing back from anybody. It was going to be nice to take a break, get out of town again, and see "Mister," as I used to like to call him.

I went up to SB on Saturday and brought over cupcakes, hoping to share them with him and his parents. I drove directly to the sober house. He was standing outside waiting for me. I ran up to him and gave him a hug and a kiss. He helped me get the cupcakes out, and we ended up sharing them with all the guys at the sober living house.

Matt told me that his parents were really busy, and he was kind of trying to stay out of their hair. I was disappointed to hear that, because I wanted to see his mom and had brought her a gift.

I went in and met several of the guys who stayed there. They were very thankful and surprised that I had done such a thing. Matt threw back one or two of them in just a couple of mouthfuls and then plated himself a couple for safekeeping next to his bed for later.

We left and went down to State Street to a coffee shop that he had taken me a few times before, Hot Spots. It's situated very close to the end of State Street, not too far from the pier. His younger brother who lived in L.A. had called and was in town, and we were going to meet up with him. Matt and his younger brother had not seen each other since before Matt went to jail. Matt's younger brother had just gotten finished with a big business project and was coming into town for a friend's wedding. I'd never met him before, even though I had been to his place a few times in Beverly Hills when Matt used to stay there. Matt asked me if I minded. I said no. *Really?* What girlfriend would stand in the way of two brothers catching up and seeing each other? I think this was just another way he showed consideration toward me and how we'd spend some of our time together.

I was kind of nervous meeting another person very close to Matt. I was always worried about what everyone would think of me. Is this girl stupid? He has a problem with drugs and just got out of jail because of another girl. No one understood, not even my girlfriends, because no one was with Matt and me and went through the things we went through, even the parts of us learning about each other and how in some ways we were for years on this same parallel road through life. That made us better understand each other and relate to one another without any judgment. And when we spent time together, it was such a good time spent—laughter, love, sharing, and kindness.

Besides, we had this strong force that kept bringing us together, and when it did, everything seemed right in the world.

I told Matt while we waited for his brother that this was their time to reunite and catch up. Matt's brother drove up, parked, and walked toward Hot Spots. Matt walked up to him, and they hugged like they hadn't seen each other in years. It was sweet to see that, because I don't recall seeing any two guys hugging with such deep emotion and love for one another. My family had hugged, and we are actually very touchy-feely sometimes, but that was something different and less intense.

After Matt's bro got himself a coffee, he came outside and sat down with us, and they caught up about everything. Matt didn't have any reservations about what was said in front of me. Since Matt had been out of jail, every time we saw each other, he shared more and more about jail and the months leading prior to him landing in jail. He'd release more information as we went, never telling me everything all at once. This time wasn't any different. I heard a little more than he probably wanted to share with me because he would look at me, looking to see for a reaction. I gave none, but he knew later I'd bring it up, just to have it be discussed and addressed.

One thing that I did notice as I acted to look through the Santa Barbara Independent newspaper was that it was clear to me now that Matt's mind was a little altered. I had brought up things we had discussed or things he went through while he lived in Beverly Hills, but it was clear he didn't remember some things—and these were things he should have remembered. Also, once when he was talking to his other brother on the phone, he had completely twisted my words about something I had shared with him. This wasn't the Matt I knew. I was thinking that there was some damage from the overdoses, the drug usage, or the psychotic meds that he had been put on in jail after he detoxed from the narcotics. But was it temporary?

It was sad, and when I had my first glimpse of it, I wondered if it was permanent damage and whether I could live with that for the rest of my life. I was really in it for the long haul, because now there was no denying that something was wrong, and I thought I could deal with it. *I had to.* I guess then I learned that I lived by a code, *through thick or thin*, but only if it's someone who doesn't hurt me physically or intentionally.

We ended our visit with Matt's younger brother. Matt's brother and I had wrapped up the meeting with some positivity, telling Matt how he could do it all again. He could build businesses to be successful again. He could get the car of his dreams again. He had to sell it when he was in jail, which really bummed him out. We also told him that he could do whatever he wanted again, just as long as he stayed clean and focused, never giving up. It didn't matter that everything was gone, we said. He could rebuild his life once again.

Matt thanked his brother, and when we were walking to the car, he was so pumped by what his brother said to him that he went on and on about it. When we drove away from Hot Spots, I was a little hurt and mentioned to him how he totally took in what his brother was saying, but I had been telling him the same thing forever. I said, "Why do you acknowledge what he is saying and don't realize I've been telling you that for the longest?"

He said, "Baby, I totally listen to you, and if I hadn't, I wouldn't have been with you all this time. I love that about you."

I still felt unheard, as if I was just talking out of my ass to him all this time. In the end, it didn't matter to me where it came from, so I let it go. All that mattered was that he learned to believe it. He needed to believe it.

We went back to our motel in Carpinteria and hung out for a bit. This was a weird weekend, and I felt it all weekend long. I felt some distance between us. We had made such strides in the last few months, but I was still wary at times. Whatever it was, I felt a million miles away from him this weekend.

Since he wasn't up to doing anything that evening, we went to grab some food. I went into a local McDonald's and got us something. He stayed outside because he said he didn't feel like being around people. He spent most of his time talking and texting his other brother. He said his brother was spiraling out of control, like he himself had been a year earlier. Matt was very concerned and worried about him.

There were also a few times during that visit, like at Hot Spots and then later at the motel, that Matt would cut me off before I could say anything about certain things. It was obvious he was scared that I was going to bring up the difficult conversations. This was one of those times when he didn't want to talk about issues or reflect on anything. I wasn't even necessarily bringing up anything. "Stop thinking; stop thinking so much," he'd say.

Back at the motel, I showed him that this hurt me. I knew he was going through so much and now worrying about his brother, but he didn't need to react in such a way, especially to me. I know and understand addicts, and this is how they react when they desperately want to use, but I still felt hurt, and it still wasn't okay.

We were on the bed together after we had eaten, and we were both on our phones, each texting one of our siblings. Afterward, I tried to say something, and he cut me off again to not say a word. Our relationship had never been where we talked badly to one another, so I couldn't believe he was snapping at me like that. I just stopped and looked at him in disbelief. Quickly, he apologized and said, "No, go on. I'm sorry. Tell me what you were going to say."

I said, "Forget it. I will not speak the rest of the time."

He said, "Please. Tell me what you were going to tell me."

I said again, "Don't worry about it."

He then totally tried to smooth things over, apologizing more and then trying to hug and kiss me and make me laugh. I didn't smile, but I did let it go until a few minutes later. We were back to talking, and he was showing me photos his brother was texting him. I went to take off his Vans so that he would feel more relaxed, and he snapped, "What are you doing?"

I couldn't believe it. I took my hands off his shoes and sat down on the other bed as if to catch my breath. Maybe I was trying not to explode or just burst into tears. It took me about two minutes to say, "Let me take you back to the sober house now."

Things obviously weren't going great, so why prolong it a couple of more hours? It wasn't like he was staying the night with me at the motel. I drove off pissed, and it was obvious. I had almost missed the on-ramp to head back to Santa Barbara.

Once I dropped him off, he didn't try to get out of the car immediately. He turned to me and said, "So, are we over?" He said it as if it was the saddest thing he ever said to someone.

I told him, "I just can't do this. Not like this. I don't know. We'll see."

Then he kissed me good-bye. I drove back to the motel still so pissed. I was now pissed at his behavior on this whole visit. I was pissed that once again I felt a million miles away from the one person I had felt closest to in the world my whole life. I was pissed that again I might need to let go and not be able to see what we could be. I was pissed that I paid for a motel room that night. Even though we had plans the next day, I went to bed planning to just call him in the morning and cancel and drive my butt home early back to L.A.

Fortunately, that didn't happen. The next morning when I was loading up my car, I saw that in the backseat of my car were some slippers Matt had bought himself for hanging out in the sober house. I felt gravity, like the universe was making me not end things like this. I called him and let him know that I was coming by to drop off his slippers but that I wanted to head back to L.A. early. I drove up to the sober house, and he was standing outside waiting for me. He hopped into the passenger seat. Now he wanted to talk! He obviously didn't want it to end like this.

I was still aggravated with him. Usually when I'm pissed, I'm silently pissed; I'm not screaming or violent. But those who know me can tell that I'm upset, sad, or pissed. Matt could tell if something was wrong; he could even hear it in my voice. He first asked how my night was, and then he launched into an explanation of his behavior. He apologized for telling me to stop thinking so much and for cutting me off when I wanted to talk about things. He said that he wanted one evening free of those things that burdened him. He told me how hard it was every morning because he woke up with this heaviness of guilt and disappointment. He felt guilty for what he had done to his family, his sons, me, and himself. He was disappointed that he had let his life end up where it was and about all the wasted years. He explained that not only was it hard to get up every morning but that it took a physical toll on him too. He said that even once he got up and did his required meeting and had something to eat that it was a struggle just to get through the day. He said that it was just hard to have this conversation with me and that once again he was so sorry for how this weekend turned out.

I just sat there listening to him, staring into his eyes. I told him that this is all I needed to hear. I told him that it was okay, that I totally understood, and that as long as he stayed off drugs, we could let the past go; all everyone wanted was for him to be sober, healthy, and happy.

He again asked, "Are we over?"

I said, "No."

He kissed me over and over, and I said, "So that wasn't so hard to discuss with me, right?"

He gave me his half smile.

I said, "Please keep talking to me. Don't shut me out."

He said, "Okay."

Just then, he spotted his sober coach outside of the house and said that he'd better go and see why he was there. He told me how he was going to meet up later with his brother to watch some football and catch up some more before his brother headed back to L.A. I kissed him, we gave each other big hugs, and I left Mister until next time.

On the drive home, I now had wished so much to have hung out with him for the rest of the day. Reconnecting like that and what I saw as another milestone we had moved beyond was making me want him more. But all was good. He needed his time with his younger brother.

I struggled getting back up to Santa Barbara the following weeks. Finances were tighter than ever, and I really needed to spend all my time looking for a job, not spending money. Matt and I talked every day at first. He sent me pictures of him just hanging out down at the beach. There was even a day he was mesmerized by all the flock of pelicans flying around and took a picture for me. I kept on making plans to go up there, only to cancel because always at the last minute when nothing was happening with securing a job interview, I'd decide not to dip into my savings.

October 22, 2011, was the last time I did this. My sister's son was in his freshman year at University of Santa Barbara, and she and I were thinking of sharing a motel room. UCSB was having a family weekend, and that is why my sister was going up there. Matt was so excited that I was coming. Unfortunately, a few days before, I realized I couldn't afford to. Matt said he understood, but I knew when he'd be disappointed or sad that things couldn't work out as he would like them to. This was one of those times. I heard it in his voice, but I just couldn't do it.

After this moment and for the next two weeks, things seemed all right between us, but after then I realized things weren't okay. He began to call less and less. I'd get funny texts again, like they were rushed, or he'd not respond at all for a couple of hours. And then they started to reveal two things—one, that he was mixing up my texts with those obviously from other girls, and two, there were a few texts that were so inarticulate that he was obviously under the influence again. Matt had a tendency to shortcut certain words and have typos here and there, but these texts were like he barely knew the English language. I had seen these before when he was living in Beverly Hills and then later right before he entered rehab. I couldn't believe it.

I called him out on it. He tried to explain himself. He said that he did not know what I was talking about, even when I pointed out a number of elements in his texts that didn't add up. I wasn't buying any of it.

The next morning when he called, I let his phone call go to voice mail because I was too upset. He left me a message and texted me. I texted him back and told him that the girl, if there was one, didn't matter; what mattered was that he stopped using. He couldn't lie to me about using. I texted him that the only thing that his family and I cared about was him and his sobriety and he needed to stop doing this to himself. He texted me back, "Okay." I left it at that.

I was quite upset after that. We had come so far, and now the possibility of "us" was gone again. Later, someone who heard about our story said to me, "Addiction kept you apart." There were other girls, but he knew I wouldn't let him give up trying to fight this disease. Addiction had hurt me all my life, and it was continuing to do so. It wasn't Matt, exactly, but he was the vessel.

A few days after those last texts, I wrote a letter to him. He knew when he left jail that it was his last chance with me and now he ruined it. I told him in the letter it was over, wishing I'd stick to it, but knowing I probably wouldn't. Now here I was, writing my good-byes to him. I told him to delete my number, delete my e-mail, and to delete me out of his life. I wrote him about how mean he was to do this to me *again!* Part of the letter were words of encouragement but me telling him how mean he was was the harshest thing I can recall saying to him out of that five-page letter I sent him, along with sending him back all the lovely letters he had written to me in jail. I was devastated that he was doing this again, to me, to us!

My last text to him was to get his address at the sober house. He gave me the address, but about five days later, the letter came back to me. He had missed one number of the street address, which I then fixed and resent back to him. I re-mailed it on November 8; that was a Tuesday, late in the day.

12

Good-Byes

On Thursday, two days after I resent my letter to Matt, my parents came to visit. They were still living in Arizona but were moving back to California. They were going to look at apartments in San Diego but wanted to stop and see Oliver and me first. They arrived that evening, and we all went out to eat. I was still skeptical of my mom and having a relationship with her. The money she sent me made me think of possibly having some kind of contact with her again; it made me feel like she cared. Time had passed, and I was thinking of possibly giving her another chance. Besides, I knew that if I wanted a relationship with my dad, I'd still have to maintain some kind of relationship with her, because my dad was tied to her forever. A relationship with my dad was important, because the last ten or fifteen years of our relationship was the best it had ever been. We had respect toward one another and could have deep conversations without it ever turning into a fight.

When they came to visit, it was actually nice. We actually spoke a lot about what had been going on with me for a few weeks. They really seemed like they understood for the first time that my life, raising Oliver without anyone's help and all that I had done with putting myself through school wasn't easy. Now, when I was forty-one years old, they wanted to help me. They asked me what I wanted to do, and I showed the photography websites that I adored. I wanted nothing more than to do my passion, photography. They saw the tears in my eyes and heard me choke when I spoke about it. They offered me more money to buy a camera so that I could start taking pictures professionally, which was my dream. I insisted that I couldn't. I refused because they had to move back to California. My father was almost seventy-six years old and unemployed. My mother hadn't worked in more than two decades and was seventy-four. They had no retirement plan. All they had was the money from selling the house in Lima and some money that my father had from stock that he sold off once he was fired at his last job. It was more than likely that my dad wasn't going to find a job, especially in that economy and at his age.

I told them that they needed to hold on to whatever money they had and that I would eventually be able to buy my professional camera once I found a job and got stable.

I was more concerned about them, even though I was struggling. I had been unemployed for over a year, and I still had only received $13.33 in child support from the guy who fathered my son, but I knew I'd make it on my own through this challenging time, like I always had done before.

By the time my parents left on Saturday, all was good. I was still upset about Matt, but thankfully, they had distracted me for a bit. And my mom and I hadn't had one bad moment during her visit. That was huge!

All was still good until the following Wednesday morning, November 16. Oliver had stayed home from school. I watched him lying in his bed while I checked my e-mails in my bed, and I saw an email from my mother. I couldn't believe it! It was a drunken, crazy, long e-mail. Even though we'd had a good visit, I was reminded how mean and thoughtless she was and that her problem with alcoholism and whatever mental problems she had would never go away and were just getting worse. She was saying things that were like her to say when she was drunk but that no child should ever hear from a parent or a loved one. What I did was copy all my sisters on my response, with her e-mail at the bottom, and this is what I wrote:

> After reading the 1st part of your email, I went to look at Dad's FB page – couldn't finish reading your entire email. But, I wanted to see what you were talking about.
> YOU ARE CRAZY (STILL) OR DRUNK!!
> I DO NOT NEED YOUR HYSTERICS, YOUR PARANOIA & JEALOUSY RIGHT NOW!!! I am going through ENOUGH!!!
> Do what you want.
> Stay away from me.

When they had visited me just days earlier, they saw me in tears. I had spoken to them about how I was struggling to find my way. After responding to her e-mail, I didn't hear from her or my dad. I'm sure she covered her tracks, and because my parents used the same e-mail address, I'm sure she deleted any trace of these e-mails. She had told me and two of my sisters in the past that she'd delete any e-mails to my father if she didn't want him to look at them.

The only responses I got were from Paoletta and Guadalupe, and they were behind me 100 percent. Candelaria was not computer savvy, but I did send it to her husband so that he could read it to her. I wanted my oldest sister to understand why I was done with our mother. Her behavior was nothing new to any of us, but why did we—why did I—need to take it anymore? Just because she is my mother? That is an earthly title: we are not spiritually bound together and don't need to be. Who could condemn me if they knew our history?

I called my oldest sister to let her know that it was very important that her husband read that e-mail to her. I had her on speakerphone while my sick sixteen-year-old son watched and heard it all unfold. My sister told me to ignore my mother or just delete the e-mail—to accept it because she was *my mother.*

I couldn't anymore. I couldn't do that to myself or to my spirit anymore. I got off the phone, clearly upset, and was reminded again on how dysfunctional this all was. I'm not perfect but any means. I do have struggles. I clearly have issues, because I'm the only one that has never been married or even close to it. But I'm trying to change my life, how it is lived, and how it's affected. This was toxic, and it needed to be over! I was *finally* done with her for the last time after receiving her e-mail, and nothing could change that.

We all have continued the pattern of fighting and not immediately making up that was established by my mom and her sisters. While growing up, the four of us girls did bond together and at times against our parents. The most poignant and heartbreaking moment was when my two oldest sisters physically fought my dad; that was the biggest physical fight I have ever seen in my life.

We fought against the dynamics of our home life. We knew that how we were being raised and treated was wrong, or at least we didn't agree with it, and at an early age, we learned to rebel against the violence and some of the stupidity of our parents. *Do as I say, not as I do.* We'd feel like all we had was one another. But as sisters, we also had our own fair share of physical and/or verbal fights among ourselves. In the last twenty years, these habits and behaviors have continued, and some family members wouldn't speak for months or years for a number of reasons. When Guadalupe went to Chicago to have a medical procedure while living in Cincinnati, for example, she stayed with Candelaria and Paoletta. Candelaria was taking care of her, and some disagreement broke out. I never got a clear story; all I'd heard was that there had been an argument and that Guadalupe got physical with Candelaria, and Candelaria couldn't believe Guadalupe was so ungrateful. Candelaria had been taking care of her like our mother should have been, and all she got back from her was a physical fight. Similarly, following an awakening by Guadalupe after the birth of her first child, Guadalupe didn't speak to Paoletta and our parents for more than eight years.

I definitely had my disagreements or verbal altercations, but I never really discontinued speaking to anyone because of it; I had been the only one in our family who kept a neutral ground, never taking sides but always understanding all sides of the situation. But at the end of 2011, at the age of forty-one, I discontinued contact with my parents, though it wasn't really because of a fight; it was a choice because I finally understood why it was necessary for me to cut ties with them. From the moment I received my mother's belligerent e-mail, I realized along with discontinuing my relationship with my mother, I had to also unfortunately do the same with my father; my father and mother came as a package. My father sometimes forced it, saying, "But she's your mother." I knew now I had to part ways with him because she'd always somehow get back into my life, or he'd allow her to come back into my life. I couldn't continue on with this behavioral, dysfunctional cycle.

For a few decades, I had been changing and pushing myself forward, wanting to evolve. What I had been shown about how to speak to and treat your loved ones and how to live your life was wrong. I'd be in constant conflict almost every time I saw some of my family, because there was this disconnect between how I saw things and how they saw things. It was as if they just wanted me to accept everything as it was, but I couldn't. Sometimes when we'd get together, I'd revert to the angry, negative teenager they remembered and was always trying to point things out or bring up the past. They didn't get to witness who I really had become.

Two days later, on Friday, I had to regroup, because I finally had a job interview. My interview was at 11:30 a.m., and I was getting ready. Oliver had only stayed home one day and was back at school.

At about 9:45 a.m., my phone rang, and I walked over to my bed where it was to see who Caller ID indicated was calling. It was Matt's mother. I had no clue what she would be calling me about, but within two seconds of answering her call, my heart dropped.

Matt had died of a heart attack early Monday morning, November 14, at the sober house. She was surprised that I hadn't heard. She apologized to me that it had taken her so long to call me.

We spoke for as long as we could and then had to hang up because we needed to break down. I already had half of my makeup on and kept trying to refix it because of the tears that were flowing. I was devastated.

Somehow, I made it to the job interview, but afterward, I couldn't wait to run to my car and let everything out that I was holding in for that hour. I sat in my car in the parking lot, sobbing, and I realized how I couldn't be alone at that moment.

I didn't want to go back to my apartment, so I called Jonathan and asked if I could go to his house because something terrible had happened and that I didn't want to go back home until at least Oliver was there. He said, "Definitely."

Now, finally, I was able to share everything to Jonathan about Matt and me. He now heard the truth about why we had been off and on for so long. That the addiction kept us apart without letting us see what could happen between us. I sat on the floor of his upstairs office, crying. The man that Jonathan thought had changed me and had wanted to meet because of it was now gone.

After about half an hour of crying to Jonathan, I went down to their living room and just cried and cried. I was just wasting time, waiting for Oliver to get home or my girlfriend Nicole to come over after she was done with work. I had quickly called her to let her know that Matt was dead and that I needed her, asking her to come over. She had asked me if there was anything I wanted her to bring; all I could say was a two-liter bottle of Coke. Of all the times when anyone else would be drinking themselves silly, I asked for soda. Sugar is my vice and was what made me feel good at times.

Around 4:30 p.m., I left Jonathan's. I thanked him for being there for me when I didn't know who else to turn to. He said, "Anytime."

When I got home, I told Oliver what had happened and mentioned to him that Nicole was coming over. Nicole came over around 5:30 and sat on my bed with me, listening to me talk and cry. For the past year, she had not wanted Matt and me together anymore. She didn't like his addiction and had even referred to him as a junkie. But she was so kind to me at that moment, and the judgment she'd carried for a year was no longer there. She had compassion and a little bit of sadness for Matt and me.

Thankfully, it was Friday, and I still didn't have a job. I was in my bed all weekend crying, feeling like I was at one of my lowest points in my life. I was shaken, not knowing how I was going to get through it. A week earlier, things were good between my parents and me, and Matt was alive, so even though we were "off" again and I was upset with him, there was always hope. Now I had lost my best friend and our possibilities, and I had let go of any attachment or relationship for the last time with my parents. My life always seemed to happen like that; when it rained, it poured! I felt like my life was crumbling because also I was still living as a jobless single mom without child support—or any kind of help—and now all this happened. How I didn't find myself in a bar somewhere in the middle of the afternoon, I don't know.

The following week, I managed to take Oliver to school every morning and sometimes pick him up after school instead of him taking the two city buses he'd typically take home. By Monday, also I got back to still looking for a job. On Tuesday, I took my son to the DMV to get his ID. While he was in line waiting to get his picture taken, Guadalupe called me. On Friday when I'd heard the news about Matt, I had texted her, Paoletta, Nicole, and Melanie to let them know. I hadn't heard from Melanie or Guadalupe yet, so I had to take this call from Guadalupe.

I walked outside of the DMV, and she started talking about dad and how she didn't hear anything from him in regard to my mother's belligerent e-mail. I interrupted her and said, "Matt is dead." She asked me what had happened, and we talked for about ten minutes, and then she said she needed to listen to a voice mail that her soon-to-be ex-husband left her when we were talking. She said that it was about him picking up their kids, and she needed to know when he was going to do that. She said that she'd call me later that evening so that we could continue talking. That was a Tuesday.

It was Thanksgiving week, and Oliver's birthday fell on Thanksgiving that year. On his birthday, we picked up lunch and watched a movie together. I bought him a cupcake and put a candle in it. It was about all I could muster. We were going to celebrate his birthday on Sunday with a proper birthday lunch at the usual place we celebrated birthdays and Mother's Day, Le Petit Four, up on Sunset

Plaza.

The morning after Thanksgiving, I was lying in bed, sobbing and trying to watch anything on TV to distract me from my reality, and just then, Guadalupe called me. She had never called me back on Tuesday night or Wednesday or even Thursday to see how I was doing.

For years, Oliver and I had done the Black Friday sales, but we hadn't done it in two years because of my layoff. Even if all this hadn't gone down, I wouldn't have been able to do it this year because I was broke. I let Guadalupe's phone call go to voice mail. What was I going to say to her? If the roles were reversed, I would have been calling her nonstop. I listened to her voice mail, and it was all cheery. She said how she guessed Oliver and I were out doing Black Friday and that I should give her a call later. I deleted the message and threw the phone. Besides the fact that Matt just died and she knew what he meant to me, she would have known that I couldn't afford to be out shopping or at that point wouldn't care to go out and be a consumer.

Through all of 2011, whenever Guadalupe and I spoke over the phone, it was just to hear her talk about her pending divorce. She'd ask for advice but never take it, only to come back to me for more advice. Anytime I spoke to her about Matt, it seemed like she placed the phone down and didn't listen, because after rambling for a bit, I'd ask her if she was still there, and it always sounded like she would be grabbing at the phone, almost sounding like it was about to be dropped on the floor. I couldn't believe now how unsupportive she was.

I didn't return her call. I did hear from her again by text about a week later, saying that she was upset because the guy she was dating ended it. I was crying on Pacific Coast Highway going to pick up Oliver, and a song from New Order had just come on, which reminded me of Matt. At the red light, I texted her back, "Well, I'm grieving!"

She texted me, "I'm sorry. XOXO."

The next time I heard from her was a month and a half later when she left a message for me, saying, "I guess you're mad at me, but I thought I'd call you." I didn't return that call, either. I realized she had never really been supportive and was never really too kind to me. I had grown up with her being very selfish and saw that she still was. It's a one-way street with her, and if I am supportive of someone, I deserve someone that is supportive of me—at least in my worst moments—and this was about one of the worst times in my life. It's hard to put this wall between us, but I see now what our relationship is, and I just need to keep her at a distance. I finally learned what I truly meant to her.

The next day, Saturday, was Matt's service at the Hindu temple in the Montecito hills, close to where Matt and I spent a lot of our last moments together. It was a beautiful, sunny, warm day for the end of November. I was terribly sad inside, but I felt different that morning. A year and seven months had gone by since I'd first met Matt, and two years had gone by since I began making a shift toward what I considered my last half of my life and how I wanted to live it and who I wanted to have in it.

The drive to the exit in Carpinteria, which led us to the temple but could also lead us to "our" Motel 6, was an enlightening drive. I had clarity and was able to somehow see how the transition of my being had been shifting, evolving, in overdrive for the last two years. My life had been a crazy journey since my teenage years. I had traveled through very dark roads, despite wanting to try to find my way back to the essence of me and what I felt life should be all about. I had always wanted to find my way back to grace—that warm, calming peaceful place where the center of my being, the universe and my life feels right. Something out there during that drive spoke to me, like angels whispering into my ear, about what I had to do now— release and trust—and that it would all be okay.

On that drive up to my best friend, my ex-boyfriend's, service something also made me realize that my parents' life was their journey and that it was okay now to let go. I was done being a part of it, because it just held me down, and it was okay to finally step out of their lives. I saw how my parents' life was their own journey together all along. My dad would never leave her side, and though it had always bothered most of his daughters, it was okay now. I had only a piece within their journey, their life together here on earth this time around. It was now my time to step out of that and move forward with my own journey, which I had been taking part in changing vigorously for the last several years. It was a freeing, enlightening moment, because I was finally at peace with breaking away and not feeling torn or guilty about it.

In a week's span, I went from being mad, to understanding *everything*! The clarity was remarkable. The calmness was soothing. The understanding was peaceful. What I knew for sure was that I had learned so much from being a part of their lives, but there was nothing else that it was going to teach me, good or bad.

A few days later, I said my good-byes to my father over the phone, and I told him if I never spoke to him again before he passed that I loved him and that I had no resentment toward him about what was clearly his path—that it was with her and that our journey ended here. I didn't say good-bye to my mother; I now realize that she had been gone for a long time. I love them both very much, and I was very fortunate to have mended my relationship with my father over the last decade or so when we were in touch. I hope that their next journey is a peaceful one where they can learn, grow, and cherish life and to really know what real love is.

For over twenty years, I had struggled with members of my family, butting heads. I was trying to show them the way and trying to have them see how I saw that our family unit wasn't only wrong but that we weren't who we were meant to be. I tried so hard at times that I looked like the one that couldn't get over the past. *No one, I believe, completely gets over his or her past.* They try to move forward, delete it from their memories, but it is always carried with them in their behaviors, actions, and reactions. I had finally noticed I could no longer change them or show them the way because my path, my journey, was and is mine. And it was okay now to live my own by myself.

I saw how the months leading up to my turning forty until now was a transitional period to step 100 percent into my life, my journey, and not be burdened by who was no longer in it. What mattered was me, who I was meant to be, and what my time on earth was supposed to be. It was so clear; everything made sense.

My time with Matt made sense. All those times in the beginning when I'd cry and ask whomever was out there listening to tell me why we weren't together...it all made sense now. At that moment, I felt so deeply that there was a purpose and why we were meant to be together and why I always felt I needed to stay in his life. A one-hour drive had all these things come into perspective. I was meant to be there for him in his life for the last part because he needed to reveal everything about himself and open himself up to someone who understood and accepted him—to someone who was supportive; who tried to enlightened him and have him see himself in a positive light, and to just be loving toward him. I wasn't perfect, but I tried so hard, and in the end, I saw that he was meant to be in my life also because he had some things to teach me too. I had finally met a man who was sensitive and understanding. He trusted me by sharing all the things that he couldn't share with others, and he was appreciative and thankful that I was there in his life. He was my voice of reason, we were each other V.O.R.s, as we'd like to say, when we needed someone to remind us to see the good. I always thought if he got sober and really loved me that I would have been the luckiest girl in the world. He was *The Nicest Thing I Had Ever Seen*. He taught me to be more compassionate, understanding, and sensitive toward everyone by giving out his last five dollars to some homeless teenagers and a buck and change another night to an older gentleman on State Street. He also helped me to understand my mother and how unfortunate it was that she could not find her way to peace and happiness.

His mom shared stories of his generosity at his service that others shared with her. Most of the time he put everyone else first. One day, months later, she played me the last voice mail that he had left her the day before he passed and he said that he'd be by to visit her and help out around the house after he went to court with his brother and saw his ailing grandmother. The last thing he taught me was that I was much stronger than I thought. I always thought I put people first, was extremely compassionate, and had a lot of patience, but I had never known that I had such an abundance of these traits before all the struggles we endured in this time. Maybe the year and seven months with him helped me grow into the person I'm meant to become. I just wish I could hug him one last time and apologize for that letter I last sent him. I hope he knew I was just hurt temporarily and didn't mean it. And I wish he could have read this book. He was the one who encouraged me the last year of his life to get back to writing it. I am forever thankful that our paths crossed.

Epilogue
From Me to You

I first started this book twenty years ago after an incident I'd had with my pimp in Hollywood who had worked the streets for ten years before moving the business in-house. It was the night that I first saw how off track my life had veered and I was scared. I came home and tried to understand how my life had turned out as it had. It was the lowest point in my life and I tried to make sense of it. My life had been so dark for some time and this was my rock bottom to wake me up to the fact that I needed to do whatever it was to begin changing my life or otherwise I could end up dead one day. I was one of the lucky ones to have survived.

When I began writing, I also wanted to help others so that they wouldn't make choices like I had. I had always acknowledged my childhood as being bad, but I always said it could have been worse. But, I wasn't equipped at an early age to realize that we all have choices and that we are making a choice pretty much in everything we do. Even if you are a victim to your parents or from a crime, you don't need to allow it to keep victimizing you and putting yourself in harmful situations that you may never recover from. There will come a point that you need to move through the pain and grief of what has happened to you. You don't need to get stuck in it and stay in victim mode, unconsciously self-loathing and being self-destructive like I had for too many years. You are not your circumstances nor are you cursed to live like your parents chose to. Your life, your destiny is your own. Your perspective on things—life, matters and you must be aware that your decisions and choices will guide you down one path or another. You must choose which one that will be, but always know that you have a chance to get back on the right path.

Life is too short, and there is so much beauty out there and things to experience. Just take a moment to look up at the sky, look at the trees, or check out the birds flying around. It's beautiful! It took me a long time to also find hope and faith that things could be better. Sometimes teenagers or children get stuck in the reality of being abused under their parents' roof, I ask you to please speak out, seek help, find someone to talk to, and know that there will come a time you no longer have to endure it. It *will* end. Do the most with your time, like studying in school so that once you leave you can leave for good and have the life you could only dream about!

I lived too long in a sometimes suicidal state of depression, and I also used drugs to make me feel better. That's not the way to go! I understand depression to its core and how you get so lost in it, that it never seems like life is worth it, but *it is*! You have to take the steps of talking to someone and getting unstuck from what makes your life unhappy and also change your way of thinking; I know from experience that you can allow your thoughts to only think about the negative. If you can't find someone to talk to, talk to yourself in a loving, positive manner. Give yourself positive affirmations of your great qualities. Workout—bike ride, run, skate, any activity to get those *happy* chemicals flowing in your brain. Find a friend to hang out with that makes you laugh. Laughter is medicine. Being optimistic and knowing that your surroundings or whatever is happening is only temporary helps. Stop yourself when you even start going to the dark or negative thoughts. You are beautiful, smart, and strong. There is a light at the end of the tunnel. *Trust me!*

Bask in your uniqueness. You are a gift; we all are in our own unique ways. Smile and "keep ya head up," like 2Pac wrote to me. I pass this on to you and like a homeless lady on the streets of Chicago once told me and I am telling you now, "You are too beautiful to walk with your head toward the ground; look up!" What others say about you will come and go. Try not to worry yourself about it. One day, everyone will forget the things that were said, and hopefully you can rewrite those words in your head that you are repeating. Keep anyone who judges you and who doesn't support or encourage you out of your life—or at least at a distance.

See the world, reach out to others. Give a hand. You will grow and be fulfilled in your heart. Follow your dreams. Don't let anyone tell you that you can't do that or that won't work. We wouldn't be so evolved if all the inventors, creators, and the people who are so happy working in all these diverse fields listened to the naysayers!

You have so many possibilities; we all do. Wake up every morning appreciative, because every day is a new fresh start. As long as we are living, we can do anything. Sadly, some aren't as lucky to still have a chance! Don't compare yourself with others. The grass is not necessarily greener on the other side. Pick up the pieces to your mistakes and try to do better. Don't get down on yourself when you repeat a mistake. Just try and try again. Let go of the guilt, shame, and loss. When your life is over, no one in the end will hold those things against you. Love, care, and try to understand as much as you can. You will always be evolving.

I let others mistreat me for too long. There are going to be people out there in the world who do not serve you, so the sooner you recognize it, the better. Distance yourself from them. I learned that even though I had been hurt emotionally, physically, and mentally, I still didn't need to fill my life with anger, hostility, and just plain meanness. We are here for such a limited time, and the last thing you should do is spend time being unhappy and hurting yourself or others just because you have been hurt. You should just fill yourself up with the beautiful moments that touch your soul.

I share my story for you to understand me and how I'm still trying to evolve, despite everything. I could have given up a long time ago. I feel I even did at times, but eventually, I learned that is not the choice I want to make anymore. I've learned so much about life, myself, and the things that happened to me. I know for sure that we are all meant to evolve and that doesn't stop until we take our last breath.

By sharing my story, I'd like you to realize that you too can change your path and not succumb to the illness of victimizing yourself one way or another. I am not perfect nor is my life. This all takes time and you might find yourself, like I have, taking two steps forward and one step back. But stop and realize this—have trust in yourself that you will do better next time. Every day, every moment is a new start to make a change. The cycle from your childhood doesn't need to continue with you. You deserve better. Your children, future children, and generations to come deserve better. I'm always evolving, and I believe if I can do it, you can do it too. I have hope in you. You just have to learn to love life, find hope and most of all *love yourself*!

Much love,
Grace

Regarding some of my dear friends and family...

Tammy, after years of being lost, got her life on track and completed her bachelor's degree and received her master's degree from a great university here in California. She rarely drinks and no longer uses drugs, which she was doing when I moved in with her. She has light contact with her mom and has a good relationship now with her father. She is an inspiration as someone who has moved forward beyond what challenges others placed upon her.

Leah finally moved to Los Angeles a few years after I had moved back. After leaving Oxnard, she went to a university, completing her bachelor's degree. I am proud to say that she is doing well, works a lot, and—from what I see from being friends with her on Facebook—is very happy.

Melanie moved away from Oxnard before I did. She traveled, living in various parts of California and Arizona. She lived for a bit in Venice Beach, California, when I was living in Hollywood, and we hung out a lot, rollerblading and roller-skating when she lived there. She has done well. She is a hairstylist and is living a sober life. We stay in touch but have not gotten together except for one time after Matt passed.

As far as my parents go, I still don't speak to them. I have seen them once when I had a graduation lunch celebration for my son when he graduated from high school, but that is it. They have called fewer than a handful of times, just to speak to Oliver. They are respecting my wishes, and I hope that one day they will truly understand and accept my choice.

I talk to my sisters once in a while. I don't know how our relationship will be after this book is published, because I am opening a lot of wounds that they do not want to acknowledge, face, discuss, or deal with. I just hope one day they will understand why I had to do this. I love each of them because of the history we shared together and the times they were there for me when we were children. I do not carry any bitterness towards them, but I do acknowledge how our relationships are now. We are just very different individuals and I accept that. I hope they still love me and forgive me in the end.

About the Author:

Grace Lozada resides in Los Angeles, California. She works and donates as much as she can to the causes that have affected her and Matt's lives. She looks forward to moving to Santa Barbara one day.

Made in the USA
Charleston, SC
14 October 2015